T0361123

Routledge Revivals

Rural South Asia

First published in 1983, *Rural South Asia* examines questions of change and development in terms of linkages between localities and the outside world. The authors examine the response specifically to the introduction of a 'modern' features of production, the importance of physical, cultural and economic communication, and the impact of various development efforts. This book will be of interest to student of South Asian studies, history, economics and agriculture.

Rural South Asia

Linkages, Change and Development

Edited by Peter Robb

Routledge
Taylor & Francis Group

First published in 1983
By Curzon Press

This edition first published in 2023 by Routledge
4 Park Square, Milton Park, Abingdon, Oxon, OX14 4RN
and by Routledge
605 Third Avenue, New York, NY 10017

Routledge is an imprint of the Taylor & Francis Group, an informa business

Publisher's Note
The publisher has gone to great lengths to ensure the quality of this reprint but points
out that some imperfections in the original copies may be apparent.

Disclaimer
The publisher has made every effort to trace copyright holders and welcomes
correspondence from those they have been unable to contact.

A Library of Congress record exists under ISBN: 0700701605

ISBN: 978-1-032-61751-0 (hbk)
ISBN: 978-1-032-61760-2 (ebk)
ISBN: 978-1-032-61754-1 (pbk)

Book DOI 10.4324/9781032617602

COLLECTED PAPERS ON SOUTH ASIA NO. 5

RURAL SOUTH ASIA
LINKAGES, CHANGE AND DEVELOPMENT

Edited by
PETER ROBB

CURZON PRESS

First published 1983

Curzon Press Ltd : London and Dublin

© Centre of South Asian Studies, SOAS 1983

ISBN
0 7007 0160 5

ISSN
0141 0156

Printed in Great Britain by
Nene Litho, Wellingborough, Northants.

CONTENTS

Contributors   vi

Preface   vii

1   Introduction: The External Dimension in
    Rural South Asia
    Peter Robb   1

2   The Plantation System and Village Structure
    in British Ceylon: Involution or Evolution?
    Eric Meyer   23

3   Wage-Gathering: Socio-Economic Changes and
    the Case of the Food-Gatherer Naikens of
    South India
    Nurit Bird   57

4   Economic Dislocation in Nineteenth-Century
    Eastern Uttar Pradesh: Some Implications
    of the Decline of Artisanal Industry in
    Colonial India
    Gyan Pandey   89

5   Rural Labour in the Bombay Textile Industry
    and the Articulation of Modes of
    Organization
    Dick Kooiman   130

6   The Role of the Broker in Rural India
    Walter C. Neale   163

7   Two Karnataka Villages and the Outside
    World: Internal Characteristics, Movement
    Linkages, and State of Development
    H.G. Hanumappa and John Adams   179

8   'Decentralized' Planning in a Centralized
    Economy: A Study of Sarvodaya Programmes
    in a Taluka
    Ghanshyam Shah   204

9   International Rice Research and the
    Problems of Rice Growing in Uttar Pradesh
    and Bihar
    Paul R. Brass   229

CONTRIBUTORS

Professor *John Adams*, Department of Economics, Maryland.

Mrs *Nurit Bird*, Department of Social Anthropology, Cambridge.

Professor *Paul Brass*, Department of Political Science and School of International Studies, Washington (Seattle).

Dr *H.G. Hanumappa*, Institute for Social and Economic Change, Bangalore.

Dr *Dick Kooiman*, Institute of Cultural Anthropology and Non-Western Sociology, Free University (Amsterdam).

Dr *Eric Meyer*, Centre d'Etudes de l'Inde et de l'Asie du Sud, Paris.

Professor *Walter C. Neale*, Department of Economics, Tennessee.

Dr *Gyan Pandey*, Centre for Studies in Social Sciences, Calcutta.

Dr *Peter Robb*, Department of History, School of Oriental and African Studies, London.

Dr *Ghanshyam Shah*, Centre for Social Studies, South Gujarat (Surat).

PREFACE

This volume results from an international symposium
which I organized in December 1980 under the auspices
of the Centre of South Asian Studies at the School of
Oriental and African Studies, London. Further papers
from the same symposium and an earlier meeting in June
are being published separately under the title *Rural
India: Land, Power and Society under British Rule*
(Collected Papers on South Asia No.6).

The present book comprises those contributions
which bore particularly on questions of change in relation to economic development. The intention is to concentrate on linkages between localities and the outside
world, and in general between what may be defined as
intrinsic to a given society and what may be called
external. The essays are illustrative of the subject;
this volume does not pretend to be a survey and has no
pretensions to being regionally or thematically comprehensive. Four papers, those by Eric Meyer, Nurit Bird,
Gyan Pandey and Dick Kooiman, examine the response of
South Asian societies specifically to the introduction
of 'modern' features of production: plantations, foreign
imports or capitalist industry. Four more papers treat
aspects of external linkages in particular relation to
economic development: that by Walter Neale on the role
of the money-lender as 'culture broker', that by H.G.
Hanumappa and John Adam on the physical communication
between villagers and nearby towns, and those of Ghanshyam Shah and Paul Brass on recent development efforts
and different responses to technological advances.

The conference and therefore this publication would
not have been possible without the financial assistance
of the Projects Committee at the School of Oriental and
African Studies, and that assistance is gratefully
acknowledged.

The presentation of the papers has been standard-
ized to a point but absolute uniformity has not been
attempted. The use of italics has been avoided as far
as possible, for example after the first appearance of
less common but repeated words. A problem arises with
transliteration where words are or were current in Anglo-
Indian usage (in English): to apply strict conventions
to such words is to give them a misleading 'indigenous'
quality. I have therefore left all transliterated words
in the forms used by the different authors.

P.G.R.

INTRODUCTION:
THE EXTERNAL DIMENSION IN RURAL SOUTH ASIA

Peter Robb

The symposium from which this volume is drawn had the
title 'The external dimension in rural South Asia:
linkages between localities and the wider world'. It
was concerned to focus attention on processes of integration and exchange between the levels of government,
central markets or regional and metropolitan culture,
and the level of the villages of South Asia. The essays
which follow treat aspects of these questions in their
own way. Several continuing themes may be discerned.
First there are methodological points. The papers show
a clear preference for making assessments according to
function rather than form, and on the basis of a complex
of roles or a society in the round. As a consequence
two general conclusions seem possible: that the 'traditional' systems may not be seen as a set of hierarchical
isolates, for linkages of various sorts are not peculiar
to so-called modern societies, and that the categories
of our analysis - such as 'political', 'social' and
'economic' - are misleading because Eurocentric, conjur-
ing up distinctions and divisions which do not exist in
South Asia. Divisions there are, of course, but the
categories which they provide are mostly hybrids ('socio-
political', 'socio-economic' and so on) according to our
terminology. Secondly the papers provide some substantive hypotheses. They recognise that communities differ
in their response to stimuli, that in general adaptation
is preferred to transformation, and that imperfect linkages are an important inhibitor of or barrier to change.
    We may dispose of the methodological points first.
The paper by Neale encapsulates them: he examines the
moneylender, by which he means the 'external' bania
visiting the villages to trade, according to his function and not his reputation, as a broker mediating between different economic cultures, and he stresses that
the bania did not operate wholly in the economic sphere
or seek economic rewards above all others. The more
detailed papers embody similar ideas. Hanumappa and
Adam stress the variety of relationships and the multi-
plicity of function for institutions and actions in the
villages they study. Meyer, on Sri Lanka, begins by
trying to understand the traditional ecosystem, and thus
abandons the idea of static or closed villages which was

1

implicit in accounts of areas of perpetual cultivation
and permanent occupations: he sees the interplay between
'outfield' reserves of land and 'infield' paddy fields
and gardens. Nurit Bird, too, stresses the pattern of
work, consumption and trade in the life of the food-
gatherers before they became involved with labour on a
plantation, and Pandey pushes back in time the market-
involvement and dependence on intermediaries of the
weavers he studies, while also judging the impact of
trade in manufactured goods in terms of the rural economy as a whole. Kooiman adopts Neale's strategy in
analysing the functions of the 'jobber' who provided
labour for the Bombay mills in terms of the services he
provided. Shah's essay exemplifies the discontinuity
between rhetoric and practice, between the Gandhian 'decentralization' which he sees as yet another in the
series of strategies intended to defend the supposedly
isolated village from outside influence on the one hand,
and the practical needs of and constraints upon development agencies or the desires and expectations of local
people on the other hand. Brass's questions too are
very much of the genre 'how does it work?' in preference
for 'how does it look?'; his explanations of the relative failure to improve rice yields in Bihar depend upon
the connexion between agricultural profitability and
ecological constraints, especially problems of water
management.

The studies thus tend to emphasize pre-existing
conditions and often enough resistance to change. To
Meyer the essential feature maintaining the balance of
the society was the flexibility provided by chena cultivation, that is, occasional crops of paddy and millets
on so-called waste land. This was destroyed by plantations, land-grabbing and government policy. The villager's response was to substitute other sources of income and flexibility, for example by opening his own
plantation or more commonly by trading with or working
for the Europeans with their Tamil labour force. Bird's
tribals, similarly, take from the plantation, its wages
and the market, those features which best suit their
previous life-style. Pandey's weavers, too, fit into established patterns. Pandey, anxious to distinguish between the impact of British trade on different sections
of the population, argues that in the seventeenth and
eighteenth centuries even lowly textile producers were
already involved with entrepreneurs who captured most of
the profits, and that the fortunes of different production centres fluctuated even then from time to time.

Thus Pandey sees the loans and advances made under the
East India Company and to a lesser extent the subsequent
rise and fall of weaving communities as partially continuing the past: the region and its trade were already
open to whatever damage was inflicted on them by the ad-
vent of European manufactures. Moreover, faced with the
challenge, people did not suddenly change their habits:
factory-products could be readily substituted for most
of the finer qualities of cloth but not for coarser handloom (the demand for which continued into the present
century), and local manufacturers of fine cloth attempted to save themselves by cornering the market wherever
imports could not compete, and ultimately in cotton
saris for local sale.

A second conclusion is that adjustment is usually
preferred to revolution. Kooiman's jobbers were newcomers, urban-based, dependent for their position on
knowledge and physical strength. To the employers they
were both contractors for and managers of labour. But
to the workers they were patrons, the 'mukadam' or traditional leaders. They were not of the village but they
were from it, in the sense of recruiting through kinship
and common origins and of reproducing, in the factory,
conditions which accommodated to the understanding of
the villagers. They were recipients of bribes or tri-
butes; they were creators of vertical solidarity. Just
as the mill-owner abrogated to the jobber the right to
hire and fire, so the workers gave up any pretensions of
entering a wage contract or combining as a class. The
jobber was, in short, a culture-broker in the sense that
Neale uses the term: he provided for capitalist enterprise a 'non-capitalist' face in the villages, and for
the worker both a channel and a filter. Meyer's villagers required different aptitudes to meet the challenge
of the plantations and therefore there was some change
in the people who were successful, but none the less
their involvement with a capitalist system may be represented merely as the substitution of one outfield for
another; its function for the village had not changed,
and therefore the underlying structure remained the same.
Bird makes this explicit with the notion of 'pre-existing pattern' by which she accounts for the continuities
to be found in the customs of the Naikens, and which may
be seen to be the equivalent of the cultural conservatism described in all the papers. In stressing the
importance of function, Bird reminds us, as Neale does
also, that social, economic and other features do not
exist independently of the uses to which they are put

and the ways they are perceived. Integration with the plantation or the money economy did not imply for a Naiken what it would imply to a North American: Bird's concept of 'wage-gathering' is thus not paradoxical, because she does not understand wages to imply the system of values and customs which surrounds their payment in some other societies, but rather sees them as an objective feature whose functions are peculiar to the society in which they occur. For the Naiken indeed the wage is not a currency at all - that role is filled by debt - but a substitute for forest-products, and it is gathered when needed just as they were in the past.

The dynamic element in these explanations is also important, and central to some of the papers. Change, it is clear, is not a necessary consequence of contact, for contact of some sort is a perennial feature. Change is a necessary consequence of the right mix between an innovatory contact and a receptive society, or between internal needs and pressures and an appropriate input. The extent to which defence is possible, as in the substitution practised by Meyer's villagers, Bird's tribals and Pandey's weavers, depends on the ability to accommodate a change of content within existing structures, and that will depend, for example, on the degree to which the 'outfield's' characteristics are or are not peripheral, and in general on the nature of pre-existing arrangements. The Naikens did not 'develop', because the plantation represented a change with which they could cope, and also because they were not predisposed to seize upon the opportunities for economic maximization which it could have provided. Pandey's weavers were protected to some extent not by isolation but by the persistence of old tastes, the inappropriateness of some of the finer cloths for some of the consumers, and most of all by the continuing need for surplus income and the opportunities provided as an adjunct to cotton-growing. Indeed the claim is that weavers had probably always operated at or about subsistence level and that the true losers to foreign competition were probably those agriculturists who needed to supplement inadequate incomes from cultivation; they substituted migration. On the other hand, the weavers in some communities were not disposed to change their ways by producing in factories, even though they had long been involved in the market and dependent on middle-men. Here, I think, and in contrast with Kooiman, the 'de-industrialization' argument runs into difficulties. Arguably change would become endemic rather than epidemic, at the point at

which intolerable conflict arose between the weavers'
self-image and sense of identity, and the conditions
with which they had to fit in. So too the half-way
house represented by the jobbing system discussed by
Kooiman is possible precisely because such a crisis had
not occurred: the village may have been 'subordinated'
to the factory but if so it was not because of the dominance of the capitalist mode of production but in the
sense that villages were made to serve certain purposes
for the mills, chiefly as labour pools; and indeed, on
the contrary, the existence of the jobbers rendered the
mills imperfectly 'capitalist', prevented them from
undermining village society, and even perhaps caused
them to perpetuate existing social relations.
       In seeking fuller explanations of dynamic processes,
these papers look first at the linkages themselves.
Neale argues that the lack of suitable brokerage may
have rendered ineffective some attempts at modernization
and development. Hanumappa and Adam, concerned to analyse the 'hiatus between ... infrastructure and ...
village structure', believe external connexions to be
instrumental in development. Their two examples, one
'growing' and one 'declining' village, admit of differences of opportunity (proximity to towns, availability
of water) but suggest that these are not sufficient
explanations of the differences of performance. Rather
the range and nature of outside movements may be correlated with the economic position of the villages and of
individuals within them. The differences may have had
underlying causes, as for example in the caste composition of the villages, one of which had a large number of
tribals and the other a large number of the locally-
dominant caste; but however the differences in receptivity originate they are, it is claimed, instrumental
in development or decline. Other essays too take up
this point by looking beyond the substitution and adaptation which we have seen as the initial reaction of
non-receptive communities. Kooiman sees the adjustment
represented by the jobber as a transitional arrangement:
the interchange occurred at first without any concur-
rence of customs or attitudes between the parties, and
the worker remained migratory, attached to his village
which he sought to re-create as far as possible in the
unsanitary chawls where he preferred to live: but, as
the discussion of trade union development shows, this
worker could be harnessed through the jobber into new
forms of association, and vertical solidarity could be
translated into without being superseded by horizontal

mobilization. The fact that 'pre-existing patterns' are not at first disturbed does not mean that fundamental changes never come, merely that they are delayed. Kooiman's jobbers came to need or to want what outsiders could offer them, the political brokerage of administrative skills and the articulation of grievances in a political idiom; ultimately the jobber and the village could be superseded, by means of the linkages which were in existence or created.

Shah's account leads in the same direction. He shows how a development agency is dependent on external forces however committed it may be to internal uplift. The need for capital formation and certain political pressures invite centralization; but more than this much of the response to the external which distorted the Gandhian ideals was derived from the local people themselves. When the agency tried to emphasize agriculture and crafts in their school they found people demanding English and science, as vehicles for an escape from the status of manual workers and farmers. Cooperative preparation of papad, a vegetable product, flourished because it provided jobs for women who would not work in the fields, but its commercialization offended the Gandhians. The picture is of a tension between internal and external forces, certainly, because the development workers were unable to change the pattern of land-holding, the customs and attitudes which created local conditions, or the decisions of governments and aid programmes which provided the external inputs: thus the technocratic improvements evoked a ready response but were not to the advantage of small and marginal farmers, while the development of the dairy industry, diamond-cutting and paper-manufacture was dependent on the demands of external trade. But the picture is also of a tension that is being resolved, for Shah concludes that internal resistance has weakened as the external forces, particularly integration with the market, become stronger. The Gandhian ideals were first compromised and then rejected : so this agreeably sardonic essay reveals.

Such arguments have wide ramifications, for Gandhi's view of the Indian village was not an original one. Many years ago Daniel Thorner, in an appreciation of Henry Maine, remarked that his 'ideas may have been modified in a number of respects but they are very far from having been completely disproved or entirely displaced',[1] and this is still true, not just among Gandhians but generally. The essays in this volume however belong to a trend which has brought displacement nearer.

Criticisms of Maine's egalitarian *ur*-community and of
single-line evolution have been well-digested, but the
present tendency is also to question the extent to which
village structure was, in pre-modern conditions, largely
or essentially unaffected by outside influence, or that
communities were 'left to modify themselves separately'.[2]
There is little autochthonous development to be found in
the pages of this volume, and also little sense that the
character (as opposed to the extent) of the most important exchanges between the village and its environment
has altered in the dramatic sense in which Maine believed. It is true that in an essay which was before
our symposium but which has been published elsewhere,
Gilbert Etienne rejected the 'village republic' ideal on
the basis of the lack of dynamism in the model, arguing
that any system of production has its 'inner rationale'
so that there comes a time when its 'maximum productivity has been reached'.[3] But this rationale so far as
it is reflected in this volume seems to be the result of
exchanges between external and internal conditions: it
is itself a source of the dynamic, for conditions are
constantly changing. Etienne proposed population pressure as an example (perhaps *the* example) of the crisis
that generates advances in technology and a change in
the system of production, or else leads to some catastrophe which preserves the existing system by a demographic check. But other essays suggest that change may
result or be avoided through a range of influences, at
once wider than this because reflecting the ways in
which the village is embedded in its environment, and
narrower because specific to each case.

We are groping then towards a fundamental explanation of historical change. We appear to accept the
pre-eminence of ecology over culture without denying the
resilience of the latter. It is after all only as a
theoretical construct that we see behaviour resulting
merely from man's accommodation to physical conditions,
that we attribute entire social structures to pre-deter-
mined responses, in the way that the origins of *bhaia-
chara* communities have been traced to insecure agriculture.[4] The last paper in the collection makes this
point clearly. Brass denies that lack of enterprise
explains the failure to increase the productivity of
rice cultivation in north and east India, and refers
instead to problems which specifically affect paddy in
many parts of Asia. The peasant, to Brass, is a
rational producer who rejects the additional input
required for high-yield varieties in situations of high

climatic risk. But Brass does not ignore cultural
explanations altogether. He emphasizes the importance
of understanding ecological *and* human factors; and in
the cultural sphere he notices particularly the impact
on goals of a farming system geared to subsistence and
not marketing. The size of holding is an important
factor here, as is the ability to enjoy surplus, but so
too are cultural preferences, though none of these is
immutable. Indeed diversity is a theme for Brass and others.

In treating particular examples the papers in this
volume have thus, it seems to me, some common conclusions. I shall attempt here to expand upon these points,
to relate them to the questions with which we began, and
to assess their significance. The interpetation will be
my own, but based on the aspects of the papers already
described. When I was asked to clarify the starting-
point for our discussions, I explained that I sought a
range of factors likely to be significant, mechanisms
likely to operate, characteristics receptive or hostile,
where there is externally-induced change. It seemed
necessary to ask how internal and external worlds relate
in general, to encompass continuity as well as change.
There were two different kinds of question. The first
was one of definition, which is, in South Asia, peculiarly complicated by point of view and assumptions: variations and contradictions present more than the familiar
problem of deciding what is general and what is specific.
We have to distinguish between reality and rhetoric. We
can, for example, easily see the difference between
varna theory and the practical operation of a jati. But
how can we be certain that we are not, in our analyses
of rural society, merely repeating the equivalent of a
Brahmanical view? Moreover we cannot escape our defin-
itions: our terminology must be general to the extent
that we wish to communicate with others and relate our
findings to theirs. In the last century the drawing
of the boundaries depended upon certain preoccupations
about society, evolution and race: thus we had tribes
and castes as the imposed categories of analysis. Today
we see that all the boundaries - the very study of ethno-
graphy, the idea of locality or the identification of a
region - depend upon distinctions as difficult and arbitrary as those which historians have long worried about
in the case of periodization.

Our first problem therefore was to describe and
delineate externality and internality. We might, for
example, map out the extent of operable relationships,
find out how far regional influences extend, how wide

are the networks within which a village is placed, and
which aspects of life are subject to the general trend
and which to particular variation. These are in the
last resort questions of fact. The second problem,
however, concerned interrelation - not just the identification of a shift in the external environment to which
internal change might be a response, but the interaction
of one culture with another or between general and specific aspects of a single culture. The interface between internal and external is a point of movement, of
exchange and causation, whether we are analysing change
or stability, for the first results from exchanges which
tend to subvert and the other from exchanges which tend
to confirm. And here the questions (what mechanisms
determine which it is to be?) were wholly ones of interpretation. The problem goes deeper than merely choosing
one or even a set of 'causes' when all seems interdependent. If there is no road, except the examination of
the particular case, along which to seek the relative
importance of factors that were generating or resisting
change, it is a road that leads into familiar cul-de-
sacs. It is agreed, perhaps, that change and continuity
result from a mix of internal conditions and external
environment. Go beyond this assumption, to questions
about what the mix is likely to be, and agreement ends.
We may see this in development terms: at some stage
sufficient of either incentive or opportunity will induce change, but it is difficult to define the suffi-
ciency. Just as we ask at what point lack of incentive
will be overwhelmed by magnitude of opportunity, we have
to consider when it is that internal forces are sufficiently favourable or external sufficiently dramatic, to
induce change.

Hence it was that at the outset I asked for the
independent examination of the ways things interact.
Broadly speaking, are there kinds of institution which
are resistent to change or kinds of influence which are
bound to prevail? The inquiry had already moved on,
therefore, from those old controversies about the nature
of the village community which depended on the theoretical establishment of original forms in order to understand how relations 'ought' to be (before changing or
protecting them). We were concerned rather with the
terms on which various forms develop and decline, with
what I made bold to call a 'systematic study of connexion'. It was not to be expected that any symposium
would address itself wholly to the questions with which
it began; but the essays presented here have, it seems

9

to me, consistently abandoned any idea of a kind of moral supremacy for past or original social forms, discarded indeed any idea of isolation in which a single original form could appear and be sustained over time, and turned instead to the roles played by various forces at any time, moving societies in different directions from diverse starting-points. Moreover, to my mind, the essays reinforce certain conclusions, in particular that change will be induced within a society either when influences are so strong as to produce an environmental revolution, in which case change may be said to be independent of the social or value system, or when influences are so appropriate as to be readily accepted, in which case change might be said to be dependent on the existing culture.

One lesson of the papers is thus that we ought to escape the obsession with the cultivator in his isolated village. A second lesson is that our terminology still needs attention, damaged as it is by the observation of how groups function and interact. The return of the peasant to South Asian history has been rightly hailed,[5] by a great and greatly lamented exponent of this trend, but sometimes it seems as if it is a nineteenth-century view of the peasant that has come back. The term may imply the isolated and independent subsistence producer who is so much at home in those isolated villages. But who is this peasant? Is he the small-holder of the Mali type who grows vegetables for a limited market? Is he the surplus cultivator whose attention quickly turns to those 'capitalist' activities of rent-collection and usury? The term supposes an equilibrium in landholding and land-use which perhaps did not exist, and a broad and important section of the population on which we should be concentrating our attention. A peasant role no doubt existed, but perhaps it was not wholly identified with a single group, differentiated internally only by relative wealth and independence.

Furthermore, we are led to ask whether or not this *is* the role on which we should concentrate if we are interested in change. An economy and equally a society or a polity depend (I would argue) upon connexion, and it may be seen (as suggested by Walter Neale in this volume) that there are two roles which may be played in this regard in the South Asian countryside. There is brokerage, whose importance depends on the ability to translate, to be different things to different men, and there is patronage, the key to which is the supply of necessities in return for services. The underlying

feature of the one is exchange, and of the other dominance or dependence. Here too we have to attend to the
role and not a type or an individual. The money-lender
who takes coin from the town and makes it available to
the cultivator (for rent or revenue-payments) is acting
as a broker. He may also be a patron if he supplies
seed and food grains in return for control over the disposal and sharing of the harvest. The prosperous cultivator who lends cash or grain or draught animals to
his fellow-cultivators, in return for their labour in
his holdings, is also performing either or both of these
roles. Our analysis of connexion therefore depends not
on the use of categories such as bania, dominant peasant
or zamindar, but on examination of the impact and operation of those who performed certain roles, regardless
of their status.

These observations lead us on, or so it seems to me,
to those further lessons about the nature of change
already discussed. Our conclusions may be taken as
representing a new stage, in contrast with some of those
of the past. Not just in recent discussions but since
the debates of the nineteenth century, 'colonialism' has
cast a long shadow over 'development'.[6] Thus are postulated indigenous structures and external forces, the
latter seen as having penetrated the former.[7] Such
interpretations inhibit understanding, for in their Euro-
centrism they imply a whole series of further conclusions: that movement comes from outside not just in the
sense argued here but in the sense of across continents
and cultures, and that internal or indigenous features
are bound to be weaker than external or foreign ones, a
weakness that results from isolation and segmentation, a
strength that is attained and transmitted through improved communciation. Refinements of these ideas -
Furnivall's pluralism or Boeck's dual economy [8] - have
tended merely to add sophistication to the old dichotomy between East and West, fatalism and rationalism,
sufferers and actors. So too Marx bequeathed to his
followers an imprecise but potent image of backward Asia:
of primitive communism, a despotic political and social
system derived from communal property; of isolated communities where all divisions of labour (and those into
producers and controllers) were unalterably fixed, in
stasis, for want of class conflict; of a milieu in which
production for consumption prevailed over production for
wealth, only the latter demand being insatiable and thus
dynamic. Nineteenth-century debates and also some of
those conducted more recently, are dominated by a model

for which Adam Smith was ultimately responsible, one in
which development resulted from the displacement of inefficient peasants by landlords and capitalists, and of
fragmented economies by more integrated ones. Some con-
demn the process; others object to its being interrupted.
Only the heterodox argue that because social groups and
economic roles were interdependent - the merchant or
money-lender or zamindar needing the cultivator as much
as the cultivator needed him - there was no certainty that
the predicted development would take place and no safe
identification of individuals with the Smithian or indeed
the Marxist categories. Of course we can hardly, today,
escape Smith or Marx, any more than our predecessors
could; and we are bound to measure economic progress in
comparison with the rise of the capitalist economies of
Western Europe: certain kinds of economic change presup-
pose particular changes in the means of production and
the allocation of resources. But we can allow the
theory to take us in rather different directions from
those in which it has taken many people in the past: in
particular we need not assume that inefficient peasants
are necessarily displaced by the operations of capitalists and proto-capitalists; or that integrated economies
necessarily take the form of those which exist in Europe;
or that, indeed,localized, 'traditional' economies are
static isolates, unlike capitalist or centralized-
bureaucratic economies. We are encouraged to avoid the
assumption that one set of characteristics implies
another. We are encouraged, moreover, to endorse the
assumption that there are, in all societies, internalized
features, which tend to reinforce existing patterns, and
that change depends on the resolution of an equation in
which the two variables are the resilience of the internal features and the strength of the external, subversive
pressure. The argument is that the inate tendency in any
society or system is towards stability, to variation
within a specific range, and that development is generated by the breaking of the mould. All societies constantly experience interchange between the internal and
the external, in this sense of the terms, and the status
quo is itself therefore a long-term movement. But
equally some societies are more open to influence than
others, or in some periods are more exposed to influence.
All evolutionary theories propose some necessary or
likely progression; we postulate various results from
the fortuitous matching of pressure and response.[9]
     It may seem that the argument is circular, dependent
on the particular definition of 'internal' and 'external'

features; rather, I would argue, the terminology, which is not wholly satisfactory, is not material to the general conclusion. What is essential is first acceptance of the idea that every society represents an optimal formulation in respect of its environment. Take for example the concept that there are appropriate customs of inheritance. It is true that the absence of primogeniture may be said inevitably to involve fragmentation of rights in land, though not necessarily of working units; this is the case provided the rights are individually heritable and regardless of any increase in population. But we may reasonably argue that if this fragmentation had been seriously disadvantageous then some other expedient would have been adopted; and that perhaps on the contrary joint and equal inheritance had beneficial effects on the provisional of agricultural labour, especially for rice cultivation and in general where rainfall followed the Indian pattern of monsoon and drought and thus prevented a steady demand for work, or that it played its part in unifying the family's and the clan's claims over land in conditions of political insecurity or variable cultivation. The British of course tended everywhere to provide someone with a definite legal title over specific pieces of land and to guarantee that title for an individual and his heirs. For various reasons, moreover, land gained in value. The opening up of waste land and of alternative employment, and the slowness with which British laws came to be effective in practice in rural areas, may have masked what was happening, but it is clear that steadily the incentives for solidarity in land decreased and the advantages of separation grew. Family quarrels or opportunism thus led increasingly to the expression of the fragmentation of rights in terms of a sub-division of land. The development may even have been exaggerated because the poor were most vulnerable to the famines and epidemics which kept down the overall population, while those who had most land were most affected by a rising birth-rate and possibly an improved survival-rate: their cultural patterns, especially the age of marriage, still depended on the expectation of early death. Partitions may also have had debilitating effects, in the longer term, especially on productivity (though a debate turns on this question). None the less, however, the change may be seen as fitting with our general model: it is produced by a sufficient change in external conditions, and partition or fragmentation, however motivated, represent *responses* as much as did joint inheritance; this

13

observation does not depend on the resultant pattern of
land-holding continuing to be effective, though of course
effectiveness must be judged overall by the widest social
and economic criteria, and what seems detrimental inertia
for the many, in terms of the total economy or some moral
judgment, may well represent continuing advantage or the
minimising of disadvantage for the few, those able to
effect change.[10]

   That societies represent optimal compromises is not
to say that they result wholly or largely from rational
or utilitarian decisions, or indeed to imply any significant
degree of human control: often enough what is meant
is merely 'making the best of a bad job'. But the argument
is that the compromises will be sought and that they
will persist until conditions change. The stimulus for
such change may seem at times to be internal, coming from
an innovating farmer, for example, but general or significant
application of new methods or technology implies
an input whereby an idea is *brought in* and *taken up*.
If, as I argue, men are mostly content to imitate and are
not striving constantly to improve methods or even to
avoid effort then a catalyst is needed to prompt widespread
response to innovation: it may be leading individuals
who provide linkages to outside information or
resources, and by their own example demonstrate advantages;
or it may be the pressure of need, from some demographic,
climatic, economic, political or ideological
change which has altered the ground rules on which existing
practices were based. It does not seem to me fruitful
or possible to single out any one of these types of
change as prime mover in theory: for any significant
movement they are likely to appear in combination, and
their relative impact depends on the nature of the
society on which they impinge - concentration on connexion
rules out single causes or mono-directional
change. By the same token, moreover, while change may
be seen as resulting from some impetus, outside the
range of exchanges promoting continuity, it may not be
seen as necessarily induced by outsiders; it is arguably
more likely to result from reactions by insiders.
The point is merely that societies tend to reproduce and
not to reform themselves, but that it is difficult for
customs or attitudes to persist unchanged in an environment
in which they are disfunctional.

   There will be, however, an element of lag, differing
from society to society. In the short term customs may
show great and even enhanced resilience, and this may be
distinguished from persistence in the face of damage as a

result of, say, a preference for social over economic
goals. We approach what our discussions showed to be a
hotly contested issue, however, when we argue that
societies differ in their conservatism or adaptability.
One side of the argument, indeed, stresses objective
factors in such a way as to suggest that any cultural
emphasis is a crude reiteration of nineteenth-century
racial stereotypes. But let us, for the sake of argument, admit that there are differences between groups of
people in their aptitude for certain tasks: it is hard
to imagine that anyone will wish to adhere to the very
extreme position that no such differences exist. (Are
we to say, for example, that there will be no differences
in economic performance between a group whose ethic
favours agricultural labour and one which considers it
demeaning?) We might go even further and suggest that
the Indian social system, with its self-perpetuating and
self-regulating jatis, is peculiarly designed to ensure
continuities in social attitudes.[11] Let us, then, postulate the existence of, say, 'good' cultivators. It is
logically inescapable that equally 'good' cultivators
will perform equally well in any given conditions; in
such a theoretical case objective, physical factors will
be the sole determinants of relative success. We must
ask, however, not only whether all cultivators are
equally good, but, given the social, political and economic structure of different regions, whether equally
good performers are everywhere equally well-placed to
perform. In Bihar, for example, it might be said that
strategic agricultural decisions generally lay with
those who were, culturally, least well-disposed to
direct involvement with agriculture, and that therefore
while a Bihari Kurmi, say, might be thoroughly a match
for a Punjabi Jat, in industry, competence and enterprise, he was less able to increase his productivity and
profit, and unable to effect improvements regionally.
Thus I would not argue against the importance of objective factors, and might well accept that the social
system and mores of dominant groups in Bihar and Bengal
derive from long experience of surplus agriculture in a
fertile region, or, now that population growth has
removed this advantage, that the problems in the area
are due as Brass suggests to the objective difficulty
there of water-management.[12] But I would argue that
receptivity to change does depend very much on attitude
and aptitudes, and that these play a vital role in
economic performance.

The importance of external linkages may be said

therefore to rest on their role in development, but
more fundamentally on the extent to which they determine
or define the character of all societies. They illustrate, what is more, the tendency for substitution or
adaptation on the one hand, and the need for an appropriate match between input and receptivity on the other.
To examine the nature and function of linkages is,
indeed, to invite complex explanations. It was easy,
for example, to characterize the impact of European
rulers and traders on an India made up of self-sufficient communities: to open them up to the world was to
introduce qualitative change. But what of the communities found in the pages of this volume, communities
already bound up with the world, selecting among the
influences which impinge from time to time and reacting
with them? We are dealing with quantitative change
perhaps, or with adjustments, matters difficult to
interpret. This difficulty also is reflected in these
pages. Kooiman is inclined to accept that 'indigenous
agriculture' was at variance with and has submitted to
the exigencies of imperial rule and the world market;
but his account is open to a different interpretration
at several points about which he seems wary. He shows
that the mills were neither exactly capitalist nor
wholly an enclave in a 'traditional' economy, and therefore approaches the conclusion that what has emerged
today is a new amalgam and not the submergence of one
system by another. He sees the jobber as a capitalist
agent and as a form of labour organization continuous
with unionization; but equally the conclusions might be
drawn that the jobber was a means whereby villages dis-
tanced themselves from an industry in which they wished
to partake; and that the unionization to which he gave
his support was thereby different in character from
unionization elsewhere. Kooiman sees the villages as
being exploited by an industry which did not pay a family
wage, though the example of wages in Ahmedabad, with its
different pattern of labour, rightly makes him uneasy;
Pandey too quantifies contributions to some villages by
migrants: one might even try linking rural change to what
millworkers remitted home. Finally he treats the
workers' use of their wages and in particular their
indebtedness to the jobbers as examples of their being
disadvantaged by inclusion in an unfamiliar kind of
economy; but the example of Bird's Naikens suggests that
the use of debt as a currency may represent on the contrary the continuation of an economy that was familiar.
Similarly Pandey, the other writer who deals explicitly

with the question of imperial impact, is bound to be
somewhat equivocal in his assessment. He has to prove
not that weavers ceased to be independent and prosperous
for he knows they had long been dependent and poor, but
that they suffered a reduction in their circumstances.
He is led to conclude that they were left producing
coarser cloth and that this was less profitable to them;
he does not have the space to expand this point but of
course it is a difficult one to argue if we are talking
about weavers who were already on a subsistence level,
their profits being taken by intermediaries. Whether
cheaper goods are less profitable therefore depends not
just on establishing that they are produced with a
smaller margin of profit, allowing for the different cost
of materials and labour, or with a smaller quantity of
profit, allowing for the different scale of production
and consumption, but on establishing that the producers
themselves are able to enjoy less of the margin than
they did with the finer grades in the past. Profit is
not the same as value, to be sure; but how much more
difficult is our assessment when we know that the enjoy-
ment of profit by the producer is largely a matter of
status and politics because of the linkages within the
community and beyond it. By the same token the judgment
of any decline in an industry or in the economy as a
whole is fraught with difficulty: can we say that imports
or any of the other changes mentioned by Pandey - migration, subdivision or fragmentation of land, indebtedness
- are necessarily net depressors of the economy? They
are not as certainly as they were when we began with the
image of a stable, sealed community.

Milton Singer, in summarizing a symposium on occupational cultures, has concluded that a 'traditional'
system is not necessarily a major obstacle to modernization, though innovators may (only may) be deviants
from their culture; that modernization does not require
a 'modern' ethic; and that existing cultures may be displaced or adapted but not according to whether that culture is ascriptive or achievement-oriented, parochial or
cosmopolitan.[13] If the analysis in the present volume
does not make our way clearer through all questions, it
does help, it seems to me, with some, and in particular
perhaps the rather subtle, paradoxical and even ultimately verbal distinctions which Singer has made. His
views certainly differ from ours, but what is more
interesting perhaps is that he and his contributors also
appear to accept that the nature of a culture, apparently
in its specific features rather than in its normative

17

aspects, does influence its reaction to change, and that modernization depends upon the pre-existence of 'functionally-appropriate' cultures or flexibility in inappropriate ones. Thus Richard Fox argues that India was not inherently unprepared for capitalism but was only thought to be so because, in the nineteenth century, the British reduced a wide range of commercial activity to the level of the lowly bania, and because of what Fox considers a false Weberian dichotomy between commercial and industrial capitalism: industrialization may, according to this account, be induced *within* a 'bazar' economy and mentality.[14] But Fox, it appears on closer examination, is not denying the importance of appropriate culture, merely denying the necessary instrumentality of one culture, that of the Protestant ethic. How far do we agree? Certainly we seem to accept that there is more than one road to change and more than one kind of development. We conclude indeed that all cultures are 'appropriate', in the sense described, and, by implication at least, that development depends on the availability or adoption of goals which favour it. On the other hand, Neale's arguments can hardly be matched with Fox's speculation that the bania was merely the debased survivor of a more vital commercial life, for he had long performed necessary functions from his particular niche, and for that matter traders and money-lenders certainly remained differentiated in the nineteenth century even if not precisely as in the past. And to me it is improbable that different sets of cultural characteristics may be appropriate to a single kind of development, as might seem to be implied in Singer's conclusions. If it is agreed for the sake of argument that the Protestant ethic helped produce European-style industrial capitalism, then it is hard to argue that another radically different ethic will produce it also. (It might of course be argued that the ethic is irrelevant but that was not the point being made.) Where we seem to be at one, is in asserting that, given (as said) that there is more than one kind of development, then certainly some ways of increasing productivity, providing industrial labour, coping with a market economy, and so on, will be more suitable to some societies than others.

The idea of historical movement at different rates is akin to but less static than Braudel's idea of time: identifying the movement with external forces is, to my mind, a consequence of that model. The present discussion leads, therefore, if its conclusions are true, to the replacement of history's dialectic with dialogue.

In place of the supposed co-existence of different cultures, or of 'great' and 'little' traditions, or of opposed modes of production, we are left with a continuum through which the manner of exchange is all-important: this, it seems,is an external dimension which may not be quite the one with which we began but which is worthy of investigation.

We return to the assertion that it has tended to be assumed that the isolated Asian village provides a tabula rasa in a certain sense, in terms of trade and the input of ideas and technology, whereas it is of course already within a web of social and economic linkages and inter-actions. In development terms this is a conclusion of hope rather than despair: marry the appropriate input to local culture and conditions and, as in some of Shah's examples, prosperity will increase. Less optimistic, on the other hand, is the emphasis in these pages on the preference for substitution over transformation. It seems to me that this is strong evidence for the conclusion that cultural features are subsequent to but more resilient than ecological ones (if one separates them out for the sake of theory); or, to put it another way, for the existence of yet another distinction between internal and external - the external world of activities and production against the internal world of attitudes, hopes and, by extension, social customs. The former seem to change quite readily, but not the latter: cultural lag seems the ultimate conservative. Thus it is that practices may change within the mould of custom, as seen repeatedly in this volume, while the mould itself is rarely broken. Rather it decays. By this token, development must often be a slow process of attrition whereby those social features appropriate to change wear away those which are not. In a perfect world there would be sufficient wisdom, knowledge and resources to create environmental upheavals wherever they were necessary to neutralize cultural or ecological constraints on improvement. In reality prosperity seems attainable, in the short run, only by those fortunate in their physical, social or political conditions; they will not of course be the same people or regions for ever.

The objection which I am making, in terms of recent studies of rural Asia, is not just to the idealistic tradition which sees the peasantry as embodying values which the urbanized, industrial, individualistic modern world has lost (a line stretching from Rousseau, through German romantics and British jurists and Russian populists, to some of today's anthropologists).[15] It is

equally to the alternative view of the peasants as
apathetic, fatalistic and predisposed against change
(by contrast, implicitly or explicitly, with self-maxi-
mising economic man in his Western habitat). The
suggestion is that it is an error to treat the peasants
as a distinctive category apart from the rest of humanity
until disturbed by 'modernity'. There *is* a trend, a
third approach, which sees the peasantry as rational
decision-makers: it tends to replace 'they are less
advanced than ourselves' with 'they are just as mean-
natured as we are', and often implies that the fault
is not in themselves but in their stars, in their feudal,
imperialist or capitalist overlords. The arguments in
this book suggest, however, that, once we look at the
context, at rural societies' links with a wider world,
the peasantry may be found to have a common share of the
rational and the irrational, and all societies may be
seen to differ in ways specific to themselves, resulting
from the mix of cultural and physical conditions in which
they exist. We leave behind, therefore, the supposedly
inevitable consequences of isolation or subsistence, the
disabilities or advantages peculiar to a single genus,
rural Asiatic society. In the same way, and indeed in
order to achieve this perspective, we leave behind some
of the assumptions of our Euro-centric sciences: it is no
accident that, for example, Brass in his essay decries
not just inept or ignorant cultural explanations but also
Malthusian arguments which are used to justify inappropriate development strategies.

Robb, 'The external dimension in rural South Asia'

1. 1951; reprinted in Daniel Thorner, *The Shaping of Modern India* (Bombay etc. 1980).
2. Henry Maine, *Village-Communities in the East and West* (London 1871); also quoted in the third edition (1876) by Thorner, op.cit., p.263. It is true that Maine did argue that 'the stable part of our mental, moral and physical constitution is the larger part of it': see *Ancient Law* (London 1870), pp.116-17. I shall follow this line of argument below. But Maine also believed in a necessary evolution from joint to several property, from less to more 'civilized' societies, and it is to this belief that I refer here. See also Clive Dewey's Cambridge Ph.D. dissertation (1976).
3. Gilbert Etienne, 'Asia's Rural Development with special reference to India: the village and the outside world', paper presented to the conference on the external dimension in rural South Asia, SOAS 1980; see *Kurukshetra* (New Delhi, April 1979).
4. See Eric Stokes, *The Peasant and the Raj* (Cambridge 1978) pp.4-9.
5. Stokes; ibid., pp.265 ff.
6. See Peter Robb, 'British Rule and Indian "Improvement"', *Economic History Review* 2nd series, XXXIV, 4 (November 1981).
7. See for example H.C. Brookfield, *Colonialism, Development and Independence: the case of the Melanesian islands in the South Pacific* (Cambridge 1972).
8. J.S. Furnivall, *Netherlands India: a study of plural economy* (London 1939); J.H. Boeke,*Economics and Economic Policy of Dual Societies as exemplified by Indonesia* (New York 1953).
9. The argument here is not intended to be strictly functionalist and certainly not wholly quantitative. It is something of a compromise between the two extremes recently described by Lawrence Stone, between historical writing that is descriptive, focused on man and specifics, and that which is analytical, focussed on circumstances, collectivities and statistics. Stone suggests that many historians now believe the 'culture of the group, and even the will of the individual, are potentially at least as important causal agents of change as the impersonal forces of material output and demographic growth'. ('The Revival of Narrative', *Past and Present* 85, November 1979.) The conclusion

is not apt, it seems to me, for peasant studies. I
would argue that, for the changes which affect
peasants, the will of a single individual (amongst the
peasantry) is insignificant even 'potentially', whatever that means, while both the culture *and* the
material conditions are crucial, and also interdependent. Feelings or states of mind matter, but not more
than other factors, from which moreover they can hardly
be divorced. Perhaps we seek to understand the *personal* forces of material output and so on - which is
not far, surprisingly, from a dictum of Trevor-Roper's,
quoted with approval by Stone, that we should study
not circumstances (and, I would add, not man) but 'man
in circumstances'.

10. These questions are discussed further in the
companion volume (see the Preface, above), especially
by Neil Charlesworth.

11. I am indebted for this remark to James Manor.

12. See Stokes, op.cit. pp.228-242. The point of
course is that the answers (apathy, casteism) given
repeatedly to explain Bihar's impoverishment are not
really answers at all - they are repetitions of the
question - whereas answers may lie in ecological factors, probably compounded by political ones. A possible British government role is discussed in a paper
of mine in the companion volume and is generally
suggested by the comparative neglect of the region, in
terms of official expenditure; see Stephen Henningham,
*Peasant Movements in Colonial India. North Bihar 1917-
1942* (Canberra 1982), pp.16-35.

13. Milton Singer, ed., *Entrepreneurship and
Modernization of Occupational Cultures in South Asia*
(Duke University 1973), pp.13-15.

14. Richard G.Fox, 'Pariah Capitalism and Traditional Indian Merchants, Past and Present', in Singer,
op.cit.

15. See James C.Scott, *The Moral Economy of the
Peasant: rebellion and subsistence in Southeast Asia*
(New Haven 1976), in comparison with Samuel L. Popkin,
*The Rational Peasant: the political economy of rural
society in Vietnam* (Berkeley 1979), and the review of
both by Jonathan Lieberman in *New York Review of Books*
XXVIII, 16 (22 October 1981). In the present volume
only the paper by Pandey seems much influenced by such
sentiments: they led him to celebrate the weavers' sense
of 'community' (p.116) which he also described as lost
(p.114), and to add a moral gloss to the change in the
nature of migration which he discerns in his period.

THE PLANTATION SYSTEM AND VILLAGE STRUCTURE IN BRITISH CEYLON: INVOLUTION OR EVOLUTION?

Eric Meyer

A controversy has arisen in Ceylon since the 1930s regarding the impact of the plantation system upon the village ecology. The nationalist elite, with a view to attract the votes of the Kandyan peasantry enfranchised when the Donoughmore proposals were implemented in 1931, tried consistently to make out that the plantations had a very detrimental impact on the villages: the highlands were forcibly taken away after 1840 and the villages became hemmed in by the estates as a result; with the felling of forests, climatic changes occurred, water courses became irregular, paddy-fields silted up. At the same time, a foreign enslaved immigrant population (mainly low-caste Tamils) was forced into the midst of the native Kandyan population, a tool in the hands of the British imperialists.

The British tried their best to defend their policy, on the grounds of economic development which according to them benefited the whole population. Sir Hugh Clifford, the Governor in the late 1920s, argued the case in public, but the Land Commission nominated by him, though moderate in its conclusions, nevertheless blamed the plantations for the plight of the Kandyan peasantry and recommended that the spatial growth of the plantations be altogether stopped and that the trend be reversed, with a priority for peasant agriculture. Some of its recommendations were implemented before independence, with D.S. Senanayake as Agriculture Minister.

After independence, the controversy was revived in its academic and its political aspects as well. On the academic side, several reports in the 1950s tried to substantiate the thesis of a regression in the peasant section; but during the following decade, some Ceylonese historians (especially Michael Roberts and also Lal Jayawardene) exposed the weakness of the nationalist thesis and tried to minimize the extent of the ecological change in the subsistence economy; they insisted on the responsibility of population growth for stagnation, and suggested that in the alienation of the peasantry, the Ceylonese landed class played a major part.

The political issue was closely connected with the

23

twin question of the take-over by government of the
foreign-owned estates, and of the fate of the Indian
immigrant population. The Bandaranaikes' Sri Lanka
Freedom Party favoured an immediate take-over which it
eventually implemented in 1972 and 1975, in some measure
to take up the challenge of some of the young rebels of
1971 who went so far as to advocate the suppression of
the plantation sector and the expulsion of the immigrant
labourers. The policy of the present Jayawardene
government is to bridge the gap between the plantation
and the village, but the problem is far from being
solved, and the communal clashes of 1977 have rather
clouded the issue.

The aim of the present research is to ascertain
some historical facts at the local level. I have mainly
relied on the colonial records of the districts and of
the Land Settlement Department (in Ceylon, settlement
meant the delimitation of Crown and private property and
had nothing to do with taxation), and have supplemented
the archival information with the study on the spot of
some villages and plantations. I had to select a test-
district: Kegalla, on the boundary of the rubber, tea
and coconut areas, was found to be best suited for my
purpose, but as the Land Settlement Department was set
up too late to carry its activities there, I have extended the research to the Ratnapura and Kurunegala
districts which were major fields for settlement work.
The research is not completed and the following remarks
must be taken as hypotheses in the process of being
tested.[1]

The classic essay by Clifford Geertz on Indonesia
has paved the way for the study of colonial impact in
ecological terms.[2] But the relations between the plantation and the village in Sri Lanka are distinctly
different from those prevailing in Indonesia. According
to Geertz, two ecosystems existed side by side in this
region. In Java, paddy cultivation was predominant, and
the plantation system was forced into the paddy-cultivation cycles by the so-called culture system, which
compelled the peasants to grow by rotation on a fraction
of their lands a plantation crop, usually sugar, in lieu
of a land tax. (The indigo plantations in north Bihar
studied by J. Pouchepadass and by C.M. Fisher present an
interesting variant of the Java case.)[3] In outer Indonesia, especially Sumatra, the dominant ecosystem was
based on slash-and-burn cultivation of temporary fields,
and there the plantation structure was inserted as a
cyst in the available space without being integrated

as a rule into the peasant structure. In short, in
Java it was rather a matter of time-sharing or contest,
in Sumatra of space-sharing or contest. According to
Geertz, while the sugar economy forced the rice sector
of Java into a process of intensification without
modernization (called by him *involution*), the rubber and
tobacco plantations in the outer islands brought about
a development which extended by virtue of the spread
effect to the smaller producers.

But in the wet zone of Sri Lanka there existed a
single ecosystem combining the two types distinguished
by Geertz. Every village was, more or less, a minia-
ture Indonesia, with a rice-producing centre and a periphery of temporary fields. The plantation structure,
though it encroached on the periphery alone, affected
the system as a whole.

In fact, the typical pattern of land use in the hilly
wet zone was tripartite. The valley bottoms were with
few exceptions occupied by paddy-fields; they were surrounded by a belt of residential gardens permanently
cultivated with fruit-trees; and the gardens were themselves surrounded by an area made up of temporary fields
('chena' in Anglo-Sinhalese), of secondary forest (sometimes called *landu*) and in the remotest or highest
localities, of primeval forest (*mukulana*). The whole
'outfield' was included by the British in the ambiguous
category of 'waste land', though it played various
essential functions in the village ecology. The lands
farther from the paddy-fields were used as hunting
grounds, pastures, and for gathering wild fruit and
other forest produce like jaggery (obtained from the
kitul palm), creepers, fence sticks and the like. In
the chenas two different kinds of crops used to be
grown: after the first burn, the more fertile and wet
tracts could be cultivated with hill paddy (*el-wi*)
followed the second year with millets (*kurakkan*, *amu*),
while the less favoured areas were planted with millets
only; all were abandoned after two or three years for a
period of rest of seven to fifteen years according to
the local conditions.

The frontier between the garden belt and the chenas
was constantly moving on; the villager was a micro-
pioneer encroaching step by step, when required by population growth, on the temporary field area to convert it
into more or less permanent gardens; most chenas and
gardens bore the same name with a different suffix: for

25

example: Kitulgahawatte / Kitulgahahena (the garden /
the chena of the sugar palm tree). On the other hand
the frontier between the gardens and the paddy-fields
was much more rigid, the hill slopes being rather rarely
converted into paddy fields as compared with the situation prevailing in South East Asia (except in Uva and
along the main passes leading to the heart of the Kandyan country). [4]

The proportion between the outfield area and the
infield area was extremely variable. In some districts,
like Kurunegala, the colonial administration considered
as normal a ratio of three (chena) to one (paddy) and
settled high land on the villagers according to that
rule. But ratios as high as ten to one could be found
in poor villages, especially in the more hilly tracts of
Sabaragamuwa and of the border between Kurunegala and
Matale, where certain communities (notably the Vahumpura
caste) lived mainly on chena culture and forest resources. [5]

The social perception of this geographical pattern
was intense. The villagers viewed the paddy area as the
sphere of stability, security and legality; everybody
knew the limits, the ownership, the value of each plot.
A family would not as a rule alienate its paddy-fields,
but only mortgage them (*ukas*) or give them out to fellow
villagers on a sharecropping basis (*ande*) - two forms of
alienation of use without alienation of right which
were basically identical. [6] By comparison, the highlands were considered as the realm of mobility, of im-
precision, of casual activities, of enterprise, and also
of illegality (from the point of view of the authorities). There the arbitrary powers of the local leading
families (from which the headmen were drawn) had free
play, with little interference from the kings or the
colonial administration of the early days. One might
argue that the headmen as a class derived their wealth
from the paddy-fields and their authority from the
control they exerted over the margins of the village
territory.

In fact, chena cultivation was by no means a
secondary element in the village economy; in the dry
zone where paddy cultivation was highly unreliable it
was clearly the basic element. But even in the wet
zone, where the rains could be depended upon, it played
a major role. Chenas provided the flexibility necessary for the survival of the ecosystem; they helped in
some cases, to make good the loss of a poor paddy harvest; they could yield a surplus to provide for cere-

monial expenses. Moreover they acted as a safety
valve: they afforded means of subsistence to marginal
individuals (such as young couples not yet settled in
village life) or to marginal communities (such as
hunters, food gatherers, sugar-palm tappers).[7]

The legal status of the villages had some bearing
on the condition of access of the villagers to the
highlands; during the Kandyan period, and up to the
1830s, there were three categories of villages. The
koralegam, by far the most numerous, were also the
smallest as a rule; most were inhabited by the Goyigama caste (numerically and hierarchically dominant).
The villagers were recognized as having full ownership
of their fields and gardens. But after 1840 the
British Crown asserted, at least in principle, its
rights over the highlands, including the new gardens.
The villagers were supposed to pay a tithe when they
cultivated their chenas with *el-wi* (hill paddy), receipts were issued and a register (*wattoru* register)
was kept in the district office, and this came to be
considered as a register of title deeds in highlands
when the colonial administration began to check the
claims of the villagers especially after 1870. But as
no tax was paid on millets grown in chenas, the major
part of the outfield was not covered by the *wattorus*
and could be confiscated by the Crown.

The *gabadagam* (royal villages) disappeared as such
during the 1830s, but the Crown tried up to the end of
the century to assert its full ownership of the whole
of the highlands, the paddy-fields and old gardens
having been sold to villagers or headmen in the 1830s.
These large and well-populated villages were quite
often inhabited by peasants belonging to the Duraya
castes who had a low status and were deprived of any
control over the local power network which was entirely
in the hands of the Goyigama headmen.

The third category was more composite: it included
temple villages (*viharegam* and *devalegam*) and seigneurial villages (*nindagam*); their privileges were preser-
ved in theory, but after 1850, the investigations of
the Temple Land Commissioners and of the Service Tenure
Commissioners resulted in the contraction of the extent
of highland under the direct or indirect control of the
feudal aristocracy; while the peasants who used to
cultivate 'recognized' Temple or Ninda lands retained
their access to unrestricted chena cultivation, subject to the goodwill of the landlord, those who used
to chena 'rejected' Temple or Ninda lands (often Duraya

or Berava villagers) lost their security because they
had never paid any tax and could not establish any title
over their chenas.[8]

Invasion of the village territories

During the first phase of the plantation growth (circa
1840-1855) land for coffee was alienated according to a
process from which the Ceylonese were almost altogether
excluded.   The first areas to be absorbed were the
upper slopes of the highlands occupied by primeval
forest or pastures taken over by the Crown under the
Waste Land Ordinance of 1840. The planters selected a
tract suiting their needs; they filed an application,
then bought the land from the Crown at depressed prices;
quite often they occupied the land and felled the forest
before the purchase actually took place. The villagers
sometimes obstructed the surveyors or the planters, and
during the 1848 rebellion, which was not unconnected
with the off-hand behaviour of many up-country planters,
some estate buildings were burnt down. But the headmen
soon discovered that they could derive handsome profits
by countenancing the spread of the plantations, owing
to their position of middlemen between villagers, officials and planters and their traditional control over
the highlands. However the headmen were not the only
possible middlemen: at the same time, many low-country
Sinhalese and Muslim traders, carters and carpenters
came into the picture, and they gave a decisive impetus
to the spread of native coffee plantations.[9]
     Between 1855 and 1875, for want of sufficient
forest land, coffee planters began to make inroads in
the chena areas, and the roots of a conflict appeared
between the Crown, the planters and the Kandyan families who retained authority at the village or district
level. The appearance of a high land market heralded
the second phase of the plantation invasion. In the
Kandyan provinces, the grain tithe was often commuted
long before the compulsory commutation system was established in 1878. The headmen were usually responsible
for the assessment as well as the collection, so that
when a peasant was penniless or on bad terms with the
authorities, the headman combined to extort a mortgage
or a highland transfer in his favour. As soon as these
areas became valuable because of demand from the planters, these paper titles came to be eagerly sought after
by middlemen who bought undefined amounts of chena land
without at first taking possession.
     Meanwhile the colonial administration began to

realize that in the areas still untouched by the plantations, the extent to which chena cultivation was carried
on would impair the prospects of Crown land sales to
planters - a sizeable source of revenue. The district
Revenue Officers, especially in Kegalla, Kurunegala and
Matara, tried to check chena cultivation, often in a
ruthless manner: in the words of Fr. Saunders, then
Agent at Kegalla, 'this form of cultivation must be put
a stop to'. The new policy resulted in near-famine conditions, and after 1873 the authorities adopted a more
conciliatory position in a test region, the Three Korales (i.e. the southern half of Kegalla). A settlement
was first made according to the land registers (1873-
1879), but the difficulties of the task and the dissatis-
faction of many villagers led a new Agent, Ievers, to
evolve a scheme of block settlements: the highlands of
each village were partitioned in two blocks, one for the
Crown, the other for the villagers.[10]

A decisive turning-point occurred between 1880 and
1890, when the collapse of coffee ruined the British
planters and those villagers who had become more or less
dependent on the new product, while at the same time the
compulsory commutation of the grain tax (eventually
abolished in 1892) made the need for ready cash all the
more pressing. In Kegalla, the Crown lost no time in
selling its compact blocks to planters in search of new
land to experiment with tea, and the Three Korales became for a decade or two the scene of a dramatic speculative fever. The villagers were soon the prey of a
host of land-grabbers and sold out for paltry sums the
chena blocks shortly before settled on them; the planters, eager to extend their estates, hired the services
of land-hunters such as traders and tavern keepers in the
mushroom bazaars of the Kelani Valley, of low country
carpenters employed to build the factories and lines, of
headmen enticed by the prospect of bribes, and of petty
lawyers of Kegalla and Avissawella, outdoor proctors who
thrived on the land cases multiplied by the development
of the land market and the boundary disputes to which
the settlements gave rise. In spite of a fresh settlement made after 1890 to curb the massive alienation of
private chenas, it was too late to check a process started by the government policy itself and countenanced by
the chief headmen of the Three Korales, the Ratemahat-
mayas Ekneligoda and later Meedeniya.[11]

The same process of land-grabbing affected most of
the wet zone. In the up-country, especially Matale and
Uva, the land-grabbers were the European planters in

search of tea or cocoa land; in Kurunegala, their
example was followed by Ceylonese speculators anxious to
invest in coconut land; in Ratnapura and Kalutara, the
rubber boom created an extensive speculation after 1900;
and in the Matara district of the Southern Province,
trafficking in land became in the 1890s a prosperous
local industry carried out by Ceylonese from the coast
in collusion with the headmen of the interior. In the
strategy of land-grabbing, the contest for the appro-
priation of the value created by the intrusion of the
plantation system became especially eager when the
rubber and coconut booms followed the tea boom at the
turn of the century. Ceylonese planters as well as
European planters tried to buy land as cheaply as possible, because an extensive capital of cheap land was,
with the exploitation of cheap labour, the key to the
maximization of profit, especially in rubber which
could not pay within the first ten years of planting.
On the other side the colonial government after years
of laissez faire viewed with concern the near exhaus-
tion of the Crown lands in the wet zone and the threatening pauperization of the local peasantry. The middlemen were amassing enough capital to open their own
plantations and pose as respectable members of a growing
middle-class. Many Kandyan aristocratic families were
selling or leasing to planters their rights over the
highlands, with less and less regard to the needs of
their tenants and dependants.

The new Waste Lands Ordinance of 1897 and the subsequent establishment of a Land Settlement Department
were an attempt on the part of the colonial authorities
to check land speculation; the new policy took shape at
a period when European land-grabbing was practically
over and when Ceylonese land-grabbing was at its worst:
it was easier for government to take the side of the
poor peasant against the mischievous Ceylonese specu-
lator than against the powerful British planter. By
that time the rising Ceylonese elite had not a sufficient bargaining power to oppose the new policy. But
after 1915 the nationalist movement made it the target
of virulent attacks and the Ceylonese bourgeoisie pre-
tended in its turn to take the side of the peasantry
against the Land Settlement activities. The Land Commission reviewed the whole question, and according to
its recommendations, the territorial extension of plantation agriculture was definitively stopped and all
available land in the wet zone reserved for village
expansion: but such a conversion could not have taken

place had the Settlement Officers not saved thousands of acres from the clutches of land-grabbers, and had the Great Depression not killed the speculative fever of the 1920s.[12]

The disruptive impact on the village ecology

Wherever the villages have been hemmed in by plantations, the ancient agrarian regime has been shattered and a kind of ecological revolution has taken place. It is not yet possible, for want of local monographs, to assess the phenomenon island-wide, and the following remarks are limited to the Kegalla district.

The north of the district (the Four Korales) was well provided with paddy lands, but the commercial activity created by the Colombo-Kandy road and the heavy density of population led to the early disappearance of the self-sufficiency in rice (probably circa 1860). The south (the Three Korales), where human settlements were usually small and widely dispersed, was largely dependent on chena cultivation (especially hill paddy), but had small paddy fields as well; while in the north chenas were also universal.

The more sparsely-populated parts of the district were the first affected by the early settlements of the 1870s and '80s and by the subsequent development of the large tea and later rubber plantations. Most of the small villages of the Three Korales were taken in the storm of the large-scale land speculation, and reduced to their tiny paddy-fields and their narrow garden belts. Their demographic growth was not however stopped and very few cases of deserted villages are on record, while many such cases are to be found in Kurunegala at the northern fringe of the coconut areas; it appears that their inhabitants found alternative resources more or less related to the proximity of the plantations. In the more densely-populated parts, the growth of the plantations which occurred later (after 1900) did not affect the demographic growth, which continued at a rapid pace, but the restriction of the areas open to village expansion led to a dramatic overcrowding after one or two generations and subsequent unemployment. The localities where the villagers were able to take in their own hands their economic development were those where the absence of large plantations left the more enterprising free to convert their chenas into commercial crops (instead of subsistence gardens): Kinigoda Korale (northern-most of the Four Korales) is a typical case of such an evolution.[13]

31

The impact of the plantations on the village ecosystem is very complex. In the Kegalla district, the
silting of paddy fields was very extensive during the
first years of the opening of the plantations - tea in
the 1880s and 1840s in the Three Korales, rubber in the
1910s in Beligal Korale (the most western of the Four
Korales). Most of the small irrigation and drainage
channels on the border between the lower slopes of the
estates and the village paddy fields were temporarily
choked up. The only benefit for the cultivators was the
free provision of manure washed down with the silt. But
while in the nearby Kalutara district extensive areas
appear to have been abandoned, in Kegalla less than 50
acres went out of cultivation for good, and in most
cases these were paddy-fields already irregularly cultivated. The alleged drying up of springs is rather
difficult to prove; but so far as I have been able to
ascertain the facts at the micro-level, it seems frequently to have occurred in the areas where tea plantations came into direct contact with paddy-fields, and
to have been rarer where the villages kept their garden
belt intact, and where rubber plantations replaced the
chenas. (This consistent differentiation should be
tested over a much larger sample than mine.) I have
also met several cases of planters diverting water
courses for their factories (especially before 1900).
Another trouble frequently alluded to was the reduction
in the number of buffaloes resulting from the restriction of the grazing grounds in the highlands. Michael
Roberts has argued that for the coffee period no proof
can be produced of the responsibility of plantation
growth for the alleged retrogression of paddy techniques, and his main argument is that buffaloes were not
generally used in the Kandyan provinces: this might be
true of the terraced paddy-fields up-country, but does
not seem to have been the case in the numerous fields
in the bottom of the valleys in the Four Korales. In
general, the relation between the number of buffaloes
and the growth of plantations cannot be established on
a statistical basis.[14]
The only clear feature is the very frequent
occurrence of cattle trespass on estate land - a major
cause of ill-feeling between peasants and planters,
even if it had no serious consequences on paddy cultivation, which remains to be proved. The problems
resulting from the contact between the territory of the
village and that of the plantation were of a political
as well as economic nature. The villagers used to fence

their paddy-fields and to let their cattle graze freely
over the rest of the village area. When forests and
chenas were converted into estates, the animals continued to wander in their favourite areas which were not
enclosed as a rule, and developed a taste for young tea
leaves. Some plantation workers, especially beef-eater
Paraiyars, used to hunt the animals in the estate or
even to lift them in the villagers. These border incidents became the source of strained relations between
village headmen and planters; the peasants blamed the
planters for not enclosing their estates, while the
planters, resting on their western notion of property
and for some of them literally obsessed by agoraphobia,
resented as intolerable any presence of 'native elements
in British territory' (in the humourous words of W.E.
Davidson, a Civil Servant of that time); most of them
would not speak a word of Sinhalese (though they spoke
Tamil), many considered the village as a strange land,
the hotbed of lawlessness, where 'their' coolies were
led astray, attracted by illicit arrack and toddy
taverns and by gambling dens. Some of them got the
idea that the development of small village plantations
was in every case the result of the theft of seedlings
in their nurseries, and the planting lobby obtained from
the colonial authorities the. right to make use of cor-
poral punishment on the spot. Many superintendents
refused to let the villagers use footpaths and cattle
tracks across the estates, but they never scrupled to
widen their access roads to the detriment of the village
gardens; the peasants sometimes retaliated by closing
to the plantation workers the paths across the fields.[15]

When they were blamed for all these troubles, the
planters used to retort that the estates brought prosperity to the villagers, and that the traditional system of chenaing the highlands was no less damaging to
the fields. (The argument is not borne out by the
facts: chenas were almost never cultivated on the slopes
just above paddy fields, the peasants being careful to
reserve a garden or forest belt, and the very principle
of chena cultivation was to allow the rapid growth of a
secondary vegetal cover, while the practice of clean
weeding by the plantations led to the unavoidable
erosion of the slopes.) An Assistant Government Agent
of the 1920s, Hobday, epitomized the argument: 'After
all, it is the capitalist who makes good use of the
land, and the peasant who spoils it; the best off is
the man who supplements the small returns of his paddy
land and chena with good pay from a neighbouring

estate.'[16]

The major change in the village ecology lies in the almost complete disappearance of chena cultivation in the plantation areas between 1890 and 1930, while the pace of population growth accelerated: the traditional ecosystem lost its flexibility at the very moment when it became more necessary. The fact has been overlooked by most scholars who focused their attention on the paddy sector and did not take into account the vital part played by the highlands in the village economy (at least in Kegalla). But what is still more important is that such a revolution did not lead to a dramatic regression, nor to an involution on the Javanese lines. Some will argue that the chenas were not really essential after all. My own view is quite the opposite: the Kandyan villagers adapted themselves by looking for resources which provided flexibility similar to that of chena cultivation.[17]

Towards a new economic system

The opportunities were not the same everywhere. In some cases, the villagers were able to get full benefit from the change; in others they could not recoup their losses; but in most they had to build up a fragile equilibrium out of complementary resources.

In the areas where land sales by the Crown or the villagers themselves to outsiders had not been extensive, and where land speculation had not broken out, the more enterprising villagers converted their chenas into small plantations. The operations of land settlement were instrumental in this adaptation, provided that there was a ready market at hand for the sale of the products.

A detailed study of the peasant bidders at the 'sale and settlement' auctions at the beginning of this century would likely reveal that a process of 'kulakization' was on its way in such areas: only a fraction of the peasantry was able to seize the opportunity, and the difficulty of financing their purchase led these enterprising villagers to mortgage their lands to moneylenders, especially to Nattukottai Chettiars who were very active in the Kurunegala district (around Narammala, Kurunegala, in the hinterland of the coastal strip between Negombo and Madampe, and to a lesser extent in the Southern Province and the Kandyan highlands). This new class was not however strong enough to overcome economic crises: between 1880 and 1890, the great bulk of the village coffee gardens disappeared; and later thousands

of small coconut and rubber plantations which had
sprung up since 1910 were caught in the dramatic 1930s
depression.[18]

Kinigoda Korale, in the Kegalla district, provides
a typical case of such an evolution. One of the most
backward and unhealthy areas of the district, with a
high incidence of malaria, a majority of villagers belonging to the depressed Batagama and Vahumpura castes,
a heavy rate of crime (especially cattle stealing on
the border of the Kurunegala district, and homicide
resulting from drunkenness), it was entirely transformed at the turn of the century as the result of an
endogenous, indigenous development. External conditions were provided by the presence of the Colombo-
Kandy railway: a large slice on both sides of the line
was reserved for the fuel supply of the engines, so
that the government abstained from selling Crown land
till coal replaced wood; by that time, the new Land
Settlement policy was well established, and most of the
area, being free from the larger European plantations
and from the devestating activities of the Ceylonese
land-grabbers, could be settled on lesser Ceylonese
entrepreneurs and on villagers around 1910. At the
same time, the station at Rambukkana provided an ex-
cellent outlet for the local produce: a purely indigenous trade network sprang up around it, and Muslim
traders and Sinhalese merchants from the Karawa and
Batgama communities fought fierce battles for the control of the market. The villagers first converted
their chenas into banana, then into coconut plantations, with no other incentive than the demand; some
of them became rich enough to purchase at very high
prices the land put up by government 'for sale and
settlement'. But after 1910 the expansion of the small
plantations slowed down because it met its physical
limits, and banana cultivation was affected by the
'bunchy top' disease. A process of concentration
appeared, and Kinigoda was a vulnerable area, with a
heavy population pressure and signs of increasing
landlessness, when the Great Depression brought coconut
prices to an unremunerative level; several village
colonies were established for the landless after 1931
on the initiative of the local M.P. But when on the
top of the depression a severe drought took place in
1934, the area was the first and the worst affected by
the deadly malaria epidemic of 1934-1935.[19]

In other areas, the chenas were planted up by the
villagers with rubber (for example in the central part

35

of the Kegalla district) and even with tea (for example
in Kotmale, south of Kandy, and around Balangoda, east
of Ratnapura) when in the 1920s Ceylonese entrepreneurs
set up numerous bought-leaf factories. The extension
of these small-scale plantations can be gauged from the
returns of the Tea and Rubber Controller during the depression, and the diaries of the officials detailed for
the task.[20]

But in most cases, for want of space and of capital,
the loss of the chenas was not balanced by a sufficient
development of village-owned plantations, so that a complex economic system evolved, based on the diversification and the more or less casual nature of the resources
resulting from the presence of the plantation. The
village economy did not merge into the plantation economy, rather it borrowed from it what was necessary for
its survival, and this limited symbiosis came to be as
essential to the new village equilibrium as chena had
been in the ancient ecosystem. The system was and is
still based on three sources of income: paddy cultivation, in many cases involving the yearly rotation of a
plot between different members of the same lineage,
according to their position in the genealogy (*tattumaru*);
garden produce, quite often marketed, especially in those
areas where the Indian immigrant plantation workers were
numerous (the spectacular development of the Sunday markets after 1910 is largely the result of this tendency);
and last, casual or regular jobs directly or indirectly
provided by the estates, such as felling the jungle,
tapping rubber, weeding on contract, cutting timber,
even tea picking, and the whole range of activities
derived from coconut and its manifold uses.

The territorial extension of the rotation system
(Kalutara, Kegalle and Ratnapura are its main areas)
has never been satisfactorily explained. I venture to
suggest that this distribution has something to do with
that of hill paddy cultivation, and with that of rubber
which in most cases replaced hill paddy: lineal rotation
cannot be a workable proposition if there is no alternative resource for the coparcener who has access to the
paddy field only once in two, three or even more years.
Hill paddy was in the ancient system a good substitute
(much better than millets); imported rice purchased with
the earnings of casual labour replaced it in the new
system.[21]

The social impact

The social changes brought about in the villages by the

intrusion of the plantations are quite difficult to
ascertain, and the following remarks are an outline
derived from the study of Kegalla; detailed studies of
other areas are required before one can reach definite
conclusions at the national level.

At the district level, the structure of power does
not seem to have undergone such a radical transformation
as is often assumed. It is true that many leading families in the Kandyan areas were wiped out during the
nineteenth century, and that the control by the British
of the highlands, through the 1840 Ordinance and the
settlements effected by the Temple Land Commissioners,
deprived them of one of their traditional sources of
authority. In the Three Korales, the fate of the Eheliyagoda family is a case in point; the policy initiated
by F. Saunders (see above) checked the extensive felling
of forests by local villagers whence Eheliyagoda Dissawa,
the local chief, used to derive handsome profits in the
1860s (the timber was sold to Moratuwa carpenters or to
Colombo merchants). But if one leading family replaced
another, the system remained basically the same: though
a faithful servant of the British, and an outsider from
the neighbouring Ratnapura district, the chief headman
who succeeded Eheliyagoda, Ekneligoda, was eventually
dismissed because he was involved in underhand dealings
with the European planters and the Ceylonese landhunters
during the speculative fever of the 1880s in the Three
Korales. His successor, Meedeniya, who ended his career
with full honours, was a man of more humble birth who
owed his position to the protection of the local Revenue
Officers, but though he was appointed in the Three
Korales explicitly to clean up land matters, he was in
his turn involved in land speculations in the very
areas where the Eheliyagodas possessed villages. [22]

The immediate subordinates of these chief headmen,
the korales, who were all local men, usually got their
share of the spoils, because they had the knowledge of
the local situation (an essential requirement for the
success of the land-grabbing strategy). In spite of
several casualties usually attributable to the vicious
circle of drunkenness, indebtedness and crime, most
families overcame the trial.

At the village headman level, however, the establishment of the planters' raj over the highlands had
more serious consequences. Some of the headmen were
employed as middlemen by the planters and pocketed
commissions for each sale of land by villagers to estate
owners; others recruited village labour for the

plantations. But they were not powerful enough to
haggle with the planters like the chief headmen, they
could not speak English in most cases, and they were in
the hands of their superiors who could and did report
against them to the Revenue Officer with every chance
of being believed. Study of a small area south of
Kegalla reveals the contrasting fate of the two leading
families of adjoining villages. One tried to rely on
its traditional influence (it even possessed a small
seigneurial estate) in order to act as intermediary between the villagers and the planter. It entirely collapsed during the 1930s and left the district to take
up land in a dry zone colony intended for landless
villagers. The other family, though of an inferior
status, was able to reinforce its power and wealth. It
began by planting coconut or rubber on small plots often
bought at government sales, and then took over much
other land, including the major part of the other family's paddy-fields. As a next stage the family's sons
were educated in order to become clerks in the local
administration; they have now reached a level sufficient to send their brightest son abroad. Another has
become a successful local trader. Clearly it was more
profitable to emulate the planters than to traffic with
them.[23]

In the same village, the ordinary peasants seem to
have reacted to the intrusion of the plantation in different ways. In 1862, this small locality was inhabited,
apart from the leading family, by six lineages (four
Goyigama, one Batgama, one Berava). One hundred years
later, the same families are still there, with a few
newcomers: a group of Goyigama families related by
marriage to each other and to the original leading
family which has left the village, and including a son
of that family who came back a few years ago to live in
the crumbling dwelling of his ancestors and earns a
livelihood by cutting timber; a Goyigama lineage settled
in the outskirts of the territory, entirely landless
and dependent for work on the estate or outside the
village; two very poor Batgama landless nuclear families
with only casual employment as timber sawyers; and one
well-to-do Batgama group from the neighbouring village,
enriched by small plantations and minor jobs in the
government service, who have started buying land in the
village, including some originally belonging to the
leading Goyigama family. When the tea and rubber plantation was established in the 1900s, most of the families
sold their chenas through the leading family and also

through a well-known town proctor. The Berava lineage sold its paddy-fields as well and became dependent on estate employment at an early stage: most of its members became full-time estate workers while continuing to reside in the village, and they have rather improved their lot. The original Batgama lineage on the contrary has stuck to its fields, which are not sufficient for its subsistance but still provide a sizeable proportion of its resources. Of the Goyigama lineages, the smallest in 1882 has not multiplied locally; the largest was already marginal one hundred years ago, with tiny paddy-fields and extensive chenas: it has certainly suffered from the growth of the plantation which has arrested its spatial expansion, and the main resource of its present ten households is provided by estate employment; except for one member who has succeeded in getting access to the university, the group is impoverished as a whole and has lost a large slice of its lands to outsiders. The two other lineages have kept their paddy-fields, which are held under the rotation system and are quite insufficient as a result of population growth; but they have reacted in two opposite ways to the presence of the plantation: while one of them makes a point of not working on the estate (caste pride is among its motives) and tries to find urban jobs for its sons, the other is fully engaged in estate work and insists on its children learning Tamil. In the particular case of this village, the peasant response to the growth of the plantation appears far more complex than one might assume. For example, caste is a factor which certainly has an impact, but I am not sure that a clear-cut pattern will appear at the national level. In Kegalla, Kurunegala and Ratnapura, the lower castes seem to have been in a weaker position to withstand the land speculation activities, when their members were tenants of feudal lords or temples; but in other cases, as in Kinigoda or around Kadugannawa, the enterprise of some of their members enabled them to make the best of the opportunities offered by the new system, while many of them, undeterred by caste pride, may have improved their lot by salaried work which meant freedom from feudal dependence. [24]

In any case, the main beneficiaries of the new system were the middlemen and the investors, and most of them were outsiders from the low-country who had come to try their luck up-country, some during the coffee period, others at the turn of the century. The decisive role played by up-country enterprises in the growth of a

Ceylonese elite of low-country origin (Sinhalese as well as Muslim) has been clearly demonstrated and need not be discussed here.[25] I may add however that at the local level similar tendencies were at work in the small towns and roadside bazaars, and I suggest that the present emergence of the trading class is somehow related to small-scale land speculation during the first half of this century.

The settlement of very numerous Indian immigrant communities in the neighbourhood of most Kandyan villages is a social fact of the first magnitude in the history of the island. The history of the contact or non-contact between the immigrant and the native community is still in a large measure an unexplored field, for want of documentary evidence and of local monographs, while the inside history of the coolies begins to be better known.[26]

The reasons for the import of Tamil labour by the British coffee planters have been discussed elsewhere. The function of immigration was not only to ensure a sufficient number of labourers, but also to provide an uprooted labour force easy to control. In fact, the only serious objection raised by the planters against the employment of local villagers was that they refused to live in the lines and left the estate to look after their own interests when the occasion required; what planters called instability or indiscipline was just the refusal to be drawn into the 'new system of slavery'. But soon after the beginning of the tea boom and also during the rubber boom, the planters found that Indian labour was becoming scarce, more expensive, and more difficult to control. By that time the recruiters-cum-overseers had accumulated capital and an authority which enabled them to haggle with the planters over the supply of labour, while the new administrative requirements in the matter of social provision (health, and housing) increased the cost of labour. As many villagers by that time were looking for complementary resources, estate labour, especially rubber-tapping, became more popular. After decades of rather limited contact, villagers and planters began to need each other. In the larger tea and rubber estates where Indians were employed, the percentage of Sinhalese rose to ten per cent around 1930, and almost twenty-five per cent fifteen years later. Up-country the estates retained an overwhelming majority of immigrants and in the low-country coconut plantations local villagers predominated, but most mid-country estates, where rubber is the main product, often

in association with tea, evolved a socio-economic
pattern combining immigrant and villagers. There would
be a nucleus of resident immigrant labour, mainly Indian
but with some low-country Sinhalese, mostly from the
Matara district. At a periphery would be Kandyan Sinhalese commuting more or less regularly between the village
and the plantation; among these commuters were more than
the average of young people, of women, and of members of
the lower Kandyan castes: marginal they were in village
life, marginal they remained in the plantation structure.
But I maintain that their activity was nevertheless
essential to the equilibrium of the village, and in a
growing number of cases to that of the estate.

As far as the Kegalla district is concerned, it
appears that no serious social problem resulted from the
presence of numerous Tamil-speaking Hindus, with a majority of Untouchables among them, in the middle of Sinhalese Buddhist villagers with a Goyigama majority. It
might be argued that these relatively peaceful relations
were in fact not relations at all, or that local incidents remained unnoticed. This last argument is hardly
convincing: the Revenue Officers were quite sensitive in
the matter, and a comprehensive perusal of their diaries
(in the case of Kegalla) from the 1860s up to the 1930s
yields only a few cases.[27] When supplemented with the
meagre evidence collected from other diaries and published sources, they suggest that, up to the 1930s,
there was a cerain amount of antipathy and sporadic
incidents of very limited extent, but that the relations were far better than those between villagers and
Sinhalese workers of the plumbago mines or Coast Moor
merchants. The most common occurrences were of cattle
lifting and shooting on the part of the Indians, while
the coolies who had to pass through the villages (mes-
sengers, beef coolies and so on) were sometimes waylaid
and robbed of their gold earrings, or otherwise harassed.
In addition, the few Kandyans who came to reside in the
lines were regarded by the villagers with a kind of
joking contempt, so much so that to live in the plantation and to be a Tamil were considered as one and the
same thing: some of these Kandyans actually lost their
socio-cultural identity by conforming to the dominant
model, adopting Tamil names, customs and language.[28]

But if Goyigama-Tamil relations did not reach a
critical stage before the late 1930s, it was not because
there was no contact between the communities before
them. I have already mentioned the market relations
soon established between estate workers and the small

41

village producers ready to sell them fruits, vegetables
and drinks: coolies were supplied only with rice by
their masters (except in the larger estates where shops
were opened and workers sometimes allowed a small garden
plot), and they used to barter a portion of it against
materials for curry. When 'bolting' became more common
after 1900, many indebted fugitive coolies found shelter
with the villagers or the shopkeepers of the roadside
bazaars and became regularly employed on the small
native plantations, where their skills were much appreciated.[29]

However, social relations remained limited, and
intermarriage extremely rare, except in the province of
Uva (this curious anomaly should be investigated in
depth). But endogamy was in the nature of the prevailing caste system, and had never prevented caste groups
from integrating themselves as a body in the Sinhalese
social structure. It was not the first time that
Indians had been established in the midst of the Sinhalese areas of the island; the case of the Karawa fisher-
men is well known, but two other examples are more
relevant to our point. The Salagama caste, originally
a South Indian community of weavers, was systematically
employed by the Portuguese and the Dutch to peel cinna-
mon, then the major export product of Ceylon, under a
system of compulsory delivery which amounted in fact to
compulsory labour. And, in the Sinhalese kingdoms,
numerous groups were attracted from India by the kings
and landlords to serve as 'soldiers and husbandmen',
with the status of bondsmen; these immigrants came to
be known collectively under the name of Durayas, and
even if they were placed at the bottom of the hierarchy,
they were fully accommodated within Sinhalese society
(many kings and landlords were themselves of more or
less recent Tamil origin). But under British rule, for
the first time in the history of Ceylon, the integration
process was altogether arrested. As in other countries,
the reason for segregation may be found in the plantation system itself, in which direct control of production
was based on absolute control of the worker, which under
British superintendents was much more effective than any
control which had been exercised in the royal or feudal
villages over low-caste bondsmen. The planters wanted
a submissive, punctual, amenable labour force; they
therefore tried consistently to shut it up in the estate
and encouraged in every respect its traditionalism,
according to the general pattern in force in most of the
planting and mining areas of the colonies. It is for

example symptomatic that, in spite of the facilities
given to missionaries in the island, no large-scale
attempt was made to convert the coolies. Another feature of plantation life helped to maintain the separate-
ness of the immigrant community: when tea replaced
coffee, women came to be employed in equal if not superior numbers to men, with the result that immigration
became a family affair and that the sex-ratio of the
community made endogamy a matter of course. A last
significant factor lies in the suddenness and size of
the migratory movement, which was quite different from
the earlier small-scale immigration, and which led to
the concentration of a critical mass preventing amalga-
mation with Sinhalese society.[30]

A turning-point in the relations between immigrants
and villagers was reached between 1930 and 1940, the
result of outside influences. Among them, the first
place must be given to the general tendency to communal-
ism (affecting caste relations as well) following the
granting of universal franchise and limited self-rule
under the Donoughmore constitution. Although only a
fraction of the Indians was enfranchised, Sinhalese
politicians began to view them as potential allies of
the colonial power, and some found that they could make
use of the age-long resentment of the Kandyans against
the take-over of their highlands by the planters, and of
the contempt in which they held the Tamils. Both aspects were merged into a queer image portraying immigrant coolies as the agents of British imperialism.
But other less-known factors were at work, and three of
them should be mentioned here. One is the role played
by enriched Tamil overseers in some areas, notably Uva,
where they began to lend money to Kandyans and to buy
village land as well as existing estates; the trend
should not be overestimated, but it was enough to arouse
the bitterness of the Kandyans. [31] Another is the
attempt on the part of government and of some planters
to increase the intake of Sinhalese labourers on
estates. Incidents worsened when, in the face of growing discontent among Tamil workers, linked with the
unsettled conditions brought about by the Great Depression and the subsequent rise of trade unionism, certain
superintendents tried to employ Sinhalese workers as
black-legs. On the top of it, the stoppage by India,
for political reasons, of the free migration between the
two countries, precipitated strikes on an unprecedented
scale in 1940.[32] Another cause of dispute was the purchase by the government of estate land on which to

settle landless villagers, especially in Kegalla: it
happened that the Tamil workers were ruthlessly
evicted when they tried to resist.[33]

What happened next is well-known: after independence, most of the immigrants became stateless, and in
1964 a 'repatriation scheme' was set up; the nationalization of the larger estates in 1972 and 1975 accelerated
the pace of emigration, and the bloody pogroms which
occurred immediately before and after the 1977 elections
on several estates created a panic, especially in mid
and low-country estates. The resulting desertion of
many plantations by the Tamils is perceived by some
Kandyan villagers as a kind of social decolonization,
while the official policy of integration betwen village
and plantation provides a certain number of jobs,
usually distributed on the basis of political recommendations. However, a nucleus of workers of Indian
origin is likely to remain in the larger estates, and
they are to be given Ceylonese citizenship. How these
will merge into Ceylonese society is another question,
the issue being clouded by the increasingly tense relations between the Jaffna Tamils and the Sinhalese. But
at the local level, in the particular area where I have
carried out my observations, anti-Indian feeling appears
to be a product imported from the towns and bazaars,
whence came the rowdies who killed and burnt in 1977.
The local Kandyan villagers and Tamil estate workers
get on rather well in the estate or the shops.[34]

Involution or evolution?

The impact of the plantation system on village structure
in British Ceylon cannot be characterized as an involution on the Javanese lines. The paddy sector never
revealed the labour-absorbing capacity ascribed to it
by Geertz, nor have the two sectors operated like water-
tight compartments as assumed by the champions of the
dualistic theories first developed by Boeke in his analysis of the Javanese economy.[35]

After a traumatic phase which revolutionized the
ancient ecological regime, the village sector and the
plantation sector came to depend upon each other. The
absence of duality was revealed during the depression
years of the 1880s and the 1930s, when the so-called
village sector was affected by the drying-up of the
whole range of marginal resources drawn from the plantation sector. One might even argue that the very elas-
ticity of the village economic structure was ensured by
what the village could borrow from the plantation system.

The difference between Ceylon and Java may be
explained by the fact that in the ancient regime, elas-
ticity was already marginally ensured by the peripheral
extension of chena cultivation and not by the intensification of paddy cultivation at the centre. When space
ran short as a result of the simultaneous growth of the
plantation-controlled areas and of village population,
the peasants did not rely on the intensification of
paddy cultivation to make good the loss of their lebens-
raum. At this crucial stage, several other factors may
have operated. Paddy cultivation was certainly depressed by the plantation system: ecologically (through
silting for example) and moreover economically. On the
labour side, the attraction of wages in cash diverted a
substantial number of peasants, especially the young,
from paddy cultivation usually paid for in kind. On the
income side, the massive imports of Indian and Burmese
rice by the planters to keep down their labour costs,
depressed the price of local paddy and made it unremunerative for the Ceylonese peasants. They were altogether
kept out of the market, which was entirely controlled by
Indian traders. The dispersion of ownership in paddy
land and the large extension of the sharecropping system
may have been contributing factors: the only two districts which exported a notable rice surplus, Hambantota
and Batticaloa, were quite outside the plantation area;
but they were also those where property was more concentrated. While in other respects the village economy
experienced an evolution, a fragile development jeopar-
dized during each depression, in the paddy sector there
was stagnation; but not 'involution'. The only similarity with the Java case lies in the complication of the
system of land tenure so as to preserve the access of
almost every villager to paddy cultivation, often viewed
as a criterion of village citizenship; but Geertz may
well be wrong when he consistently associates in his
concept of involution complication and intensification.
        The case of Burma as analysed by Michael Adas pre-
sents some similarities with that of Ceylon, in so far
as in both countries there was an indigenous development
in the commercial sector, which was ultimately jeopar-
dized by the impact of the Great Depression and the
collapse of the British imperial economic system. [36]
But the great difference between Ceylon and Burma lies
in the fact that the rice frontier in the Irrawaddy
delta could progress unhindered by a foreign body; and
also that paddy technology was familiar to the Burmese
peasant and that this export commodity was at the same

time a food staple. In Ceylon on the contrary, out of
the three main agricultural exports, only coconut was a
traditional food product, and it was coconut indeed
which represented the main field for indigenous expansion. As regards rubber and tea, village expansion was
in competition with estate expansion, the latter being
better equipped to overcome market depressions. In
these respects, the external constraints prevailing in
the wet zone of Ceylon appeared less favourable to indigenous development than in Burma. I cannot follow N.
Shanmugaratnam, the author of a recent paper on the
subject, when he describes 'the peasant cultivating tea
or rubber [as] an anachronism, a relic in the new world
of estates'. Such a peasant was a product of this new
world and was able, during the periods of prosperity and
where the larger estates left him room for expansion, to
make the most of his situation. Between 1922 and 1934,
the acreage of rubber holdings of less then ten acres
doubled; they accounted for 21.6 per cent of the planted
area in 1934 against 13.8 per cent in 1922. The growth
of the largest estates (those of more than fifty acres)
was much slower (twelve per cent) and their share of the
total area actually diminished from 67 to 57 per cent.[37]
But, as in other countries, the small producer in Ceylon
was wholly dependent on a structure and on a market over
which he had no control: in the 1920s, the expansion of
small-scale production progressed out of proportion with
demand in all the Asian producing countries, and became
a powerful if not decisive factor in the subsequent depression. At the same time, at the local level the non-
peasant owners of small estates were growing in numbers
and left little chance to the genuine kulak. In that
historical context, I agree with Shanmugaratnam that it
was impossible even for the peasant cultivating tea or
rubber to become a 'dynamic small-scale capitalist' farmer, because, all things considered 'the plantation system did not permit the evolution' of such a class 'from
the ranks of the peasantry'.[38]

Meyer, 'The plantation system and village structure in
British Ceylon: involution or evolution?'

Abbreviations

AGA Ke   Diary of the Assistant Government Agent
         Kegalla (SNLA lot 30)

ASO   Diary of the Assistant Settlement Officer
         (LSDR)

CO   Colonial Office Records

LSDR   Land Settlement Department Records, Colombo

SLNA   Sri Lanka National Archives

SO   Diary of the Settlement Officer (LSDR)

The paper is based on research in the SNLA and LSDR,
with some information derived from the British colonial
archives, Public Record Office, series CO54. A small
portion of the local records is still retained in the
district offices; I have explored those of Kegalla. I
have also carried out a study of a small area in that
district, especially a village that we shall call
'Hallinda'. The section of this paper concerning the
period 1925-39 is developed in Eric Meyer, 'Dépression
et malaria à Sri Lanka, 1925-1939: l'impact de la crise
économique des années 1930 sur une société rurale dépen-
dante', Doctorat Ecole des Hautes Etudes en Sciences
Sociales, Paris 1980.

   1. For the historical background, see K.M. De Silva
ed., *History of Ceylon*, vol III (Peradeniya, Sri Lanka
1973) especially pp.89-164. I. van den Driesen, 'Plantation Agriculture and Land Sales Policy in Ceylon, the
first phase, 1836-1886', *University of Ceylon Review* XIV
(1956) pp.6-25 and XV (1957) pp.36-52 inclines towards
the nationalist thesis, which is assumed in the *Report
of the Kandyan Peasantry Commission* (Ceylon Sessional
Paper 18 of 1951) and in N.K. Sarkar and L. Tambiah,
The Disintegrating Village (Peradeniya, U. of Ceylon
1957). L.R.U. Jayawardena, 'The Supply of Sinhalese
Labour to Ceylon Plantations, 1830-1930 (Cambridge Ph.D.
1963), Michael Roberts, 'Some Aspects of Social and
Economic Policy in Ceylon 1840-1871' (Oxford, D.Phil
1965) and 'The Impact of the Waste Lands Legislation and
the Growth of Plantations on the Techniques of Paddy

Cultivation in British Ceylon, a critique', *Modern Ceylon Studies* I (1970) pp.157-98, are strongly critical of the nationalist point of view. The colonial policy is defended in Sir H.Clifford 'Some Reflections on the Ceylon Land Question', *Tropical Agriculturist* LXVIII (1927) pp.283-307. N. Shanmugaratnam, 'Impact of Plantation Economy and Colonial Policy on Sri Lanka Peasantry', *Economic and Political Weekly*, XVI, 3 (Bombay, 17 January 1981) is interesting for its systematic Marxist approach, but from the historical point of view, it lacks first-hand data. See also note 38 below.

2. Clifford Geertz, *Agricultural Involution: The process of ecological change in Indonesia* (Berkeley and Los Angeles 1963).

3. J. Pouchepadass, 'Planteurs et paysans du Bihar, 1860-1920' (Paris, Doctorat Ecole des Hautes Etudes en Sciences Sociales 1978), and Colin M.Fisher, 'Planters and Peasants: The ecological context of agrarian unrest on the indigo plantations of North Bihar' in Clive Dewey and A.G. Hopkins, *The Imperial Impact* (London 1978) pp. 114-31.

4. On the ancient village ecology in Ceylon wet zone, see R.Pieris, *Sinhalese Social Organization, the Kandyan period* (Colombo 1956) and H.W. Codrington, *Ancient Land Tenure and Revenue in Ceylon* (Colombo 1938). On chena cultivation, there is a very extensive documentation in the colonial records, which cannot be cited here in full; its techniques are best described for Kegalla in the Diaries and Administration Reports of the Assistant Government Agents (see especially AGA KE 14 August 1884) and its importance can be measured by the recourse to the original findings of the AGAs and Forest Settlement Officers (especially Ievers and L.W. Booth) kept in the Kegalla office, which I am exploiting village by village. At the island level, there is a wealth of information in the P.R.O. (especially CO 54/345, for 1859 and previous years), in the Administration Reports of the Central Provinces and of Kegalla, Ratnapura and Kurunegala districts before 1880 (those for the years before 1868 are among the most interesting, for example Sabaragamuwa 1864, but are not printed as such: they may be found as appendices to the Reports on the Blue Books sent to London and printed as British Parliamentary Papers, or in a manuscript form in the CO 54 series). See also the Ceylon Sessional Paper XV of 1873. The diaries and final village reports of the Land Settlement Officers, after 1898, are also very suggestive; among countless references see for example SO 21 November

1900 and 20 November 1901, concerning the Morawak korale of Matara district.
    5. On the proportion between 'infield' and 'out-
field' see Pieris, op.cit. p.48; AGA Ke February 1884;
Administration Report Kegalla 1868, p.32 ff. Jaggery
making was widely practised by the Vahumpura caste but
not only by them; see CO 54/746, enclosure to despatch
756, 21 December 1911; ASO Rasaretnam, January 1933
(Kurunegala district); AGA Ke, January 1861, 16 June
1892. For Ratnapura district (a very large village,
Bambarabotuwa, surveyed at the end of the 19th century)
see Frederic Lewis, *Sixty Four Years in Ceylon* (Colombo
1926).
    6. The sociology of paddy versus chena cultivation
in the dry zone has been recently analysed by James Brow,
Vedda Villages of Anuradhapura (Seattle 1978), p.104ff.
On *ande-ukas* systems of land tenure, see G. Obeyesekere,
Land Tenure in Village Ceylon (Cambridge 1967). My view
is mainly based on Kegalla settlement village cases, and
the Certificates of Quiet Possession files of Kegalla
(SLNA lot 30); see also note 22 below.
    7. Most authors hold that chena cultivation, at
least in the wet zone, is marginal and unessential
(Jayawardena, op.cit.; Roberts 1970, op.cit.). I main-
tain that in the wet zone (1) many hilly villages were
mainly dependent on chena, and (2) in the valley it was
marginal, but still essential. Most villages in the
Three Korales fall in category (1), and most in the Four
Korales in category (2). See AGA Ke 15 December 1864,
SLNA 30/449 and 59/1352 (C.Q.P. Wattagedara file), 59/958
(Kelani Forest Reserve File), CO54/635 (Stanmore to Sel-
bourne, 16 January 1897), and references in note 4 above.
    8. On the legal status of Kandyan villages, see
R. Pieris, op.cit., and Sir J D'Oyly, *A Sketch of the
Constitution of the Kandyan Kingdom* (Colombo 1929): this
text is perhaps based on documents collected by Molli-
goda Adigar ca. 1820, see CO54/137 folio 367-9. On
gabadagam lands, see findings of the Forest Settlement
Officer (L.W. Booth), on village Dorawaka, Kegalla district records (another copy in LSDR). On chena cultivation in feudal villages, see Administration Report of
the Service Tenures Commissioner 1870, p.286 (J.F. Dick-
son). Many cases of exploitative relations are recorded
(in Kegalla, the case of Ratwatte Basnayake Nilame: AGA
Ke 20 June 1895 ff.). The bonded community here called
Duraya is in fact a very complex group of castes (Padu/
Batgam, Panna, Velli), never appropriately described by
anthropologists; Bryce Ryan's classic *Caste in Modern*

Ceylon (New Brunswick 1953) is very defective about
them. J. Jiggins, *Caste and Family in the Politics of
the Sinhalese* (Cambridge 1979) emphasizes their importance, but often uses imprecise or unverifiable and unfortunately not historical data. A.C. Lawrie, *A Gazetteer of the Central Province of Ceylon* (Colombo 1897) is
useful. Much historical evidence is scattered in district records or local lore.

9. Van den Driesen, op.cit.; A.C.L. Ameer Ali,
'Peasant Coffee in Ceylon during the XIXth century',
Ceylon Journal of Historical and Social Studies n.s.
II (1972) pp.50-9. The earliest case of village land
sale is in Gampola (G. Bird's estate); see CO 416/3
(A.22). For villagers' attitudes see CO 54/261 (despatch of 5 December 1849), CO 54/196 (desp. 18 April
1842); P.D. Millie, *Thirty Years Ago, or Reminiscences
of the early days of coffee planting in Ceylon* (Colombo
1878) ch.XX; and British Parliamentary Papers, Reports
from the Committees, vol.XII (1850) 5 June 1849 s.3185
(evidence of George Ackland on the 1848 rebellion). The
headmen's role is clear in CO 54/282 (despatch of 5
December 1851 no.191, enclosure no.4, G.A., Kandy, to
Colonial Secretary, 16 November 1951); also CO 54/237
(despatch no.54 of 17 July 1847), and in several in-
stances in Kegalla: AGA Ke 2 November 1854, 2 October
1859, 8 January 1860, 7 September 1861.

10. For Saunders see AGA Ke 1 October 1864, and
also AGA Ke for 1864 and 1865. On famine see Administration Report, Matara district, 1868, p.233; for the
restriction of chena cultivation: Administration Report,
Ratnapura district, 1868, pp.18-22. See K.M. De Silva
(ed.), op.cit., p.130, on early chena settlements in
Kegalla. A detailed study of my own is forthcoming.

11. See note 10, and SLNA 59/178 (land sales by
villagers) and Certificate of Quiet Possession files in
Kegalla (SLNA lot 30, especially the cases of Udabage
30/574 and Padugama 30/495 which show the conflict of
interest between the Crown, the planters, the speculators and the peasants.) Also SLNA 45/1867.

12. On land speculation and land policy up to 1930,
see the very stimulating analysis of L.R.U. Jayawardena,
op.cit.; LSDR, partially exploited in ibid. and mainly on
Matara, Kurunegala and Ratnapura; and SLNA 59/178 (for
Kegalla, Uva, Matale and Kurunegala). The last areas to
to 'opened' for rubber, and where land-grabbing reached
phenomenal proportions, were the Kukul korale of the
Ratnapura district and the Kelerata (S.E. corner of
Kegalla).

13. On deserted villages in the North Western
Province, see Administration Report, Puttalam district,
1928, p. F.16; ASO Fox 3 March 1906; ASO Bassett 12 June
1929; ASO Seneviratne 4 January 1933. In Kegalla, there
are several cases of villages encircled by estates as
early as the 1880s (for example AGA Ke 9 April 1884, 18
March 1885), but only one blatant case of a plantation
destroying a village (Dabar Estate in the Kelerata): AGA
Ke 10 April 1931, SO 18 January 1930, and Land Commissioner Department Records, Colombo, file L.212).
14. On the ecological impact, see Michael Roberts,
op.cit. 1970, which I cannot discuss in detail here. He
argues that the effects of the contraction of pasture
have been exaggerated, but this is not supported by many
statements he cites himself (see also AGA Ke 13 May
1854); the idea *was* a contemporary common-place and
cannot be proved. Nor can the climatic changes brought
about by deforestation (see Millie, op.cit, ch.II, and
J.E. Tennent, *Ceylon*,II, p.206). But the silting of
paddy fields is too often reported to be easily dismissed. There are repeated references (I have at least
80 between November 1872 and July 1938) in AGA Ke, and
others may be found elsewhere, for example in Administration Reports: Matara 1927, p.C.23('a whole valley
permanently ruined in Morawak'), Ratnapura 1926, p.I.9,
and 1933, p.I.7, Kandy 1926. See also Ceylon Sessional
Papers IV and XIV, 1890 (Kalutara district seems to have
been the worst affected); SO October 1933, ASO Hunter,
March 1928, ASO Egan 11 April 1927, ASO Rajasingham
October 1933. In these cases rubber was planted on
paddy-fields; in other cases, notably near Dandagamuwa,
Kurunegala district, it was coconut: ASO Luddington,
February 1927. For a general view of the question,
Ceylon Sessional Paper III of 1931 (Soil Erosion
Committee). In AGA Ke, the most numerous cases gather
round the dates of tea and rubber estate opening, and
round 1930 when the problem attracted public attention.
15. On cattle trespass, see J. Capper, *Old Ceylon*
(London 1878), p.143; *Days of Old, or the Commencement
of the Coffee Enterprise in Ceylon, by an Old Planter*
(Colombo 1878), p.14; Report of the Committee on Cattle
Trespass (Colombo 1853), CO 54/309. Among references
from Kegalla are AGA Ke 21 February and 11 November
1885, 21 February 1886, 20 August 1890, 4 February 1900,
10 March 1902, 15 November 1914, 14 September 1916 and
SLNA 6/10990 (Petition included in G.A. Sabaragamuwa to
Colonial Secretary, 18 October 1897. W.E. Davidson (AGA
Ke 16 March 1891) was certainly the most perceptive and

able Agent in Kegalla; he later became Governor of the
Seychelles, Newfoundland and New South Wales. On border
incidents, right-of-way problems and tense planter-
villager relations see AGA Ke July and August 1884, 3
July 1885, 11 July 1891, 10 September and 8 December
1892, 2 May 1898, 29 October 1910, 30 July 1914, 1 June
1916, 17 February 1917, 28 September 1931; concerning
more precisely 'Hallinda' estate, AGA Ke 8 June 1925, 20
June 1929 and 27 October 1936, confirmed by local tradition (1979). In Kegalla, the anti-Muslim riots of 1915
were followed by the shooting of low-country Sinhalese
shopkeepers and a Kandyan headman by the European
militia which included many planters: the violence seems
related to the earlier tension.

16. SLNA L 62/1928 (Reports of the Revenue Officers
on the third interim report of the Land Commission -
Report by the AGA for Kegalla, Hobday). For a similar
analysis, see Administration Report, Matara, 1928, p. C.
34, S.157, and SLNA 59/1074 (J. Malcolmson to the Governor
of Ceylon, 10 August 1904).

17. Here I agree with Michael Roberts, op.cit.
(1970), pp.181-2, on the 'modification in the economy'
but I am sceptical that diversification 'may even be
considered an improvement'.

18. On villagers' purchases of Crown land, LSDR are
very full (and as yet unexploited). Patrick Peebles,
'The Transformation of a Colonial Elite, the Mudaliyars
of XIXth century Ceylon' (Ph.D. Chicago 1973) is very
interesting on the low country headmen. On kulaks and
land settlement see SO October 1903 and 20 December 1904,
SLNA 59/1684A (Report by SO Fox, 1 July 1906). Land for
plantain and coconut was purchased by some villagers at
more than 200 rupees an acre (AGA Ke 20 May 1899, 8 May
1903, 24 July 1906, 9 August 1907, 8 May 1908 etc.).
But indebtedness and the sources of money are easier to
imagine than to study; SOs in 1930s show that peasants
could not purchase Crown land even at reduced prices (cf.
ASO Sandys June 1930, ASO Rasaretnam December 1932), and
numerous judicial sales especially in Kurunegala district. It is hard to distinguish between peasant and
non-resident small owners among debtors, but I conclude
that the Nattukottai Chettiar are responsible for a very
large proportion of sales in the North-Western and Central provinces, especially early in the depression;
their role in expropriation should not be overestimated
in spite of contemporary anti-Indian propaganda. Later,
and also in areas where the Chettiars were not numerous,
small sums were almost invariable lent by well-to-do

Sinhalese: the expropriation of the peasantry probably
benefited the new petite bourgeoisie from which the present *mudalai* (trading) class is partly drawn. For a
fuller discussion see my thesis, and its appendices,
especially the interview with N.H. Keerthiratne of Rambukkana (1978).

19. On Kinigoda korale, see the Final Village
Reports of the area settled along the railway (LS R),
diaries of F. Lewis and L.D.C. Hugues (ASOs in the 1910s
and 1920s), AGA Ke, especially 17 November 1904, 21
September 1905, 21 April 1907, 24 August 1910. For
peasant settlement schemes of Wijeyeratne, see AGA Ke
5 September to 30 May 1931, interviews with Tissa
Wijeyeratne (1977-8) and N.H. Keerthiratne, whose
father was one of the most successful entrepreneurs of
Kinigoda (1978). On malaria, see my thesis, part III.

20. Administration Reports of the Rubber Controller
and Administration Reports of the Tea Controller, especially 1938. See also Administration Report of the eee
Registrar of Cooperative Societies 1933, ASO, Aluvihare
4 April 1930, Administration Report, Nuwara Eliya, 1925,
p.B.27-8.

21. Obeyesekere, op.cit.; M.P. Moore and G. Wickre-
masinghe, *Thattumaru, Kattimaru, Systems of Land Tenure*
(Colombo 1978).

22. For Eheliyagoda see AGA Ke 5 May 1857, 3 August
1863, 5 October 1864 ff; for Ekneligoda, AGA Ke 3 June
1893, 17 April 1894, and SLNA 30/572 and 573 (cases of
underhand dealings); for Meedeniya, AGA Ke 17 January
1904, 4 June 1923, 15 September 1925, 19 November 1925,
11 January 1927, 22 February 1927, and interviews in the
Kegalla district and Colombo, with an ex-korala of Uduwe
and with Dr N.M. Perera (1978).

23. Interviews, Kegalla district, 1978 and 1979.
For 'Hallinda' and its neighbouring estate, see also
SLNA 30/540 (C.Q.P. case), 33/7291 (Grain tax register
for 1882) and the private archives of the estate.

24. See notes 5 and 8 above, and interview of N.H.
Keerthiratne (1978): 'The depressed classes were not
given any responsible position in the country. Their
job was planting: for that there is no objection. We
had lands all over - jungle lands. We started cultivating.' (See my thesis, vol. 2, pp.79-81.) On caste
and salaried labour, there is scattered evidence in
Administration Reports, Sabaragamuwa, (for example 1868
app.A, p.25). In the Kolonna and Atakalan korales,
where the Vahumpura are especially numerous, estates
employed Sinhalese labourers from an early date.

25. See Michael Roberts' very useful 'Elite Formation and Elites, 1832-1931', in K.M. De Silva, op. cit., pp.263-84.

26. D. Wesumperuma, 'The Migration and Conditions of Immigrant Labour in Ceylon, 1880-1910' (Ph.D. London 1974) and 'Unindentured Indian Labour Overseas: Plantation Labour in British Ceylon' in *Asie du Sud, traditions et changements* (Paris, Colloques internationaux du Centre National de la Recherche Scientifique 1979) pp. 469-76; E.Meyer, 'Between Village and Plantation: Sinhalese estate labour in British Ceylon', ibid., p.459-68.

27. In Kegalla, the only recorded clashes are AGA Ke 24 June 1873 (Pelampitiya), 18 March 1885 (Gangwarily), 19 December 1891 (Dolosbage),16 August 1893 (Walagam), 25 May 1917 (Mapitigama: but involving low-country Sinhalese coolies and *not* Kandyan villagers), 10 September 1925 (Debatgama: the only serious case). However on 5 October 1914, the AGA wrote: 'The Kandyan villagers are rather fond of having a little sport (*sic*) with the T mil coolies, and it is a matter of great difficulty to bring home offences in such cases, since the headmen never fail to support their fellow villagers.' See also Mary Steuart, *Everyday Life on a Ceylon Cocoa Estate* (London 1906) p.79.

28. E. Meyer, op.cit. (1979); and see N.Shanmugaratnam, op.cit., p.79.

29. On economic relations between immigrants and villagers: Frederick Lewis,op.cit.,p.192, Administration Report, Sabaragamuwa, 1881, Ceylon Sessional Paper II of 1893, p.4 (evidence of the planter Young), *Report and Proceedings of the Labour Commission* (Colombo 1908) pp. 7, 34, 38, 329, 361, 458, 465, 597; SLNA 59/2693 (half-starved fugitive Mahratti coolies from a Ratnapura estate obtaining work and shelter in the villages on their way down to Colombo); *India*: Report of the Agent of the Government of India in Ceylon for 1934, p.19; AGA Ke 3 January 1935 ('Tamil is understood by a large majority of Sinhalese villagers'); interview with Dr N.M. Perera (1978).

30. See B.H. Farmer, *Ceylon, a Divided Nation* (London 1963); M. Roberts, 'Indian Estate Labour in Ceylon during the Coffee Period 1830-1880', *Indian Economic and Social History Review* III, 1 and 2 (March and June 1966).

31. On Tamil overseers and land see SLNA L 615/1929 (Petition of A.M.N. Banda about Idamegama in Udukinda and subsequent inquiry); SO 20 August 1928 (Maliyadda); ASO Abeyakoon 25-27 April 1934 (Diyabokadare: 'There

appears to be plenty of bad feeling in the village over these land matters. The villagers complain that as a result of their protesting against the encroachments by the estate Tamils they are not given work on the estates. The Tamils complain that the villagers are threatening to do them bodily harm and are generally behaving in a manner calculated to disturb the hitherto peaceful character of these villages'; ASO Seneviratna, August 1933.) The lists of estate owners in the *Ceylon Ferguson Directories* of the 1930s are also very suggestive. For particular cases see for example Ceylon Government Gazette 13 September 1929, p.912, and 20 August 1937, p.891.

32. CO 54/974 and 975 (very voluminous reports by the Controller of Labour, F.C. Gimson, 1940-1).

33. One such case is that of Knavesmire estate: see CO 54/988 and interview with Dr N.M. Parera (1978). On the history of these early take-overs, see Gerald Peiris, 'The Current Land Reform and Peasant Agriculture in Sri Lanka', *South Asia*, 5 (December 1975). The Kegalla district office holds very detailed files on each of these estates (Village expansion files, series LK).

34. On the riots, see 'Race Relations in Sri Lanka', *Logos* (Colombo) vol.16 (April 1978). In 'Hallinda', some villagers went so far as to give shelter to the Indians to help them escape the killings.

35. Clifford Geertz, op.cit.; J.H. Boeke, *Economics and Economic Policy of Dual Societies* (Amsterdam 1953).

36. Michael Adas, *The Burma Delta: Economic Development and Social Change on an Asian Rice Frontier* (Madison 1974). Stagnation in the paddy sector was explained thus by a Ceylonese official: 'The yield is poor where the fields adjoin cart roads; the labour spent in producing and marketing is not sufficiently rewarded. When the price of commodities rose, paddy retained its original value and the agriculturist was never well-to-do' (ASO Rasaretnam, February 1934).

37. N. Shanmugaratnam, op.cit., p.73; Administration Report of the Rubber Controller for 1938, appendix A p.T8.

38. N. Shanmugaratnam, op.cit., and see my thesis, conclusions. L.A. Wickremeratne, 'The Establishment of the Tea Industry in Ceylon, the first phase (c.1870-1900)', *Ceylon Journal of Historical and Social Studies* n.s. II, 2 (1972) especially pp.138-51, is quite useful on Ceylonese small holdings, Sinhalese labour on estates, and land sales by villagers before 1900; it uses only printed sources. See also V. Samaraweera, 'Land, Labour, Capital and Sectional Interests in the

National Politics of Sri Lanka', *Modern Asian Studies* 15, 1 (1981) was published after this essay was written, and discusses many of the same issues. I agree on the whole, but, first, I would give more emphasis to the indigenous development of small-scale plantations before 1930, and secondly, I would add, on the inherent contradiction in the position of the nationalists about land, that there were numerous cases of politicians involved in land-grabbing activities, either personally or through their family. SOs in the 1920s are full of such stories: among others, G.E.Madawela, Victor Corea and Ch. Batuwan-tudawe are called 'notorious land-grabbers' (by officers undoubtedly anxious that the colonial land policy would be upset). One, though I would not go so far, even claimed that the land-grabbing class and the political class were synonymous. Many politicians were not invol-ved - in Kegalla, E.A.P. Wijeyeratne for example - while some of the closest collaborators of the colonial regime were: in Kegalla, Meedeniya Adigar was implicated in very extensive dealings with one of the most prominent speculators of the time, A.J. Vanderpoorten. A third point: the hostility shown by many Kandyans towards immigrant Indians was not only the reflection of politi-cal attitudes at the national level; it was also, and perhaps mainly, the reaction to extensive land purchases by enriched overseers, which are mentioned in the local monographs included in the Kandyan Peasantry Commission Report. One such case in LSDR is that of the villages of north Udukinda (Uva Province), just below the exten-sive tea estates of the Kirklees.

WAGE-GATHERING: SOCIO-ECONOMIC CHANGES AND THE CASE OF THE FOOD-GATHERER NAIKENS OF SOUTH INDIA

Nurit Bird

In his 1976 Malinowski lecture Bloch critically considers the approaches to the theoretical explanation of
social change of both the Structural Functional school
of thought, [1] and the French Marxist work (mentioning
Meillassoux, Terray and Godelier). The former follows
the Durkheimian notion of the social determination of
concepts and is therefore faced with the problem that
'this leaves the actors with no language to talk *about*
their society, and so change it, since they can only
talk *within* it'. [2] The latter follows Marx's notion of
the infrastructure which is considered as 'totally
external to either rules or concepts'; changes are said
to take place at the level of the infrastructure, but
for the infrastructure 'to be a source of criticism of
the social order it means that people must apprehend it
in terms available to them and which are different from
and incompatible with those of the dominant social
theory'. [3] To an extent, and as Bloch presents it, the
Structural Functional and the French Marxist schools
follow opposite directions - 'either they see the social
process in terms used by the actors and so are unable to
explain how it is that actors can change these terms, or
they see the mechanism of change as occurring in terms
totally alien to the actors and so are unable to explain
how these mechanisms can be transformed into meaningful
action'. [4] Common to both approaches, however, seems to
be the underlying problematic issue of how external
changes, whether outside or already in the infrastructure
of the society, are transmitted into people's thought and
action or, in short, how the external changes are
internalized.

    This paper is centred on a particular case study, [5]
the features of which make it suitable both for the
demonstration of the explanatory relevance of the above
approaches, and for the consideration of the problem
underlying them. The case is that of the food-gatherer
Naikens and their interaction with the plantation opened
in their locality. It is a suitable case or 'experiment'
as it were, for four reasons. First, it offers a manage-
able scale: as is typical of a certain type of hunter-
gatherer society, the society in question is

characterized by both a very small population and a
simple culture. Second, it gives a clear-cut identifiable reaction - the range of changes undergone by
this society is outstanding: from the most primitive
hunter-gatherer economy at one end of the scale of
economic development, to the modern cash economy.
Third, there are minimal interfering restrictions -
there are favourable circumstances in that the people
have had their traditional means of livelihood relatively intact and their habitat not overcrowded, and
have therefore had a certain choice in their response
to the external developments. Consequently, fourth,
there is a control group - while some of the people
have undergone changes, part of the society has maintained to a significant extent the traditional mode of
life and can act as a control group. It is impossible
here to explore the response to the external changes in
the manifold aspects of the culture in question.[6] The
economic domain, and in particular the social relations
embedded in it, is the aspect discussed here as it is
most susceptible to changes resulting from the new economic possibilities, and is of particular relevance to
the discussion above in view of the French Marxist explanation. The scope of the paper dictates that the
main focus is laid upon this ethnographic aspect of the
case itself, and only in conclusion are its general
implications drawn.

The Naikens are a food-gathering group of about
1000 people, inhabiting forested areas in the Nilgiri -
Wynad region of South India. (In the literature on the
Nilgriris tribes they have often been referred to as
Jenu Kurumbas, but Naiken is the name used by themselves
and their immediate neighbours.) During 1979 fieldwork
was conducted among one local community of about 70
people distributed in five hamlets spread throughout an
area of approximately 5000 acres. During the latter
part of the nineteenth century, a Scottish company
cleared 500 acres in this area for a rubber plantation,
here referred to as the Gir plantation. The plantation
was surrounded by forest and was only accessible by a
steep and narrow forest path. At first the Naikens were
hardly affected. Labour was brought in during the dry
season to tap and process the latex. Naikens were occasionally engaged to clear jungle tracks and weed between
the rubber trees, but only during the rainy season.
Significant changes took place in the 1950s. Coffee
bushes, fruit trees and spices were planted, and a need
was created for weeding work throughout the year. The

cost of bringing outside labour increased as a result
of the 1951 Labour Act, and the demand for weeding
labour was therefore directed towards the local Naiken
population. The latter were in any case better than the
migrant workers at unskilled tasks in the jungle terrain.
A mud track, usable only in the dry season but nevertheless jeep-worthy, was opened, and the seasonal workers
moved in permanently with their families. From the
1960s to the 1970s some clearing and felling operations
took place in the 4500 acres of forest surrounding the
plantation, but the changes were limited in extent and
imposed only relatively minor obstacles to the viable
execution of the traditional Naiken forest-based subsistence. Over the last 30 years Naikens therefore had
the choice of either working in the plantation and/or
maintaining their traditional means of livelihood.
Indeed only some have been involved with plantation
employment throughout this period. At present (that
is, from September 1978 to September 1979) about two-
thirds of the adult Naikens studied are involved with
regular plantation work, while the remaining third still
live by the traditional mode of subsistence. The former
still occasionally practise the traditional foraging and
collecting for trade - often during weekends, holidays
and the high season for tradable forest produce. But
by and large they are integrated into the plantation
world and its wage employment; are members of trade
unions; are entitled to pension schemes etc. They can
therefore be considered as belonging to the world of
wage employment, the cash economy, and bureaucratic
industrial organization.

This analysis is concerned with the socio-economic
developments which have followed these occupational
changes in the period 1950 to 1979. Discussion is
focused on those Naikens who took up plantation employment (in the paper referred to simply as Naikens). The
changes, or lack thereof, are measured against the traditional economy still practised to a considerable extent by their present food-gatherer counterparts. Both
sub-groups profess an economy 30 years ago similar to
that of present food-gathering Naikens. This verbal
evidence is further supported by a short investigateion
conducted among an intact Naiken community in a neighbouring locality. Furthermore, the picture portrayed
by the life of the present food-gatherer sub-group, and
which is conjured up from all Naikens' accounts of the
past, accords in its broad lines with that which is
depicted both in the work of Morris, Gardner and

Ehrenfels on other food-gatherer tribes in South India,
and in the literature of other hunter-gatherer societies
especially in the work of Woodburn.[7] For brevity (and
with no other implications) the past tense and the
adjectives 'traditional' and sometimes 'pre-existing'
are used in referring to the food-gathering mode of life,
while the present tense is reserved for the wage-
labourer Naikens.

The essence of the traditional food-gatherer Naikens
can best be conveyed by using three important character-
izations of hunter-gatherer societies. The Naikens
unquestionably belong to a type of hunter-gatherer
societies which has been categorized in the literature,
by Woodburn as an 'immediate return system',[8] by Gardner
as 'extreme individualism',[9] and by Sahlins as the
'Zen road to affluence'.[10] Woodburn refers by his term,
among other features, to an immediate return for labour
and immediate consumption, both contrasting with the
intrinsic delay in return for labour and delayed consumption which characterize the agricultural system; a
lack of investment in capital or storage facilities; and
the general lack of concern about the past and the
future.[11] Woodburn describes the way of life which is
tied up with 'an immediate return' system as follows:

> Individuals and groups go out for part of most
> days to obtain their food and other requirements
> which are then consumed for the most part on that
> particular day or casually over the days that
> follow. Members of such societies avoid long-
> term commitments in using their labour, and they
> are not concerned to develop stores of food or
> other possessions; even their tools and weapons
> and other technical items used in obtaining food
> and other requirements are, in general, of types
> which do not involve a substantial involvement
> of time.[12]

Gardner covers by his term, among other features, the
lack of cooperation and competition between individuals;
'a very strong expectation for autonomy',[13] and a reluc-
tance to be controlled by others. Sahlins contrasts the
'Zen strategy' which departs from the premises that
'Human material wants are finite and few, and technical
means unchanging but on the whole adequate', or crudely
speaking the minimalization of needs to meet available
means, with the 'Galbraithian way' of the West, which
assumed that 'man's wants are great, not to say infinite,
whereas his means are limited, although improvable', or

crudely speaking the maximization of material means in
an attempt to satisfy ever-growing needs.

The change from a primitive hunting-and-gathering
economy into a modern cash economy seems a fundamental
one. But viewed away from the plantation, in their hamlets, one cannot distinguish between those Naikens who
are plantation workers and those who are still by and
large hunter-gatherers. Close familiarity with the
group also reveals that the social cohesiveness of the
community as a whole has indeed been retained in almost
every respect. Through the separate discussion and
closely magnified analysis of three areas of the present
economy - I. Production, II. Consumption and III. Distribution (money and exchange) - this statement is explored,
and the proposition argued that the changes are not as
fundamental as they seem.

Production

Naikens work in the plantation in one of two categories:
permanent employment and casual employment. The distinction between these two categories was defined in
1964 in order to protect what were then called the 'non-
act' employees, that is, those employees who were not
covered under the 1951 Labour Act with its detailed
regulations concerning work conditions and the rights
of employees. While a permanent worker was simply defined as one who is engaged in work on a permanent basis,
an important distinction was made between the temporary
and the casual labourer. The temporary worker was defined as one who is engaged temporarily for a specific
period or for work of a temporary nature not exceeding
six months; while the casual worker was defined as one
who works regularly on the estate, but not exceeding
fifteen consecutive days, and with no obligation to report for work daily. Under regulations, both the permanent and the casual labourers have the right to a minimum of
54 and 40 hours of work per week respectively for adults
and adolescents, one rest day each week and national
holidays, sickness allowance and medical facilities. In
addition, on certain plantations (including the one
studied) workers are entitled to an annual bonus calculated as a percentage of the annual earned salary of
each worker - the percentage negotiated between planters
and trade unions according to the former's profit. Unlike the casual worker, only the permanent workers are
entitled to a provident fund (created by a monthly contribution of worker and employer), and to a gratuity
which is paid to employees on retirement in accordance

with the number of years of service. Similarly, only
the permanent workers have the right to be provided
with accommodation, supplied with drinking water and
latrines; and only the permanent female worker has the
right to a paid maternity leave of twelve weeks.

Table A shows the distribution (percentages) of
employable Naikens by category of employment for all
employables; for female employables alone; and for male
employables alone. At present there are 69 Naikens in
the five hamlets within walking distance of the plantation. Old people and children excluded, there are 33
adults who can potentially work. Of these employable
Naikens 36 per cent are not connected at all with wage
work in the plantation; the remaining 64 per cent are
the subject of this paper. The majority of then (72 per
cent) are casual workers, while only 28 per cent (or 18
per cent of all employables) are permanent workers. It
is noteworthy that while 75 per cent of the men work in
the plantation, almost all of them (92 per cent) are
casual labourers, whereas only about half of the women
work (53 per cent), but more than half of these (54 per
cent) are permanent workers.[14]

To explain the general predominance of the casual
status, yet at the same time to account for the different
patterns which are reflected in the employment of men and
women, it is necessary to pinpoint other indicators of
involvement in work. Categories of employment only reflect an annual registration of workers in the plantation. They do not reflect the regularity of, or fluctuation in, attendance at work. Tables B and C provide
the actual number of workers and the average number of
days each of them worked in a month, for February and
July. These months represent two extremes in the
seasonal cycle of forest subsistence. In the dry month
of February forest produce is abundant. Soap nut can
be collected for trade; wild yam is available; and the
honey season is just about to start. During the wet
month of July forest subsistence is least viable. Tubers
and berries are hard to find; walking in the leech in-
fested and muddy forest is to be avoided. Tables B and
C clearly show that attendance during February is only
about half that of July. Table C further confirms the
findings of Table A, that is, not only with regard to
categories of employment, but also when it comes to
actual attendance at work - half of the women who worked
during these two months were permanent, whereas the
majority of men (94 per cent) were casual labourers. A
second peculiar feature however appears. Against the

expectation that the permanent workers work on average more days in a month than the casual ones, Table B shows that for both male and female, for February and July, casual workers on average worked more days than the permanent workers (for example, permanent female workers worked on average nine days in February while their casual workmates worked fifteen).

The distribution of Naikens' categories of employment is not merely a certain phase in the often presumed progress from a non-employed to a temporary, to a casual and, finally, to a 'permanent' status. A different pattern is revealed by the data. Until 1958 no Naiken was in the permanent position. From 1958 to date 27 Naikens have all been employed at one time or another as permanent; at present only six still are. Table D shows the distribution of workers according to length of permanent employment, that is Naikens who ceased their permanent term. The mean is five years; the mode is only one year. It is also significant that five of the six present permanent employees entered employment only in January 1979, while the remaining one (a woman) has been a permanent worker for the last seventeen years. It is important to look at what alternative occupations people moved to when their permanent employment ceased. Unfortunately, at present, of the 21 Naikens, seven are either dead or no longer in the area. Table E shows the present position of the remaining fourteen: four are too old to be employed; eight out of the ten employable people have moved to casual employment, while the other two ceased their employment completely. It is noteworthy that the average period of permanent employment for those moving from the permanent position into a casual one was seven years, and that they all chose to resign from their permanent status. It would appear then that over time there is a tendency among employable Naikens to move away from the permanent position, showing a preference for the casual position.

Four features thus stand out in the analysis of Naikens' involvement in plantation work, and pose queries which are to be explained. First, the majority are involved with casual labour. Second, there is a greater popularity of permanent employment among women than among men. Third, the permanent worker on average works fewer days in a month than a casual one (although over a year he works more). Fourth, there has been a tendency over time to move from permanent to casual employment. It can be suggested that the explanation for this syndrome of features lies with the management's

strategy; that is, that the management favours employing the Naikens as casual labourers rather than as
permanent workers; that if they give Naikens a permanent status their preference is shown to women; and that
when possible they dismiss the permanent Naiken employees. The combined examination of the development
of labour organization and work conditions in South
Indian plantations in general, and the development of
the structure of tasks required in the plantation in
question, would appear to cast doubt upon this hypothesis.

During the first half of the twentieth century a
significant majority of South Indian plantation workers
were immigrants to the plantation areas from other
regions. They were recruited by, worked under, and were
paid by 'maistries', having no direct contact with the
management. In the Gir Rubber Estate they worked only
during the dry season, and when the rains started went
back to their villages. Only very temporary and rudi-
mentary accommodation was offered in the plantation area
and most, if not all, workers left their families behind.
With the 1951 Plantation Labour Act the 'maistries' system was abolished. Plantation managements were invested
with the direct responsibility for their employees, and
were subjected to detailed regulations including giving
daily regular work, and hence permanent employment, and
providing and maintaining adequate housing accommodation
supplied with drinking water and latrines for all immigrant workers. From the management's point of view
therefore it has become more economic to employ local
workers. Only Naikens were local to the Gir Plantation
Estate.

There are generally three categories of tasks in
the Gir Rubber Estate: tapping; smoking and packing the
latex; and weeding. While the latter is a blanket term
for a variety of unskilled tasks, the first two are
specialized tasks. Tapping is a skill which until
recently, and still by and large today, is handed down
from father to son. Smoking and packing the latex -
locally and here referred to as 'factory' work - is a
semi-skilled task which can be taught through work but
requires regular attendance. Most of the non-Naiken
male workers are employed as tappers or factory workers.
Some Naikens were encouraged to take up factory work but
avoided it. Non-Naiken female workers tend to work as
weeders, but the majority of weeding work is done by
both male and female Naikens. Over the last 30 years
the proportional position of the different categories of

tasks within the overall plantation work has undergone changes. Essentially, until 1948-9, there was a major need for tapping and factory work, and only occasionally was weeding required. In the 1950s, with the introduction of coffee and fruit (at the expense of ageing rubber trees), came a greater need for diversified non-skilled jobs and less need for tapping and factory work. Table G shows tapping and factory work in 1948-9 as about two-thirds and weeding about one-third of the range of work required; in 1978-9 the former occupied less than a third and the latter more than two-thirds of the work performed in the plantation. It is the Naikens who are both better than the other workers in the performance of these increasing tasks, and locally available to be called upon, since the majority of the non-Naiken workers are tappers and factory workers.

The administrative personnel are well aware of a certain dependence upon Naiken labour, and express it by and large by an explicit willingness, and in many cases direct encouragement, for Naikens to take up responsible tasks and permanent positions in the plantation. Thus it is the supply of labour rather than the demand for labour which influences the actual involvement of Naikens in the work of the plantation, and Naikens themselves indeed give an explicit expression of their preferences. To understand Naikens' perception of the world of the plantation and their approach to employment within it, it is necessary to look at their traditional socio-economic structure, and within its framework to consider aspects of work in the plantation. The possible usefulness of such an examination is suggested by the above but is also hinted at by the fact that whereas other food-gatherers in South India have responded negatively to government attempts to settle them into agricultural life - attempts which were accompanied by explanations and clear material incentives -[15] Naikens who have never been approached by welfare officers happily moved into plantation work. Furthermore, as pointed out, it seems that no social gulf has opened between the plantation worker Naiken and his food-gatherer counterpart who maintains more or less the traditional way of life. In considering Naikens' work in the plantation from the perspectives of the traditional socio-economic organization it is perhaps useful to centre the discussion around six simple questions: what? how much? when? how? what for? and by whom work in the plantation is done?

With respect to the first question - what? -

traditional subsistence work included these tasks:
digging and cutting vegetal material such as roots,
bamboos and wood to be used for accommodation and
other requirements; picking fruits and berries, and
digging wild yam for sustenance; constructing huts and
making baskets from bamboo, grass and wood; and, of
less importance for the present argument, collecting
honey and other minor forest produce for trade; fishing
and, to a limited extent, hunting. It has been mentioned above that in addition to the specialized tasks
of tapping and factory work the plantation requires a
variety of unskilled tasks referred to as 'weeding'.
These include tasks which can be grouped under five
headings. First there is weeding itself, including
weeding in the plantation area, clearing paths of
shrubs and mud after the rainy season, clearing a
fire belt in the forest around the borders of the
estate, cutting the branches of jungle trees in the
plantation to regulate shade over plants (shade lopping),
and pruning coffee bushes. All these tasks involve
clearing the 'wild' - mostly vegetal material - away
from the 'tame' - the plantation. Secondly there is
picking, denoting picking coffee berries, fruits and
spices grown in the plantation, and thirdly traditional construction, including construction of temporary
sheds from bamboo; thatching with grass; construction
and maintenance of bamboo conduits; making bamboo fences
and baskets to protect young plants etc. This group of
tasks involves simple traditional technology, drawing
upon raw material from the surrounding forest. Fourthly
there is 'lines' work, the maintenance of, and unskilled
labour in assistance to the building of, workers' accommodation (locally referred to as 'lines') and latrines.
Fifth and last, there is cultivation, which includes
manuring, spraying and planting. From Table G it can
be seen that the first three categories expanded from
25 per cent in 1948-9 to more than 50 per cent in 1978-9
of the total labour required, and that they constitute
the majority of the unskilled tasks performed in the
plantation. The tasks included in these three categories, however, are in essence similar to the tasks
performed in the traditional Naiken mode of subsistence,
and are indeed the ones mostly performed by the planta-
tion-worker Naikens.

With respect to the second question - how much? -
it is certain that traditionally Naikens did not need to
go daily to collect food. Quantitative information regarding the amount of work required is not available, but an

idea of it is provided in studies of Australian Aborigines and Kalahari Bushmen, where it is calculated that on average hunter-gatherers work between two to three days in a week.[16] In the plantation regular attendance at work is required only when one is a permanent employee, and/or working as a tapper and factory worker. When one works as a casual labourer there is no obligation to attend work daily, and the casual worker can work only a few days in a week. It can be suggested that the casual employment offers the Naiken the possibility of keeping his traditional rhythm and traditional amount of labour. It fits in with this proposition, that most Naikens absent themselves from work on Monday and Tuesday, and thus usually have a four-day working week, which is not far off the recorded average number of working days per week of other hunter-gatherers.

Customarily individuals only went to work when they wanted to, to the extent, unintelligible to the protestant ethic of the West perhaps, that in some cases Naikens were observed sitting on a cold night without a fire, rather than go to the forest in search of firewood. When interpersonal pressure was put on Naikens to supply minor forest produce for trade, the result was adverse and they only avoided contact with the contractors. It can be proposed that with respect to the third question - when? - Naikens can carry with them to the plantation their customary attitude to work. Casual employment allows them the freedom to attend work only when they wish to do so. They can absent themselves from work either for a continuous period and/or for certain days, and indeed work least during the season in which forest subsistence is most viable. Similarly, I have often heard from the management personnel themselves that when Naikens know in advance that the work to be done on the morrow is not to their liking (for example 'lines' or cultivation work) they do not come to work. By pressing them to work on these and other occasions the management only finds that Naikens avoid work for a longer period than otherwise.

Also with respect to the question - how? - a similarity can be pointed out between the manner of performance of certain plantation tasks and that of the customary subsistence activities. In the traditional economy autonomy and independence were cherished. Husband and wife worked together; otherwise individuals - even those closely related to each other - worked independently and did not cooperate. There were no ties of control and instruction. There was, for example, no formal teaching

of the skills required for subsistence: if a child was
interested in a particular skill (for example the
collection of honey from big hives found in trees 70 to
80 feet high), he accompanied adults when they performed
this task and learned the skill by observation, imita-
tion, a sequence of trial and error, and finally gradual
participation. In the plantation the semi-skilled work
needs to be formally instructed and is a matter of co-
ordinated effort, closely supervised. Likewise, to some
extent, the tasks of 'lines' and cultivation. But unlike these the unskilled tasks of weeding, picking, and
traditional construction are autonomously and individually performed by members of a relatively large gang.
Although a supervisor stays with them during the day,
his supervision is not strongly felt by the workers
because of their number and the kind of tasks they perform. This similarity between traditional and certain
plantation work, explains two examples of exceptionally
positive involvement with plantation work in terms of
both efficiency and attendance. First, when Naikens
are assigned a piece-rate job, they usually perform it
in almost half the time required by them to perform
the same job under regular conditions of employment.
Second, in August 1979 a substantial number of Naikens
regularly attended work. The task they had to perform
was 'shade-lopping', and they organized themselves in
teams - the husband climbing up the tree and cutting
branches off, and the wife clearing the branches from
the ground. In both cases Naikens could work autonomously, and in the second instance, spouses could even
work together as they often did in the traditional mode
of subsistence.

In the traditional system Naikens were not concerned
with the future and did not save, invest, or store items
for possible future utilization in lean times. Their
concern was with the present, and their labour was always
invested for immediate purposes. At present, when they
work in the plantation, Naikens' weekly wages are all
spent on rice and on a few other items of provision.
(As will be discussed in the following section, their
consumption of durables has not altered much.) Having
no concern with saving for the future, Naiken workers
see no value in the provident fund and gratuity, and
accordingly perceive that the casual labourer earns a
higher wage than that of the permanent worker who makes
a weekly contribution towards his provident fund. It
is revealing that when several Naikens who were permanently employed resigned they received on account of their

gratuity and provident fund considerable sums ranging
from Rs.700 to Rs.1500. Some of them were over 60 years
of age. But invariably they stayed in their huts over
a period of several months and spent the money on foodstuffs and drinks. When the money was exhausted they
took up casual employment. With respect to the fifth
question - what for? - it can therefore be proposed that
the underlying rationale of both traditional subsistence
activities and work in the plantation is the same:
immediate consumption. It has been mentioned before
that most Naikens tend not to work on Monday and Tuesday.
The reason may well be that the money which they receive
on a Saturday often lasts until Tuesday or even Wednes-
day, and only when they need more for immediate consumption do they go back to work.

Finally, with respect to the question - by whom? -
although traditionally most subsistence activities were
pursued by both men and women, only men collected certain
types of honey and hunted certain types of game, while
women were more associated with the regular task of digging wild yam which was the staple food. Similarly in
the plantation both men and women work, but women are
regularly involved with the tasks of weeding and picking,
while men are also allocated to perform tasks such as
manuring and planting. As a result, partly because they
avoid the tasks which they do not like, and partly because they take time off to pursue traditional collecting
of honey and other minor forest produce for trade, the
fluctuation in the number of male workers is significantly higher than that of women. In the plantation
therefore, as in the traditional mode of subsistence,
women attend more regularly at work, and are there
associated more than men with the regular provision of
the new, purchased staple food.

It would appear then that a significant parallel
can be drawn between the food-gathering pattern of production and certain aspects of the plantation work. This
similarity also extends to account for the four features
(above) which emerge from the analysis of data relevant
to the involvement of Naikens with plantation work. The
tendency towards casual employment appears to be linked
with the resemblance between this type of employment and
the traditional mode of production. The casual work consists of tasks involving traditional construction, clearing the 'wild' and collecting vegetal produce, which are
similar to those of the traditional activities. The
labourer can work independently and by and large autonomously, and is least subject to control and supervision.

He can work as much as and when he wants, in direct
response to his immediate needs. Unlike the permanent
worker, his return from labour is maximized in the
present. The greater popularity of permanent employment among women (second, above) clearly relates to the
traditional association of women with the role of the
regular provider of staple food. The higher average of
working days per month of the casual labourer in comparison with the permanent one (third, above) can well be
explained by Naikens' customary tendency to avoid pressure and authority. Finally, the trend over time from
permanent to casual labour (fourth, above) reflects the
enrolment of Naikens for permanent labour by the management and the Naikens' consequent resignation, further
enhanced with the 1964 establishment of the casual
status. In conclusion then it can be argued that Naiken
involvement with plantation work, or in other words,
their new pattern of production, has to a great extent
been shaped by their traditional economic structure.
The question raised is therefore how the new items of
consumption, and the purchase rather than the gathering
of commodities, affect the traditional patterns of
consumption.

Consumption

Like other food-gatherers in South India, Naikens had
access to commodities from the outside through the
trade in minor forest produce even before they started
to work in the plantation. But they used only a limited
range of such commodities, mainly salt, cloths, tobacco
and billhooks. From the 1950s onwards - with the regular involvement with plantation work, the resulting
cash income, the intensified and constant contact with
the other workers, the opening of a forest track to the
neighbouring village markets, and the establishment of
a tea shop in their habitat - major changes in Naikens'
durable and non-durable consumption could have been
expected. However, while there have been clear changes
of the latter there has been little apparent alteration
in the former. It is impossible even at present to
distinguish by their material possessions between many
individuals who are engaged in plantation work and those
who still maintain the traditional way of life. They
all live in similar huts constructed of bamboo walls and
grass thatched roof, next to each other. The possessions
of all resemble the following inventory: a few metal
pots; metal plates; empty bottles; a cloth which they
wear and a few old clothes and rugs which also serve

when necessary as sleeping mats and carrying bundles;
a billhook; a home-made bamboo basket; possibly a metal
digging stick; occasionally an axe; beads and other
odds and ends such as wooden boxes, a broken mirror,
empty tins.

Not only do the possessions look significantly
alike, but the attitude towards them has also remained
much the same. There is little concern with the accumulation of material possessions, as the inventory well
manifests, nor any consideration for the maintenance of
things already possessed, even if only recently bought.
For example, a few cases were observed where, while
working in the plantation Naikens cut themselves, and
with no hesitation tore a strip of their new cloth to
bandage the cuts. It is important to note that in a
few cases transistors and watches entered the Naiken
huts but did not remain there long. In one example a
transistor was sold only two weeks after it was purchased, when the purchaser discovered that it was
necessary to spend money on new batteries.

In the area of non-durable consumption, especially
in their diet, clear changes have taken place. Naikens
traditionally subsisted on foraging in the forest.
Staple food consisted of nine varieties of wild yam,
which were usually cooked and eaten in the evening.
During the months of March and April jackfruit replaced
the wild yam. Leafy material and figs were occasionally
made into a spicy paste which was added to the staple
food. Honey and fruits, berries and nuts were collected
in their respective seasons, and consumed where and when
they were gathered, or sporadically throughout the day.
Very occasionally, fish and game were caught, and on
such occasions eaten at the evening meal, substituting
for the wild yam or the jackfruit. At present *ganji*
(rice porridge) is the main staple food, and is eaten at
the evening meal. Leafy material and figs are still
occasionally collected around the huts, but now accompany
the ganji. Other customary forest produce is still
occasionally consumed, especially when people happen to
notice it, for example on their way back home from work
in the plantation, and sometimes even during work when
they gather building material for the plantation. Tea
and pastries are now frequently purchased from a tea
shop opened in the plantation area (tea shop referring
to a shack in which tea, pastries, tobacco produce and
a few other items of provisions are sold). Naikens
frequent the tea shop almost daily - often more than
once - to consume these commodities.

The change from consumption which centred on the
wild yam, to the new one in which rice and items from
the tea shop occupy a prominent place, could be assessed
as fundamental. Furthermore, those who are familiar
with South India would perhaps suggest that the present
Naikens' pattern of consumption basically resembles the
consumption of other poor low-caste people, and that
consequently the change observed is in emulation of the
latter as a result of an increasing integration into
South India society. To further qualify the discussion
of Naikens' new pattern of non-durable consumption it
is useful to contrast it with that of their work mates
in the plantation who earn the same daily wage. The
majority of these are Moppala, and this name is therefore
used to refer to all the non-Naiken workers, among whom
Hindu and Christians are also included.

The staple food of Moppalas is rice, but they eat
it dry with curry and other side dishes. Porridge rice,
which the Naikens eat, is considered by them the least
esteemed form of cooked grain, and they rarely eat it.
Moppalas take their main meal at lunch, but they also
eat in the morning and evening. For Naikens the main,
and often the only meal, is eaten in the evening. Moppalas prepare their pastries and tea. Naikens, who are
particularly fond of them, never prepare pastries. They
can buy tea powder in the shop, but even tea they rarely
prepare themselves, and prefer bringing the ready-made
tea in old glass bottles from the tea shop to their hut.
There is also a difference in the sexual division of
domestic labour between Naikens and Moppalas. In the
Moppala family only the wife cooks, whereas in the Naiken family both the wife and her husband can cook. Both
Moppalas and Naikens frequent the tea shop, but not
wholly for the same reasons. For the Moppalas the tea
shop is mainly a social institution, where only men can
go and where they stay for relatively long periods; they
buy each other tea, exchange gossip, and sometimes play
cards. For the Naikens, the tea shop is by and large
simply a place from which tea, pastries and tobacco
produce can be obtained. Both male and female Naikens
visit the tea shop. Often the whole nuclear family
goes there. They either take back their purchases, or
sit separately in a corner of the tea shop to consume
them. Naikens and Moppalas also differ with respect
to expenditure in the tea shop. Table H provides
comparative details of the daily expenditure of two
Naiken and one Moppala families during one representative week. The Naiken families spent respectively six

and four times more than the Moppala family. In general, the daily expenditure of Moppalas is almost always between Rs.$\frac{1}{2}$ and Rs.2$\frac{1}{2}$. In contrast the daily expenditure of Naikens would appear to vary in direct relation to the money available to them, and in inverse relation to the number of members of the nuclear family.

The difference in pattern of non-durable consumption between Naikens and Moppalas, in spite of the similarity of the main items consumed, suggests that it may be useful to follow what has been done in the analysis of change in production patterns, and examine changes from the perspectives of the traditional socio-economic structure. It further suggests that it is necessary to conduct such an examination with reference to the fabric of culture surrounding these items as well as to the items themselves. It is useful here to centre such an examination on six related aspects of food consumption which reflect the relations between the three parameters of raw food, cooked food, and people.

The first point to be looked at is cooking equipment. The traditional cooking vessels Naikens used would appear to have been made of bamboo. These lasted only for one occasion and were prepared just before use. Raw food was put into a split of bamboo which was then placed on the fire. The external layer of bamboo caught fire at once, but the food was ready before the internal layer started to burn. For some considerable time, however, Naikens also used earthen pots and, when available, metal pots. At present Naikens only use earthen and cheap metal pots; splits of bamboo are used only for carrying water and sometimes as crockery. Every family has one or two good pots in which the ganji is cooked. The pots are left near the fireplace after the evening meal, and only the following morning one of the family (often an adolescent girl or boy) goes to the river to wash them and then place them out of the way in a corner of the hut. Furthermore it has been observed that when people move from one hamlet to another they leave their pots behind and use those available in the hamlet they move to. Thus it can be suggested that the present attitude towards cooking equipment is linked with the past attitude in its casual and temporary aspect.

The storage of provisions is the second point to be discussed. Traditionally, Naikens did not store provisions for very long, and at most kept food for only a few days. The situation at present is very similar. Even when provisions (rice and a few chillies) bought on pay day last for a few days, there is no attempt to store

them properly. They are simply put in a corner of the
hut, still wrapped in the newspaper or leaf in which
they were bought, until they are exhausted. This
tendency partly explains why Naikens do not prepare their
own tea - it requires the storage of provisions.

The third relevant point is the method of cooking.
In the past, staple food was prepared by simply boiling
the wild yam in water. Occasionally the wild yam was
also roasted on fire, but boiling was the predominant
method, and both the seasonal substitute for wild yam
- the jack fruit - and the leafy material sometimes
eaten with it, were boiled. Significantly the only
form of grain which the Naikens consume, and which their
neighbours least esteem, is simply raw food boiled in an
unspecified amount of water. Naikens do not prepare the
complicated cooked pastries such as idli and dossa which
they so much like. The traditional simplicity of cooking
thus appears to have been retained.

The maintenance of this simplicity partly contri-
butes to the preservation of the customary division of
labour in preparing the food (point four). As with the
traditional staple food, both men and women, and even
children, can prepare the ganji. The division of labour
in obtaining the food has also been retained. In the
past both man and woman could collect the food, or
occasionally obtain it in exchange for minor forest
produce. At present, both can obtain it in exchange for
money earned. The traditional independence has also
been implemented with regard to the new dietary items of
tea and pastries, since whereas Moppala women customarily
cannot go to the tea shop, Naiken women can.

Fifth is the aspect of the storage of cooked food.
Both now and in the past, the pot is normally emptied
during the evening meal. Leftovers, if any, remain in
the pot somewhere in the cooking area and can occasionally be consumed the following morning. Finally, with
regard to time and manner of eating, traditionally a main
or only meal was taken by the nuclear family together,
or by its individual members, each serving himself from
the pot in his own time. Today the situation is exactly
the same, except that ganji and not wild yam constitutes
the meal.

A certain resemblance appears between the traditional and the present pattern of non-durable consumption. To assess the nature of the changes it is useful
to distinguish between two analytical levels - that of
the pattern of cultural parameters and the network of
ties connecting them, and that of the content assigned

to these parameters. In the case of the Naikens it can
be suggested that ganji has replaced the wild yam as the
content of the parameter of staple food but with no overall change in the 'pre-existing pattern'. The first
part of this proposition, namely the interchangeability
between ganji and the wild yam, already emerges from the
discussion above. It can be further supported by looking
at the elements of 'food-gathering' in the society. At
present even the food-gatherer Naikens increase their
consumption of rice whenever they can obtain it through
trade in minor forest produce. As often as not, when any
Naiken goes to the forest, for example on a traditional
expedition of honey collection, he is likely, instead of
following the traditional pattern by collecting wild yam
as and where he finds it, to take a small bundle of rice.

The second part of the proposition, namely that
there was no overall change in the 'pre-existing pattern'
concerning food consumption, can be demonstrated by
examining Naikens' organization of food. Four clear
categories of food are distinguishable by their place
within the Naiken diet: staple food, seasonal substitutes for staple food, items supplementary to the staple
food, and others which are consumed sporadically throughout the day (Table I). These we may picture as concen-
tric circles at the core of which is the first category
and surrounding it, the second, the third, and the fourth.
In the past these four categories included respectively:
the wild yam; jack fruit and occasionally game and fish;
leafy material and figs; and, lastly, honey and fruits,
berries and nuts. At present these four categories
include respectively: ganji; wild yam, jackfruit and
occasionally game and fish; leafy material and figs;
and, finally, tea and pastries, honey and occasionally
certain fruits, berries and nuts. Thus it seems that
through the contact with wage employment, ganji moved
into the core of the food categories, wild yam moved
into the second category, and the 'tea shop produce'
entered the fourth category together with the other
'forestry produce', but there was no overall change in
the organization of categories of food and their properties. Thus while there has been no significant
change in the durable consumption, the changes in the
non-durable consumption are a matter of change in the
content of a few parameters while the 'pre-existing
pattern' as a whole has hardly been affected. But if it
is argued that changes in consumption and production are
limited, the question is raised where has the money disappeared to? How is cash integrated into the Naiken

culture?

Distribution (Exchange and Money)

There is no ground to assume that Naikens had not known
of money before they started to be regularly involved
with plantation work, but it is certain that only after
that event did they have to deal with it constantly and
to find a place for it in their economy. In the examination of contexts in which money is presently used it
is necessary to distinguish between coins and cash in
general, since coins sometimes seem to stand as a separate category of money and are regarded as a kind of
durable property. For example, when a Naiken dies, his
coins as well as his knife and pots are buried with him.
Alternatively, they are taken by friends and relatives
who wish to remember the deceased. In the most important of Naiken rituals, the souls of people who have died
during the year previous to the ritual, and who are still
free and harmful in the forest, are brought home into the
'hut of the spirits'. During the ritual, beads, and now-
adays also coins, of the deceased are put in the place
of death, and the shaman in a trance envelops them in a
cloth and carries them to the 'hut of the spirits'.
Coins in these contexts are therefore taken into the
Naiken culture without the monetary properties given to
them in the industrial economy, and are associated with
their owner, as is the case with other Naiken possessions.

To consider the contexts in whch cash money is used
it is useful to refer to three criteria often used in
the literature to define money. They are, first, a
medium of exchange, second, a store of value, and third,
a measure of value. It would appear that Naikens rarely,
if at all, use money as a store of value or as a measure
of value. They rarely possess money - when they do earn
some they immediately exchange it. They do not see the
intrinsic value of a commodity, only what money they
paid for it. They do not say, for example, that the
knife is worth Rs.15, but that they paid Rs.15 for the
knife. Naikens use money as a medium of exchange, but
the way in which they do so needs to be carefully
examined. In the capitalist system money, as a medium
of exchange, facilitates 'barter' over time and 'barter'
of any one commodity for another, irrespective of the
related requirements of those who provide the commodities
and the relative values of the goods. Naikens use money
as a medium of exchange, but not for these purposes.
They immediately exchange whatever cash money they earn.

They never save up in order to buy a durable commodity,
which they only get by an immediate exchange when they
obtain a suitable sum of money. In general they prefer
to be paid with commodities. For example, when occasionally Moppalas want to employ Naikens for work such
as clearing land and building huts, they generally find
it difficult to get Naikens to work, but have a better
response if they offer them a low daily wage, supplemented by tea and pastries during the working day, than
if they offer the same wage plus an extra sum of money
which even exceeds the value of the tea and pastries
provided. (This is another example to show that Naikens
do not see the intrinsic monetary value of these
commodities.) For Naikens cash money is almost entirely
a token which they are given, and is immediately substituted for commodities.

It is possible to suggest that it is not so much
'cash money' but its counterpart 'debt' which is the
instrumental currency for the Naikens. According to an
arrangement between them, the local rice dealer gives
Naikens rice on credit, and the plantation clerk deducts
the debt from their wages and gives it directly to the
rice dealer. The dealer only extends credit facilities
to those Naikens who attend work. Consequently it is
the need for credit facilities which directly motivates
Naikens to work and by which they are practically paid.
Naikens' purchases from the tea shop are a more revealing case. They only buy from the tea shop on credit.
The shop owner tries to extract a partial payment weekly,
but with little success. The account is settled when
Naikens get their annual leave wage and bonus, usually
sometime between July and September. A sort of seasonal
cycle in the availability of provisions is thus created.
During the period which immediately follows the 'settlement day' (as it is called locally), Naikens intensively
purchase provisions by credit. As the debts gradually
grow, the shopkeeper both increases his pressure for
partial payments and restricts further credit facilities;
so that, as the year goes on, Naikens have gradually
fewer and fewer provisions available to them. Towards
the day of settlement they get little, if any, credit;
and on the day they pay their debt, the cycle begins
again.

It is possible to relate the predominant use of
debt or credit to the long established traditional practice of trade in minor forest produce. From Morris's
work on the food-gathering Mallapantaram of Kerala,[17]
who are very similar to the Naikens, it can indeed be

77

seen that most of the traditional barter was regulated
by debt. The contractor gave some provisions to the
Mallapantaram who later supplied him with minor forest
produce, but immediately took some more provisions so
that the debt was kept open and called for further transactions. Only a simple historical continuity is established by this explanation, which is partial because it
is not interwoven with the explanation so far provided
of changes in the patterns of production and consumption,
and also because it accounts only for the fact that debt
is used, overlooking its new predominant place which is
not comparable with that of the past. A more comprehensive and structural explanation can perhaps be offered
if, following the approach employed in the above discussion of production and consumption, the use of debt
is viewed from the perspectives of the traditional food-
gathering socio-economic structure. Furthermore, it
could then be suggested that such an explanation also
accounts for the changes, back in the past, when food-
gatherers in South India entered into a relationship of
trade in minor forest produce with the surrounding
developed society, and the fact that in spite of this
contact and trade they have for centuries retained their
food-gathering way of life.

The foraging mode of subsistence meant that traditionally, like most other hunter-gatherer societies, each
individual Naiken could be self-sufficient. Transfer of
goods - even trivial commodities which could be easily
collected in the forest - was rarely practised even between those closely related to each other. An incident
observed during fieldwork may bring home the extreme to
which this point can be taken. Maran's family did not
collect firewood during the day. That night they sat
cold in the dark, and I sat with them. Maran's younger
brother, who lives only five metres away, sat near a
bright fire, with a big stack of firewood which could
have lasted for several days. When asked why he did not
borrow from his brother some wood which he could return
the very next day Maran answered that if he did so people
would laugh at him, saying he was not a 'person' if he
could not collect his own firewood. Thus only collecting
commodities from the environment would appear to have
been acceptable, while getting them from other people
was socially disapproved of. In contrast to goods, services were occasionally exchanged between Naikens, but
were followed by an instantaneous repayment. For
example, a young man who helped an older one to collect
honey would get a share of the honey. It can be said

that this 'instantaneous repayment' in itself only
served to prevent the creation of a chain of obligation and the consequent exchange of goods.

   The notion and practice of sharing would appear in
the literature to be a predominant characteristic of
hunting-gathering people, and is even claimed by some
scholars to be the very principle which makes the foraging economy viable.[18] Since it is one form of material
exchange, it is necessary briefly to examine the practice
of sharing among Naikens. Sharing was not in general
obligatory. Cases were often observed when members of a
food-gathering Naiken family ate their food, making no
offer to share it with visitors sitting with them. While
for some hunting-gathering people the notion of sharing
is extended to non-edible items (European clothes in the
case of the Bushmen),[19] Naikens only shared edible food,
mostly game, which could not be immediately consumed by
one nuclear family. But it was only rarely that big
game was caught, and even then, unlike cases where particular parts are distributed to particular categories
of kin (for example, Hadza), and perhaps to prevent the
perpetuation of exchange, there was a strictly equal
distribution, both in terms of the meat's quality and
quantity, to all the families in the hamlet. In the
traditional Naiken society, therefore, even the sharing
of commodities was minimal.

   It is possible to show that to some extent buying
on credit is not identified by Naikens as an exchange of
commodities. A debt is not tangibly comprehended since
money in itself is not used as a store of value or as a
measure of value, and since the future is disregarded.
Obtaining the commodities, and the later need to repay
the debt, are considered two separate actions; obtaining
commodities on credit therefore is conceived of as a one-
way transfer of goods. A striking example, observed
during fieldwork, can illustrate this point. Jackfruit,
which often substitues for ganji during March and April,
can be cultivated and is sold in shops. Towards the end
of the season wild jackfruit was exhausted in the immediate surroundings of the hamlet, and to obtain it Naikens
would have needed to go far into the forest. Instead
they were happy to buy jackfruit on credit for Rs.2 a
piece.

   The two transactions are considered separate but,
in addition, getting commodities on credit from shops
would not appear to be considered by Naikens as an
interpersonal transfer of goods; rather it is as if they
obtain them from the extended environment, so to speak.

This point is clearly illustrated by contrasting the Naiken attitude towards, first, services rendered by non-Naikens and, second, goods obtained from the shops. When they are rendered services by non-Naikens, still as traditionally practised among themselves, Naikens immediately make a repayment. For example, while at work Mathen felt ill, and the supervisor took him back to his hut. The very next day Mathen sent the supervisor seven eggs of wild chickens. In contrast, Naikens continuously take commodities from the shop, with no bother about the shopkeeper and their relations with him. It can therefore be suggested that, in its structural place within the culture, purchase by credit for the Naikens is not so much buying but rather something analogous to the collection of food resources in the forest. Indeed, there is a neat analogy between the seasonal availability of credit and that of forest foods. Both reach their lowest point in about the same period between July and September. Furthermore, while wages are principally paid weekly, by using 'credit' Naikens can collect food from the shops daily.

Through the selective use of debt, money would appear to have fitted in with the traditional 'pre-existing pattern', and its introduction did not disturb the web of relations within the society. There are several features which can, and often do, accompany the introduction of cash into a tribal society. First, there can follow stratification in wealth. But since Naikens have not changed their patterns of consumption - neither accumulating durable commodities nor greatly altering their attitude towards non-durable commodities - a material equality has been retained. Second, there can follow changes in the sexual division of labour. But both women and men could work in the plantation, and could buy from the shop, so that the sexes' equality and independence has been maintained. Furthermore, traditional division of labour was even reinforced, since women more than men tend to work as permanent workers, to earn money regularly, to have shop accounts in their names and therefore to be, as in the past, more responsible for the supply of the staple food. Third, there can follow differentiation in social status - either by different access to new means of production, or by changes in patterns of consumption. But neither did the latter occur (as just mentioned above), nor were there changes with regard to the former, since all Naikens could work, and since most of those who did so, chose to get only partially involved with the new means of live-

lihood (casual employment). Lastly, there can follow
changes in relations between people, when traditional
material exchanges which can symbolically tie the society
together are swept away by money. The Naikens traditionally had minimal material exchanges, and money could
even be useful for the instantaneous reciprocation of a
service (for example, often today the helper in honey
collection may be paid in money). Together, the structural similarity for the Naikens between their present
transaction by credit and their traditional collection
of requirements from the environment, and the related
fact that introduction of money did not disturb the
relations with other cultural parameters may well explain
how it was that, in contact with a cash economy, debt (or
credit) has been the one form of money which has been
taken into the Naiken economy, without much disturbance
to the 'pre-existing pattern' of the Naiken socio-economic structure as a whole.

Conclusion

It is argued in this paper that in spite of 30 years'
contact with, and some integration into, a money and
national economy, the Naiken economy as a whole - production, consumption and distribution - and the social
relations embedded in it, have retained their traditional
'pre-existing pattern'. There have been changes which
could have been considered far-reaching ones, in the
areas of production (wage labour), consumption (rice)
and distribution (money), but these are shown to amount
to changes in the content of pre-existing cultural parameters and not in the traditional pattern of cultural
parameters and the network of ties connecting them. The
explanation for this development cannot be provided
within the scope of this paper. It can only be observed
that these developments could take place partly because
the traditional base of livelihood was not destroyed
and at the same time the Naikens were needed by the
plantation; partly because of the important place of
trade in minor forest produce within the traditional
base of livelihood;[20] and partly due to a sufficiently
close fit between the traditional Naiken social structure and that of the western capitalist one.[21] In a
nutshell, it can be concluded: new items were incorporated into the Naiken economy but were treated as traditional forest resources; Naikens clearly took to shops
and the purchase of rice, tea and pastries, but through
credit 'collected' these from the environment, extended
as it were to include the shops; Naikens positively

responded to the possibilities of wage employment, but went to 'gather' wage in the plantation.

The notion of 'wage gathering' encapsulates the very argument which the case raises; and it therefore appears appropriate to link the brief discussion of the case's implications to it; that is to each component separately and to both combined.

'Wage' focuses attention upon the external changes themselves, the new items which are introduced to the culture in question from the outside. The Naiken case shows that wages and money entered into the economy, but have been taken without the economic properties attributed to them in the modern world, and are merely used as a token which is given instead of, and immediately substituted for, commodities. That is to say, the presence and certain use of new items may, but need not, indicate profound changes and modernization; or, in general, external changes cannot be assessed simply by reading into them the meaning ascribed by the new encroaching system (most often the western world).

'Gathering' directs attention to the importance of the traditional system in the interpretation of the external changes. The Naiken case shows that the traditional system influences the adjustment to external changes - an adjustment which is partial, and more important, even selective. This selectiveness is explicit, quite clearly articulated, and certainly acted out. Hence it could be said that the traditional system is influential not only in the actual adjustment to external changes, but first of all and at a deeper level, in seeing and evaluating the possibilities opened up by the new surrounding conditions. That is, to use the terminological framework within which Bloch writes, the actors see the process occurring around them in terms of their own traditional, pre-existing culture, and accordingly act. Or it could be even better expressed by reading Durkheim's own statement as if it had been written for the Naikens: 'In a word, society substitutes for the world revealed to us by our senses a different world that is the projection of the ideals created by society itself'.[22] But how then is the new input to the traditional structure dealt with, or how are the external changes internalized?

What the notion of 'wage-gathering' implies is that the Naikens manage to interpret their new experiences in traditional terms. Their case demonstrates that it is useful to distinguish between changes at two analytical levels: first, the 'pre-existing pattern' - the cultural

parameters and the network of ties connecting them -
and second, the content of these parameters. The Naikens show that it is possible for changes to occur at
the latter level alone. For example, rice was brought
into the diet but in replacement for the traditional
wild yam, taking on its role and not altering the ways
matters to do with food were organized. Again, wage
income which is almost completely and immediately
exchanged for rice has been perceived as analogous to
rice, and thence to wild yam. Thus because they 'gather'
wages, rather than earn them, the Naikens have internalized the new input which wages represent. What they
have done is to alter the content of an aspect of the
traditional culture, while the aspect itself and its
function are still defined in terms of the 'pre-existing pattern', the way that the one parameter relates to
all the others. In Bloch's terms, this is to say that
the actors talk *within* their society, but that, through
and in accordance with the grammar of their language,
they can make meaningful statements of external changes
and act accordingly. From the notion of 'wage gathering', therefore, a formula for the process of change can
be derived. It follows Durkheim's premise in seeing
social process in terms used by the actors; but at the
same time it is able to suggest how it is that the
actors change these terms.

A. DISTRIBUTION OF EMPLOYABLE NAIKENS BY CATEGORY OF
   EMPLOYMENT 1978-9

	Male and Female	*Female*	*Male*
Hamlet 1	XXXXX◙◙◙00	◙◙◙◙◙◙◙000	XXXXXXXXX0
2	XXXXXXXX◙◙	XXXXXXX◙◙◙	XXXXXXXXXX
3	0000000000	0000000000	0000000000
4	XXXXX0000	XXXXX0000	XXXX000000
5	XX◙◙000000	0000000000	XXXX◙◙◙◙◙◙
All hamlets	XXXX◙◙0000	XX◙◙◙00000	XXXXXXX◙00
Percentage	46 18 36	24 29 47	69 6 25

Key: XX Casual worker   ◙◙ Permanent worker
        00 Non-worker

B. NAIKENS' ATTENDANCE AT WORK: AVERAGE WORKING DAYS
   PER WORKER PER MONTH (1979)

	Male and Female		*Female*		*Male*	
	February	July	Feb.	Jly.	Feb.	Jly.
Casual	12	23	15	22	10	22
Permanent	9	18	9	17	0	21
Total	11	21	12	19	10	22

C. NAIKENS' ATTENDANCE AT WORK: NUMBER OF WORKERS
   PER MONTH (1979)

	Male and Female		*Female*		*Male*	
	February	July	Feb.	Jly.	Feb.	Jly.
Casual	10	15	4	4	6	11
Permanent	3	6	3	5	0	1
Total	13	21	7	9	6	12

D. DISTRIBUTION OF NAIKENS' PERIOD OF PERMANENT
   EMPLOYMENT

Number of workers	6	5	1	2	1	1	3	1	1
Years of employment	1*	2	6	7	9	10	12	14	16

*The probationary period was not completed.

E. PRESENT POSITION OF NAIKENS WHO WERE PERMANENT
    EMPLOYEES

	Unknown	*Unemployable* Old	*Employable* Non-workers	Casual
Number	7	4	2	8

F. DETAILS OF EMPLOYEES, 1958-78

	Male	*Female*
Permanent employees, 1958-78	13	14
Permanent employees at present	1	5
Employables who resigned from permanent employment	7	3
Ex-permanent employees who now work as casual workers	7	1
Ex-permanent employees who do not work at present	0	2

G. DISTRIBUTION OF TASKS REQUIRED BY THE PLANTATION,
    BY RELATIVE PROPORTIONS OF TOTAL TASKS

	1949-50	*1978-9*
Tapping	XXXXXXXXXXXXXXXXXXXXXXXXX	XXXXXXXXXXX
Weeding	XXXXXXXXXXXX	XXXXXXXXXXXXXX
Factory	XXXXXXX	XXXX
Picking		XXXXXX
Trad.Cn.*	XX	XXXXX
Cultivn.	X	XXX
Lines	X	XXX

*Traditional construction work

H. COMPARATIVE DAILY EXPENDITURE IN THE LOCAL TEA SHOP
    FOR NAIKENS AND MOPPALA FAMILIES, 1979, IN RUPEES

Date:	*29.4*	*30.4*	*1.5*	*2.5*	*3.5*	*4.5*	*Total*
Family 1	1.30	4.20	4.10	3.75	4.75	5.25	23.35
Family 2	12.90	6.15	6.55	7.00	4.70	10.35	47.65
Family 3	.80	1.02	2.20	1.70	1.17	.90	7.79

Notes: Family 1. Naiken, 2 working parents, 2 children
          Family 2. Naiken, 2 working parents, 1 child
          Family 3. Moppala, 2 working parents, 2 children

Nurit Bird

I. CHANGES IN CATEGORIES OF FOOD

	Past	Present
Staple	Wild yam	Ganji
Seasonal substitutes	Jackfruit, meat, fish	Wild yam, jackfruit, meat, fish
Supplementary	Leafy material	Leafy material
Others	Fruits, berries, nuts	Pastries, tea, fruits, berries, nuts

Sources: For tables A to G, Records of the Gir Plantation (daily registration of attendance; task-allocation).
For table H, Accounts of the tea shop.

Bird, 'Wage-gathering: socio-economic changes and the case of the food-gatherer Naikens of South India'

This paper is a version of part of a thesis to be submitted for the Ph.D. degree to the Department of Social Anthropology, Cambridge.

1. Particular reference is to A.R. Radcliffe-Browne, *Structure and Function in Primitive Society: essays and addresses* (London 1957), R. Firth, *Essays on Social Organization and Values* (London 1964) and E.R. Leach, *Political Systems of Highland Burma* (London 1954).

2. M. Bloch, 'The Past and the Present in the Present', *Man* 12 (1977), pp.278-92.

3. Ibid. In the same paper Bloch puts forward his own theoretical scheme, which for lack of space cannot be dealt with here.

4. Ibid., p.279.

5. Fieldwork was carried out from September 1978 to September 1979 supported by a College Bursary from Trinity College, Cambridge, the 1978 A. Wilkin Studentship, the 1979 H.M. Chadwick Studentship, and a research grant from the Smuts Memorial Fund. I am indebted to the above for this support. I am grateful to my supervisor, Dr Alan Macfarlane, to Mr Phillip for access to the records of the plantation, and to Mr Lakshmanan, my assistant during fieldwork.

6. This task is being undertaken in the forthcoming doctoral thesis.

7. J. Woodburn, 'An Introduction to Hadza Ecology' in R.B. Lee and I. De Vore, eds., *Man the Hunter* (New York 1968); 'Minimal Politics: the political organization of the Hadza of North Tanzania' in W.A. Shack and P.S. Cohen, eds., *Politics in Leadership: A comparative perspective* (Oxford 1979) and 'Hunters and Gatherers Today and Reconstruction of the Past' in E. Gellner, ed., *Soviet and Western Anthropology* (London 1980).

8. Woodburn, 'Minimal Politics'. In a footnote Woodburn points out that immediate return systems are not only restricted to hunter-gatherer societies but also found 'in a few highly restricted and specialized contexts in industrial societies' ('Hunters and Gatherers', p.115).

9. P.M. Gardner, 'Symetric Respect and Memorate Knowledge: the structure and ecology of individualistic

culture', *Southern Journal of Anthropology* 22, (1966)
pp.389-415, and 'The Paliyans' in M.G. Bicchieri, ed.,
Hunters and Gatherers Today (New York 1972).

10. M. Sahlins, *Stone Age Economics* (London 1972).

11. Woodburn, 'Hadza Ecology', p.91.

12. Woodburn, 'Hunters and Gatherers', p.98.

13. Gardner, 'Symetric Respect', p.394.

14. The fact that more men work in the plantation
than women is not dealt with in this paper. It can be
explained in line with the general argument but the
explanation involves idiosyncratic factors relating to
particular circumstances.

15. See B. Morris, 'Settlement and Social Change
among the Hill Pandaram', *Man in India* 56, 2 (1976);
P.K. Misra, 'Social Transformation among Food Gatherers:
a case study' in M.N. Srinivas and others, eds., *Dimension of Social Change in India* (Bombay 1977); and P.R.G.
Mathur, 'Forest Based Economy for Tribal Communities in
Kerala', paper given at the tenth International Congress
of Anthropological and Ethnological Sciences, Delhi 1978.

16. See the summary of these studies in Sahlins, op.
cit., pp.14-21.

17. B. Morris, 'Tappers, Trappers and the Hill Pandaram (South India)', *Anthropos* 72 (1977).

18. R.B. Lee, *The King San, Men, Women and Work in
a Foraging Society* (Cambridge 1979).

19. Ibid.

20. See Morris, 'Tappers', and 'The Economy and
Social Organization of the Malapantaram', Ph.D. thesis,
London 1975. This topic will also be treated in my
forthcoming thesis.

21. See A. Macfarlane, 'Modes of Reproduction',
Journal of Development Studies 14,4 (1978) and 'Demo-
graphic Structures and Cultural Regions in Europe',
Cambridge Anthropology 6, 1 and 2 (1980). I draw upon
this in my thesis and an article (*Journal of Cambridge
Anthropology*, forthcoming).

22. E. Durkheim, *Sociology and Philosophy* (New York
1911; reprint 1974). The point may be developed in two
ways: further stages in the process of change (for
example when new content enters a close cluster of cultural parameters, new linkages can be formed between
them, and a new substructure established conflicting with,
paralleling, supplementing or even replacing the original)
and more complicated cases, where the operation of parts
of the traditional system is restricted (see Meyer's paper
above).

ECONOMIC DISLOCATION IN NINETEENTH-CENTURY EASTERN UTTAR PRADESH: SOME IMPLICATIONS OF THE DECLINE OF ARTISANAL INDUSTRY IN COLONIAL INDIA

Gyan Pandey

Recent studies of 'de-industrialization' in the Indian sub-continent have helped to clarify some major questions regarding the overall impact of colonialism, although the debate on the fate of India's traditional industries begun in the late nineteenth century will not easily be closed. [1] What the nineteenth-century participants in the debate missed out, and more recent scholarship too has not been directly concerned with, is the differential impact of colonial developments on different sections of the local handicraftsmen, and the sharp fluctuations that accompanied the process of tying up India's regional economies with the metropolitan economy of Britain. It is these features that I seek to highlight in this paper, using for the purpose the nineteenth-century evidence relating to the most important artisanal class of pre-colonial India, the cloth-manufacturers, in Azamgarh and some of its neighbouring districts in eastern Uttar Pradesh. In addition, I hope to be able to indicate some of the social and cultural implications of the massive economic dislocation that came with colonialism, by reference to the more neglected aspects of the cloth-manufacturers' history and struggles: their organization and consciousness, their periodic if short-lived demonstrations of solidarity, and their resistance to various developments of the colonial period.

2

Historians writing about India in the seventeenth and eighteenth centuries have pointed to the various 'levels' of production that existed in the traditional textile industry, the regional and functional specialization in the manufacture of cloth, and the complex organization for production and marketing that had developed. A hierarchy of intermediaries, advancing loans and exercising various types of controls had evidently come to mark different stages of the enterprise (from the procurement of raw material through the preparation of yarn

and the weaving and dressing of the cloth to the stage
of transfer to a prospective consumer). By the eighteenth century the growing demands of the European
companies had added much to the complexity of the Indian
clothing business, and further separated the makers of
quality cloth both from their raw materials (cotton,
silk, mixtures of silk and cotton, or wool) and from the
market for their products. The European traders were
particularly concerned to promote productivity, stan-
dardization and variation of product, and sought to
extend their hold not only (as the Mughals had done) in
the small urban *karkhanas*, or workshops, but indeed into
rural units. [2]

Alongside the centres of fine textile production,
meant for the nobility or for sale in the distant markets, there existed all along more humble units of production, turning out coarse or medium-quality cloth for
use locally or by consumers in nearby towns and villages.
At the lower levels, it has been suggested, cloth production (from the cultivation of cotton to the stage of
weaving) was sometimes carried out within the family
unit of specific caste groups, such as the Jogis and
Julahas of Bengal. But there is some evidence of the
intervention of middlemen even in these humbler spheres. [3]

Taking as his touchstone 'the degree of division of
labour and specialisation, and the extent of capitalists'
participation in and control over marketing and production', Sabyasachi Bhattacharya has distinguished three
different levels of organization in the industry. The
first was typical of rural handicrafts: production was
dispersed, artisans worked at home often aided by family
members, and marketing was often unmediated by any trader. Here, spinning and weaving might be combined in
the weaver's household, or the weavers might use thread
already spun in the cultivator's household to produce
cloth needed by the latter. However, a good deal even
of the coarse cloth produced at this level was marketed
through middlemen. At the second level of development,
the middleman sought to ensure a regular supply of goods
of a specified standard by advancing cash (*dadan*) to the
artisan. He also invested in raw-material purchase beyond the means of the artisan in industries involving
high-value inputs, including silk textiles. The third
level saw the expansion of the work group beyond the
family unit, the intervention of one or more middlemen
in the procuring of raw material and marketing of produce, and in certain cases even the emergence of proto-
capitalist 'factories'. Bhattacharya notes that the

traditional cloth industry had units located at all
these levels, though the majority of weavers were in the
second level; but the levels of course only represent
'some points on a continuum along which the denizens of
the artisanal production system travelled (sometimes
sliding back ...)'. [4]

The work of these scholars has established, then,
the existence of intermediaries and the penetration of
money-lenders down even to the lower levels of the textile industry. One inference that follows may be noted
at once: while India's foreign trade grew and the external demand for her cloth expanded, and huge fortunes
were made by entrepreneurs in different parts of the
sub-continent at different times in the seventeenth and
eighteenth centuries, it is almost certain that all but
a small minority of the cloth-manufacturers - spinners
and dyers, weavers and bleachers - shared but little in
the profits. [5] Together with this it should be borne in
mind that the textile trade (as of that in a number of
other commodities), based as it was more and more at this
time on an expanding foreign demand, remained extremely
vulnerable.

The relatively rapid rise and decline of trade in
a particular area, like the rise and fall of medieval
towns and cities, may not have been a new phenomenon.
Babar's observation that 'in Hindustan hamlets and
villages, towns indeed, are depopulated and set up in a
moment!' [6] deserves consideration, for all the prejudices
of the conqueror, and this conqueror's deep nostalgia
for the land he had left behind. Nevertheless, what
Chris Bayly calls the 'forced' town growth of the late
eighteenth and early nineteenth centuries in northern
India was the product of a different situation - more
'settled', yet perhaps altogether more volatile. Political uncertainty and turbulence were marked in eastern
Uttar Pradesh at least until the 1810s or 1820s: neighbouring areas, in Awadh, central India and the Punjab,
remained unpacified for even longer. At the local level
this was reflected in the establishment and decay of
many small towns and *qasbas* in the latter half of the
eighteenth century, the extended jostling for power in
the countryside (which of course continued until much
later), and often violent revolt against new authorities,
British and Indian: the great uprising of 1857-59
appears, from one perspective, as the culminating point
of these extended struggles.

But there was, in addition to the problem of political and social instability, another major factor of

uncertainty. Traders, even far inland, were now deeply
sensitive to changing demands from Europe, about which,
however, they did not always have very direct or up-to-
date information, and over which they had absolutely no
control. Indeed, in a situation when war, famine and an
admittedly harsh assessment, in succession, had ravaged
much of the land, we may expect that those who lived in
the line of 'prosperity' established along the riverine
route to Calcutta, looked ever more anxiously 'outward'.
Any shift in the nature or quantum of the foreign demand
had repercussions that spread far into the interior of
the Indian sub-continent.[7] The shock-waves from Europe
spread in an expanding circle as the British consolidated their position in India. It was somewhere on the
periphery of this circle that the cloth-manufacturers of
eastern Uttar Pradesh stood at the beginning of the nineteenth century, when Gorakhpur district (then including
Azamgarh) and other parts of the region were ceded by the
Nawab of Awadh and brought under the administration of the
English East India Company.

3

In terms of the sheer scale of its cloth-manufacturing
industry Azamgarh was, at this time, one of the leading
districts of the area that came to be known as U.P.
The cloth produced here had long enjoyed a certain
regional renown: the district is mentioned in the *Ain-i-
Akbari*, along with Banaras and Jalalabad, as a cloth-
manufacturing centre of distinction. Mubarakpur, the
largest weaving town in the district when the East India
Company took over, was known for its compound cotton and
silk, *tassar* (wild silk) and wool cloths; Maunath Bhanjan (or Mau) had been famous from before the days of the
Nawabs of Awadh for its fine muslins, in the weaving of
which counts as high as 150s were used. Kopaganj, six
miles from Mau, had developed since the middle of the
eighteenth century into another major centre of textile
production. Nearby, in other districts, there were
other centres renowned for the particular kinds of cloth
that they produced. Much of what follows in this paper
is based on reports relating to the experience of the
spinners and weavers of these specialised centres. But
there are some important pieces of evidence, from the
second half of the nineteenth century, regarding their
less well-known brethren in other small towns and
villages.

Any account of the fortunes of the textile industry in eastern U.P. in the course of the nineteenth century must begin with the famous, if mistitled, Company 'investments'. In Gorakhpur and Padrauna towns, major weaving centres of Gorakhpur district just north of Azamgarh, there were, as the commercial representatives of the East India Company reported on arrival there in 1803, numerous weavers 'desirous of entering into the Hon'ble Company's employ'.[8] Numbers of them had evidently migrated from the district in the preceding 30 or 40 years, and gone to live in the Nawab Wazir's dominions in Awadh: there were 49 houses of weavers that had settled in Tanda (Faizabad district) in this way. The Company's Commercial Resident at Gorakhpur and its Reporter-General on External Commerce based at Patna, not unique in this respect (see Sleeman on Awadh in 1849-50, and the comments on Mau-Azamgarh referred to below), found in this clear evidence of the misrule and rapine that Gorakhpur had fallen prey to before the coming of the English. But in passing, the Reporter-General noticed another factor of significance in the migration of the weavers. The 49 households were induced to move to Tanda, it transpires, by 'the liberal encouragement' of a private English merchant, J.P. Scott, who gave each weaver 'a bounty of four rupees, and advanced money to enable them to purchase their looms and thread'.[9] This was said to have occurred 'about 1780': could it have been in 1782-83, the year of the great famine, or *chalisa*, in which many among the poorer classes died from starvation and which people still remembered in the eastern districts of U.P. a hundred years later?[10]

At any rate, the Company's representatives were confident that given the right encouragement, including a suitable 'investment' at Gorakhpur, such weavers could be induced to return to what were now the Company's dominions. Indeed their hopes for the future soared much higher: 'nothing appears to be wanting', as the Reporter-General put it in pleading the case for Gorakhpur, in order 'to secure to Great Britain annually' from 20,000-30,000 and, later, even 100,000 tons of hemp, sugar, saltpetre, cotton piece-goods and other articles - the produce of the Ceded Provinces, to be transported on ships built from timber provided by the forests of Gorakhpur:[11] it was an age of confidence and ambition.

The commercial residency (or factory) at Gorakhpur in fact proved to be a disappointment. In the year of its establishment, 1803, it was allowed 100,000 Calcutta sicca rupees for 'investment', of which it could use only s.Rs.15,000 by the end of March 1804. For this sum, only 280 piece-goods, valued at s.Rs.2359 had been delivered to the export warehouse by that date.[12] In 1805, the Gorakhpur residency was closed.

The Mau-Azamgarh factory, established at the same time, fared far better. Of the sanctioned sum of Rs. 500,000 (s.Rs.478,487/8/0), the residency had used well over half (s.Rs.258,356/4/0) by March 1804. Of this sum, s.Rs.50,306/4/7 was used for 'investment' in sugar, leaving s.Rs.208,049/15/5 for 'investment' in cloth. For this, the export warehouse keeper had received by 29 March 1804, 21,679 pieces valued at s.Rs.149,266/8/11; and the reports on the 10,025 pieces that had by then been 'prized' were 'very favourable'.[13]

Given the numerous difficulties that were bound to arise on 'the establishment of so very extensive a provision under the system of advances', this was without doubt a good start. The Commercial Resident for Mau-Azamgarh noted in August 1803 that the average monthly deliveries by weavers had reached a number that would provide 57,000 pieces annually. He calculated that with a little tender care, this figure could soon be raised to 78,000 pieces per annum, equivalent at a medium of Rs. 7/8 per piece, to Rs.585,000 (or s.Rs.560,000) excluding commission.[14]

Independent of the Company's investments, a large private trade flourished. The value of piece-goods annually exported by private traders from the areas under the Mau-Azamgarh and Gorakhpur Factories was thought to be about Rs.8 lakhs (800,000).[15] This consisted chiefly of very narrow cloths, said to be in great demand inland and quite unsuitable for the Company's foreign markets, but there was no reason to believe that part of this industry and trade could not be diverted to the Company's purposes. In 1804, then, while the amount sanctioned for 'investment' in Gorakhpur piece-goods, saltpetre and hemp remained at s.Rs.100,000 that for the Mau-Azamgarh residency was raised to s.Rs.600,000.[16]

In 1818 the commercial residency at Azamgarh was wound up and amalgamated with the one at Banaras. The tract continued to figure prominently in the Company's 'investments', but the allotment for piece-goods had declined considerably relative to that for other commodities, most notably sugar.[17] In spite of its reduced importance however the external demand for the region's cloth was, at the time of the termination of the East

India Company's trading position in 1833, yet to run
dry. In the mid-1830s, R. Montgomery, Collector of
Azamgarh, estimated that there were 13,682 looms at work
in the district, 10,561 for cotton and 3,121 for silk
and *tassar*. The probable produce, he thought, was ten
lakhs of pieces per annum, at a total value of perhaps
Rs.23 lakhs. Of this, cloth worth Rs.10 lakhs was
exported, leaving Rs.13 lakhs' worth to clothe the district's (estimated) eight million people.[18]
  The statement of exports and imports contained in
the Report on the Settlement of Chuklah Azimgurh prepared by J. Thomason in 1837 is instructive.[19] The
exports were:

Cotton and silk piece-goods (handled entirely by Indian traders)	–	Rs.1,000,000
Opium	–	509,700
Indigo	–	270,000
Sugar (exported by Europeans)	–	1,900,000
Sugar (exported by Indians)	–	350,000
Total:		Rs.4,029,700

The imports were:

Raw cotton	– Rs.	215,000
Miscellaneous, spices, etc	–	90,000
Grain	–	940,000
Total:		Rs.1,245,000

The Settlement Officer noted that sugar-cane (all of it
refined within the district for export), indigo and
opium were the chief 'natural products' of Azamgarh.
Comparatively little grain was grown, and grain had to
be imported from Gorakhpur, Bihar or districts in the
west of U.P. to feed the local population. The river
Ghaghra was the main channel for these imports:

  Golahs, or grain markets, are established all
  along the course of this stream, and the supplies

95

are thence poured in, as necessary, to *all the manufacturing towns in the district.*[20]

Forty years later, when J.R. Reid undertook the next settlement (or revenue assessment) of the district, a significant change had occurred. The chief exports of the district were still sugar and molasses, indigo, opium and cloth. But important additions had been made to the list of imports. After grain, the major items now were English cloth and yarn, cotton, silk, dried tobacco (*surti*), salt, metals and hardware, drugs, and leather goods.[21] British manufactures had entered this distant market.

4

By the beginning of the 1830s, as we know from other evidence, there had been a reversal in the direction of flow of textile products between the British metropolis and its Indian colony. What the consequences of this reversal were for the cloth-manufacturers of eastern U.P. it is difficult to compute with any exactness. Not only are statistics for the earlier years unavailable, the available statistics are also difficult to use. Thus J.R. Reid, a painstaking official who has left us a very detailed and valuable account of the results of his survey and settlement operations in Azamgarh district in 1877, declared it impossible, on the basis of the very imperfect returns he had, to reach a conclusion as regards the quantity and value of cloth manufactured in the district or the commodities imported into it.[22]

With all the limitations of the data, however, certain long-term trends are discernible. The traditional cloth industry was, from the 1830s, subjected to powerful new pressures which it had no way of combating. For several reasons, which I hope will become clear in the course of this paper, we must be careful not to assume that the impact of these pressures was necessarily, or primarily, reflected in the numbers involved in the textile trade. Nevertheless, some statistical tendencies might be noted.

All reports from the middle and later decades of the nineteenth century seem to agree that the spinning industry suffered a secular decline over this period. In Azamgarh, the decline of traditional spinners, like the Katuas of Mau and other specialized manufacturing towns and villages, was rapid and unchecked. More and more, as the nineteenth century progressed, English thread came to be used instead of local yarn even in the manufacture of cloth for local markets. While 'none but the more wealthy classes' appear to have worn any other than the manufactures of the district in the 1830s, it was observed at the same time that English twist had even at that early date begun to replace local thread. By the 1870s it was being noted that anyone who wished to dress 'with a certain degree of gloss' (without doubt a growing number) used English cloth or local cloth made from English yarn.[23] Filing his report on the new Settlement of Azamgarh district at the latter date, J.R. Reid observed that in Mau, where earlier thread had been spun of such fine quality that it sold for its own weight in silver, quality spinning was 'finished': the Katuas of the town now lived chiefly by shop-keeping and petty trading.[24] 'The spinning of cotton', wrote William Hoey from Lucknow just a few years later, 'has dwindled to almost nothing for it has been found cheaper to import European twist and yarn for weaving purposes.'[25]

While the reports are direct and unambigous as regards the fate of the specialized spinners of prominent centres like Mau, they have less to say about the substantial amount of spinning that was carried on, as a full or part-time occupation (especially by women), in widely dispersed households. Yet here too there are indications that the trend was similar. By the end of the century spinning was described as no more than the spare-time pursuit of those primarily occupied in other tasks and those (especially old women) who were incapable of doing any other work.[26] In the areas of cotton cultivation spinning certainly continued - in the households of the cotton-growers themselves, skilled neighbours or local weavers. So did it in many traditional cloth manufacturing districts like Azamgarh, from where Reid reported in 1877 that many of the looms were employed in the manufacture of coarse cloths from yarn 'which is spun by women of all castes in all parts of the district'.[27]

Yet the scales, even at this humbler level, were weighted against traditional spinning. Mill yarn was cheaper, finer and more even, and therefore easier to handle; and its attractiveness to weavers increased as Indian mills entered the fray to supply the yarn at still lower rates. In addition changing local tastes strengthened the case for the use of mill-made yarn. We have mentioned Reid's reference to the desire of men of 'status' to dress in English cloth or, at least, cloth made from English yarn. Reid observed, besides, that most of the low-caste labourers, 'a fair share of the lower ranks of the other classes [that is, 'castes']', and the majority of the women of the middle and lower classes still wore local cloth made from local thread. But, even for them, 'holiday attire' was an exception: festivals and other special occasions had begun to require 'a certain degree of gloss'.[28] Finally, hand-spinning was to be put under greater pressure as agents of foreign traders, and later Indian mills, extended their reach into the cotton-growing tracts and the controllers of cotton lands themselves saw a greater profit in the export of their produce.

The indigenous hand-spinning industry, then, was early on the slide. For most of the nineteenth century it was in the sphere of weaving that the real competition occurred. Here the traditional sector put up a stiffer resistance. The records show that the cheaper, coarser (and more durable) varieties supplied by the handloom weavers, as well as some of the finer cloths and unusual mixtures which could not easily be matched in conditions of factory production, for long held their own against the challenge of mill-made cloth. At the beginning of the twentieth century, at least one-third of the cloth worn in U.P. was woven by handloom weavers, and perhaps a million people (out of a provincial population of 48 million) were dependent for their livelihood on the proceeds of weaving.[29]

'A third' is, for all that, two-thirds down. Certainly, there remains the theoretical possibility that an expanding demand allowed mill cloth (foreign and Indian) to skim off the surface leaving undisturbed the market for the handloom sector.[30] Yet this suggestion fails to consider the timing of different historical events, besides taking a rather too sanguine view of the growing consumption of cloth in colonial India. The collapse of the export market, and much of the domestic one, from the 1820s or 1830s surely entailed a real loss, which was not made good until the end of the century - if then. From all the reports of the period, one gets the impression of a trade in deep trouble, uncertain of its future, surviving - but in altogether reduced circumstances.

'The weavers of Lucknow have been ruined by the import of English goods': Hoey's words written in 1880 echo the kind of report coming in from so many different parts of northern and central India towards the end of

the nineteenth century. 'The Jolahas of Lucknow are
fast leaving the city ... and seeking a livelihood in
service.' East of Lucknow, the Jamdani or figured muslin weaving of Tanda and other places in Faizabad district was under severe pressure. The town of Tanda had
approximately 1125 looms at work in 1862. The 'cotton
famine' that then struck hastened certain processes
already at work. Many weavers left their trade (and
their homes): at the end of the 1870s there were estimated to be no more than 875 looms working in the town.
And whereas before the annexation of Awadh in 1856 Tanda
had exported more than Rs.1½ lakhs worth of cloth to
Nepal, it was now said to send less than 'half that
quantity'. Jais and Rae Bareli, in Rae Bareli district,
where very similar work was done, suffered a similar
fate. In the town of Jais there were, in the 1840s, 600
Julaha families, all of whom supported themselves by
weaving. By the 1890s, no more than 200 of these
remained and only a score or so of them lived by their
traditional occupation. In Rae Bareli town too, by the
latter date, no more than one in ten of the 150 resident
Julaha families worked their looms.[31] Just over three
decades later, in 1931, the Census Commissioner of U.P.
recorded that 'the fine muslim (muslin?) weaving of
Jais, Nasirabad and other places [in Rae Bareli district]
is now ... extinct'.[32]

Lucknow, Faizabad and Rae Bareli districts were all
part of the truncated kingdom of Awadh which was taken
over by the British only in 1856. It might be supposed,
therefore, that the end of the Nawabi administration
automatically spelt the doom of the indigenous cloth
manufacturers. However, the abolition of the court was
altogether too narrow a reason to account for the decline
even of the superior fabrics.[33] In Awadh the taluqdars
and the taluqdari style remained, and indeed prospered.
In Nepal, the only Hindu kingdom in the world lives on
to this day. It was the massive influx of Manchester
goods that caused the downfall of the traditional
industry.

In Azamgarh, where English 'investments' gave a
distinct fillip to handloom production at the beginning
of the nineteenth century, we are evidently faced by a
somewhat different example. Yet here, too, the impact
of Manchester was felt before long. The fortunes of Mau
illustrate this clearly. When C.R. Crommelin, the East
India Company's Commercial Resident for Mau and Azamgarh,
first visited the pargana of Mau in February 1803, he
found that it had been 'desolated by the Zemindars'

warning one against the other under the Nawab's dominion.
'As the City of Mow was generally an object for plunder
to the most powerful party, it soon became a heap of
ruins.'[34]

The Resident drew the inevitable distinction between
the light and shade of Company administration and native
rule: 'On entering the district of Mow from this Province [of Banaras], the contrast struck me most forcibly,
the latter in luxuriant cultivation, the former a desert-
waste as far as the eye could reach; indeed I travelled
nearly two hours in my Palankeen without seeing a hut or
scarcely a vestige of cultivation, until I arrived at the
ruins of Mow'.[35] Such blanket condemnation one must take
with a pinch of salt. There is some independent evidence
of armed struggle for control of land in the region of
Mau in the years before the arrival of the British.[36]
But the more significant reasons for the decline of Mau
before the coming of the British would appear to lie
elsewhere.

For one thing, the adjacent weaving centre of Kopaganj was established and given special support in the
second half of the eighteenth century. Though Kopa was
an old village, the new town of Kopaganj (initially,
Iradatganj) was founded there in 1745 by Iradat Khan,
the Raja of Azamgarh. Weavers were brought over from
Mau, we are told, and merchants, chiefly Agrawals, were
'attracted' by Iradat Khan from various places. In 1774
the French traveller, Comte de Modave, described Kopaganj as 'a large place', with houses that had 'a better
look than those of other villages' he had passed on his
route from Calcutta and a bazar that seemed to be 'very
well filled' with printed and white cloths, pottery and
grain.[37] Then, in the great famine of 1782-83, the
population of Mau suffered greatly and 'deaths from
starvation' were recorded. If the experience of later
famines is anything to go by, weavers are likely to have
been among the principal victims. 'But the general population did not die from starvation, and wheat sold in
the Kopaganj market at 14 sers (80 tolas) for the rupee
- an unprecedented rate for those days doubtless, but
not indicative of absolute dearth.'[38] Kopaganj, still
receiving the special favour of the authorities, indeed
became the centre for relief operations: the construction of a mosque and several wells was taken up under
the orders of Mirza Ata Beg, then *chakladar* of Azamgarh,
in order to provide employment to the poor. We may
expect that many of the weavers and spinners of Mau
trudged across the distance of six miles in order to

avail themselves of this charity.

In 1803, then, the *aurung* of Mau was found by Crommelin to be 'in its infancy, there being very few weavers settled in it'. The Resident was informed that somewhere between 450 and 500 looms were at work; and judging from the piece-goods that he received from the local weavers between February and July 1803, he felt that he could get no more than 1000 pieces a month from Mau by the close of that year. At the same time, he anticipated that he would obtain 1500 pieces per month from the Kopa aurung ('this aurung is ... firmly settled. There are many weavers residing in it, and a greater increase may probably be effected hereafter'); 1500 pieces from the Maharajganj aurung, which lay on the borders of Awadh (Tanda, Nawabganj and other places in Awadh were 'full of weavers', many of whom might be expected to migrate to the Maharajganj aurung once the value of the Company's protection became clear); and 2500 pieces from the Azamgarh aurung, which had been the most productive up to July, and in which presumably lay Muba-rakpur - 'a flourishing place' at the time of cession to the Company, with an estimated population of 10,000 to 12,000, perhaps a quarter of whom were weavers.[39]

Contrary to Crommelin's expectations, Mau appears to have recovered quickly from the devastations of the late eighteenth century. It was aided of course by the restoration of the regional trade, but very distinctly too by the establishment locally of a Commercial Residency and by the East India Company's 'investment' in its cloth manufacturers, especially in the long cloth known as *sahan*. Yet, it was a fragile base for a meaningful recovery. Before long the market for Mau (and other indigenous) produce was adversely affected by the emergence of the entirely new factor of the competition from English mill-manufacturers.

By the 1830s, Thomason was already observing that the demand for the local cloth was 'much diminished' on account of this competition. The decades that followed hastened the decline. Reid remarked on the cloth trade of Azamgarh district, that, while still important, it was 'much less than it used to be'. Of the industry in Mau, he could only say that it was 'not quite dead'. His summary statement on the manufactures of the town might be said to stand for the traditional cloth industry in eastern U.P. as a whole:

> Private enterprise for a time kept up the trade of
> Mau after the abolition of the [East India] Company's

monopoly, but the introduction of English-made
thread and cloth into this country has given a
great blow to it. The place is now in a state of
comparative decadence, and many of the weavers
are said to seek a livelihood elsewhere.[40]

To what extent the number of weavers at work in the
region declined over this period is probably impossible
to establish. J.R. Reid provides a figure of 13,058
looms at work in Azamgarh district in 1877, a fall of
624 from Montgomery's estimate of 1837. But we cannot
say whether the decline from the 1837 level, when the
cloth industry of Azamgarh was already feeling the
effects of English competition, was greater or less
than this difference; we do not know the basis of Montgomery's 'estimate' or how rigorous he was.

One point may be made with certainty, however.
There were very major fluctuations in the numbers involved in the handloom industry, periods of a sharp down-
turn followed by not insignificant revival. We have
noticed this already for Mau at the turn of the nineteenth century. Another well-documented example comes
from the early 1860s, when weavers all over Azamgarh
suffered a serious set-back. The disturbed years of
1857-59 were followed in 1860-61 by famine and by
general inflation. The great increase in the price of
raw cotton, as the external demand for the commodity
shot up with the outbreak of the American Civil War,
together with the reduced demand for their products
resulting from famine and inflation, hit the weavers
hard. The number of looms at work in Azamgarh district
fell from 12,500 in 1860 to 8,680 in 1863. The falling-
off in the quantity of work actually done was no doubt
greater than these figures indicate; and the Azamgarh
experience was paralleled elsewhere.[41]

However, for Azamgarh and its major cloth manufacturing centres - Mubarakpur, Mau, Kopaganj and so on -
the reversal proved to be a temporary one. Barely a
decade after the American Civil War, Reid made his
calculation of 13,058 looms being worked in the district:
roughly 1700, 1200 and 500 in Mubarakpur, Mau and Kopaganj respectively, and between 100 and 300 in ten other
villages, apart from smaller numbers scattered all over.[42]

The ebb and flow of fortune continued on a lesser
scale in the succeeding years. At the end of the century,
we learn from a survey conducted in the 1890s, the handloom industry of Azamgarh district was certainly 'on the
decline', but it was 'still moderately flourishing' and

'a fair export trade' in cloth was being carried on.[43]
The plague took its toll: here and in other districts,
it was migrant weavers who carried the disease back
with them from Bombay and other industrial centres, and
the weaving community suffered 'terribly'.[44] But the
opening of a railway line through the district (and
through the town of Mau) in 1898 occasioned some 'revival' of trade; fewer weavers now left Mau, the District
Gazetteer of 1911 noted, 'to seek employment in the mills
of Bombay, Cawnpore and Calcutta.'[45]

The population of Mau, like that of Mubarakpur, was
said to have increased steadily in the latter part of
the nineteenth century. For Mau the census gave 11,315
inhabitants in 1872, 14,945 in 1881, 15,547 in 1891 and
17,696 in 1901.[46] Whatever the reliability of these various enumerations, Mau appears to have survived up to that
time as a trading and manufacturing centre,[47] and even
registered some growth in the last decades of the century: the opening of the railway and the establishment
here of a fairly important railway junction helped in
the process. One might even argue, on the basis of this
evidence, that the number of workers engaged in the local
handloom enterprise probably held up fairly well throughout the nineteenth century, though the early nineteenth
century evidence of progressive erosion after a short
and sharp increase in the trade would suggest a somewhat
different conclusion. But even if we suppose for a
moment that the above inference was valid, we surely
cannot equate the maintenance of steady numbers with
'prosperity', or for that matter unchanging conditions
in the industry.[48] There is striking evidence to the
contrary from Mau.

By the middle of the nineteenth century, the fine
cloth manufacturers of Mau were facing a near total
collapse of their market. Their history for the next
three-quarters of a century is the history of an anxious
search for alternatives. New kinds of goods came to be
produced. Already by the 1860s, the *dakhini pagri*
(literally 'southern turban', meant for sale in central
and western India) had become an important product in
Mau. In the 1870s, Reid observed that coarse cloths of
country-spun thread, some better cotton cloths, and some
of the silk and *tassar* cloths for which Mubarakpur was
better known, were 'still' made at Mau. At the end of
the century, while the weaving of muslins requiring yarn
from 60s to a 100 counts or more continued, with silk
being used for the weft in some cases, the *dakhini pagri*
had become Mau's 'staple product'. Many varieties of

red and white turbans were manufactured, but 'in the
majority of them the texture is loose and the cotton
used is of low counts, the quality of the finished
article being considerably inferior to that manufactured
in Bulandshahr', in western U.P. [49] Subsequent developments in western India, most notably the opening-up of
mills for cloth production, appear to have forced the
weavers of Mau to experiment in other directions; and
since about the 1920s the local weaving community has
been employed primarily in the production of coarse
cotton saris, with simple single- or multiple- line
borders, for sale in nearby markets. [50] Here was a
'sliding back' indeed. The industry of Mau had come a
long way from the flowered muslins once sought by merchants from many parts of India and the quality *sahan*
demanded by the agents of the East India Company. For
the weavers it was without doubt a much less lucrative
business.

5

The decline of the indigenous cloth manufacturing industry in the middle and later nineteenth century is reflected most dramatically in the reports from the old
established centres of quality production. This is
understandable. But some of the forces that threatened
the existence of some of these places as industrial
centres also seriously affected the lower reaches of the
cloth industry. We have noticed this already in the
case of hand-spinning. A closer examination of the
circumstances in which a part of the handloom weaving
industry survived indicates some of the adjustments that
weavers at all levels had to make in the face of the
challenges thrown up by the nineteenth century.
    Among the factors traditionally held responsible
for the survival of local cloth manufactures, one of
obvious importance was the inaccessibility of many areas
- untouched for long by railways and other modern means
of communication. Yet, as the fate of the hand-spinning
industry and of a good deal of weaving even before the
coming of the railways suggests, this was perhaps not as
critical an obstacle as it is sometimes made out to be. [51]
Banjaras and other wandering traders had, after all,
carried exotic and luxury items, as well as low-value
commodities such as salt, into distant regions for some
time before this: if there was a profit in it, we may
expect that the entrepreneurs would be available to

carry the cheap yarn and piece-goods produced by the
mills into the deep countryside.

Another factor of significance was that the mill-
made products coming from England tended to be cloth
(and yarn) of middle and high quality. The production
of coarser cloth using low counts of yarn remained primarily the concern of the Indian manufacturers. Most of
the cheaper materials required by the rural poor continued, then, to be provided by the handloom weavers,
whose products were preferred besides on account of their
greater durability. This last advantage was lost to some
extent as the finer, more even, but less durable machine-
made yarn came to be used by the weavers; but the local
cloths intended for poorer consumers appear to have
maintained their position fairly well through the nineteenth century - although, here too, there was probably
some displacement of part-time weavers by the more
specialized handicraftsmen who were forced into the production of coarser cloth.

To these factors we may add the survival of old
tastes for particular mixtures, traditional patterns
and so on,[52] plus the cheapness of handloom products
for those who could provide their own raw material. And
while the importance of the first of these declined as
tastes changed rapidly in the latter half of the nineteenth century, the second, it seems to me, proved to
be of great significance even as the century wore on.

At the time of the American Civil War, European
cloth interests expressed concern that the shortfall in
the Indian demand for their products might have been
'occasioned by increased indigenous manufacture'. The
official enquiry in what was then the North-Western
Provinces (later, the Agra province of the United
Provinces) revealed, however, that these very years had
seen

> a marked and distressing contraction of local manu-
> facture. This ... is less observable in the wes-
> tern districts, where perhaps from a sixth to a
> fourth of the looms in the cities and towns (though
> not in the outlying villages) have stopped working.
> But in the eastern districts the trade has alto-
> gether decayed, and within the last two or three
> years [i.e. 1860-61 to 1863] the falling-off is
> shown to have reached a third, and in some districts
> a half, of the looms; and even of the remainder a
> large portion are only worked occasionally.[53]

The different consequences in the 'eastern' and
'western' districts of U.P. flowed, according to
officials, from the fact that the 'eastern districts'
(including all of Banaras and Gorakhpur Divisions, and
Awadh) grew little cotton, whereas the crop was grown
on a large scale in the 'western districts' (including,
in this classification, Allahabad district and Bundel-
khand). Of the cotton they produced the cultivators of
the 'western districts' were reported to be retaining
for domestic use a quarter to a sixth, even in this
period of inflated demand and soaring prices for the raw
material. From this, then, the women spun the thread,
and weavers were hired to make specified kinds of cloth.
'It seems to be in this way', the government report
noted, 'that a large proportion of the population in the
western districts are supplied with clothing'.[54]
What this enquiry brings home is that handloom
production survived in these years of crisis, not in the
tracts that were away from the railroads but in the areas
where cotton was grown and where it was, consequently,
still available to men with meagre resources. Thus, in
a period of marked inflation, it was not so much the
lack of penetration of wider market forces and, with
them, of European manufacturers, but the availability of
the raw material at an accessible price that ensured the
continuation of the traditional industry.[55] In districts
such as Azamgarh and Ghazipur, Gorakhpur and Banaras in
eastern U.P., too, any cotton grown for local consumption
may be expected to have helped the weavers survive. Yet
here, even in the pockets where cotton was cultivated on
a significant scale, the weaker position of the tenant-
cultivators vis à vis the landowners and other exploiting
classes would have rendered more difficult the possibility of retaining much of the produce for local use.[56]
Consequently the contraction in handloom production was
'marked and distressing'. And all over U.P., even in
the western region, weavers in the larger towns, 'unable
to provide the capital required to purchase material for
their trade', forsook their looms.[57]
Those that survived in the trade appear to have done
so by a further reduction in their margin of profit. It
was found in 1863 that the imports of foreign yarn had
contracted sharply from the position of a decade earlier.
Many weavers reverted in this era of rising prices to the
use of local yarn (of low counts) and the production of
cheaper, coarser cloths.[58] It was a sitaution evidently
loaded with contradictions. The weavers of Mau told the
Commissioner of Banaras in 1863 that 'they would make

the finest quality [cloth] cheaper than the coarser, as
the latter required more cotton thread.'[59] The scarcity
of the raw material reduced the value of their labours;
and weavers in Mau and elsewhere were forced to accept
work on much less advantageous terms than before. Indeed, many who had so far succeeded in retaining a measure of independence were now brought under the closer
control of the moneylender.

Thus H.D. Robertson, Collector of Saharanpur, wrote
of the 'rather remarkable change' that had occurred in
the weavers' social position as a result of the rise in
cotton prices at the beginning of the 1860s.

> Formerly the weavers in this district generally
> purchased the thread on their own account, ulti-
> mately realizing the profits from the sale of the
> manufactured article. Since the rise in the
> price of the raw material, it appears that the
> weavers have, as a general rule, been unable to
> do this, and that they have consequently now assumed
> the position of daily labourers, employed by shop-
> keepers and merchants who supply the thread and make
> their own profits on the cloth. The zamindars and
> even cultivators are also turning their attention
> to this new source of profit by engaging the weavers
> as labourers for the manufacture into cloth of a
> portion at any rate of their cotton crops. The
> weavers naturally feel this change has rendered
> their position by no means so independent as was
> formerly the case.[60]

There had been periods of heavy demand and high
prices for raw cotton earlier in the century, such as
the phase after the end of the Napoleonic wars in Europe
when prices reached a peak in 1818-19;[61] but the exceptional circumstances of the early 1860s were not to be
repeated in the decades that followed. Indeed, while
the prices of foodgrains and most industrial crops
appear to have risen in the late nineteenth century,
the price of raw cotton seems to have been relatively
stagnant - in part, no doubt, because of the sharp increase somewhat earlier and the generally expanded area
under the crop. From time to time, however, there were
wide fluctuations.

> The trade in cotton and its price have been subject
> to wide fluctuations owing to variations in the
> supply and demand, [commented J.A. Robertson in a

summary statement published in 1908]. In the third
year of the American War the index [of cotton
prices; 1873 = 100] rose as high as 229, and in
1899, when the crop was a failure [sic] and American
cotton was extremely cheap, it fell to 59. The
latest rise ... [followed] on the gigantic speculation in American cotton; ... the price of January
1904, gives an index of 103, and during the same
month the figures for yarn and cloth are 74 and 85
respectively.[62]

Whatever the prevailing price at a particular moment, there are indications of an increasing centralization and control over the disposal of the cotton produce,
as mill agents and agents for exporters penetrated further into the cotton growing tracts and improved the
mechanism for the extraction of the raw material in the
latter half of the nineteenth century.[63] Thus, while
the lower price of yarn would certainly have benefited
many weavers, other weavers (as well as spinners) would
presumably have been deprived of the customary access to
their raw materials. Seasonal fluctuations in supply and
demand could scarcely alter this situation: they probably
contributed only to the prevailing sense of instability.
    With all this, the generally inflationary trend of
the period and the increasing severity of the competition
they faced in the urban and rural markets tended to drive
the handloom weavers more and more to the wall. Certainly by the end of the century their poverty and their
dependence were being widely remarked on. As one parti-
cipant in an industrial conference held at Naini Tal in
1907 put it,

> In the majority of cases the weaver at present lives
> a hand-to-mouth existence; his method of working,
> the appliances used by him, and the amount he has
> to pay to the money-lender to obtain money to pur-
> chase his materials, cut down his earnings to such
> a narrow limit that they are barely sufficient to
> supply his daily wants.[64]

'With the decline of the weaving industry', to quote
another report of the same period 'and the natural growth
of population' - a popular but simplistic explanation -
'the struggle for existence is severe'.[65]
    It was an index of the extremely depressed condition
of the weavers that time and again in the nineteenth century, when a region was struck by famine or some other

calamity, they were among the classes found to be most
in need of special relief or charity.[66] The weavers
had been forced 'to give up their looms and take to the
pick-axe and the shovel', wrote an official from Lalit-
pur district in Jhansi Division during the crisis years
of the American Civil War. In this sparsely populated
tract, where it had earlier been difficult to obtain
labourers for works of any kind, it was now found that
whole families of weavers 'flock to get work, and ...
many have left the district'.[67]

We have other kinds of evidence, too, pointing to
the deteriorating condition of the weaving community as
the nineteenth century wore on. 'Fifty years ago he was
far better off than he is now'. This was the view expressed in 1888 by Raza Julaha of village Usia in Ghazipur district, when the Government of India ordered a
country-wide enquiry to establish whether or not the
poorer classes suffered from a 'daily insufficiency' of
food. Raza was about seventy. His family consisted of
his wife, two married sons, their three wives and three
small children. Like many other weaving households,
this one possessed no land. Raza and his wife were now
too old to weave. The older son had left for Calcutta
a few months earlier in search of employment and 'since
his departure had not been heard of'. The second son
could weave no more than five yards of cloth a day: in
any case, as Raza observed, the consumption of country
cloth had greatly diminished on account of the import
of European piece-goods. The income of this son was
supplemented a little by the earnings of the women when
they got work at harvest time.

> I question [wrote the Collector of Ghazipur] whether
> such a family as this does not often know what the
> meaning of a fast is, and whether their daily meal
> is so regular and sufficient as it should be. A
> few such families could undoubtedly be found in
> every populous village.[68]

The profits to be obtained from spinning and weaving at any time in the nineteenth century are hard to
establish. 'It may be said with certainty, however',
C.A. Silberrad wrote at the close of the period, 'that
it is rare to earn more than 1 anna a day by spinning or
$2\frac{1}{2}$ annas by weaving, while in many cases the earnings
are much less'.[69] Raza's son appears to have been paid
an anna for weaving five yards of cloth, that is, a day's
work.[70] In Allahabad district, a decade later, Silberrad

found that rural weavers earned on average three pies
per yard and 4½ pies per yard (that is, one quarter of
an anna and just over one third of an anna) respectively
for weaving yarn into coarse fabrics known as *gazi* and
garha, and six pies (½ anna) per yard for weaving a
dhoti.[71] These rates compared very poorly indeed with
the 1½ to 2 annas daily that a casual labourer could earn
about the same time.[72] The weaver's problem was that he
was a poor competitor for agricultural labour where so
many sturdier men from the untouchable or other cultivating castes were available for the job. Hence, although
in severely straitened circumstances, many handloom
weavers carried on; looms were sometimes 'kept up merely
in order that the children may not forget how to weave'.[73]

6

It is perhaps necessary to reiterate that the mass of
spinners and weavers had probably never shared in the
prosperity derived from the textile trade. Their depend-
ance, too, was often of long standing. It will not do
to exaggerate the changes that the late eighteenth or
the nineteenth century brought in these respects. Yet
while survival at subsistence, or slightly above subsistence level may not have been a novel experience for
many artisans, the decline of spinning and weaving and
other artisanal crafts in our period removed important
sources of supplementary income from the villages at a
time when supplementary incomes were direly needed. The
significance of the decline of traditional industry might—
be better appreciated if the industry is situated within
the context of the rural economy as a whole.
    An idea of the importance of spinning and weaving
and other traditional crafts in the economy of the rural
poor can perhaps be gleaned from George Grierson's Notes
on the district of Gaya in Bihar. In the 1880s, Grierson conducted a detailed inquiry into the economic condition of cultivators in Gaya, recording statistics of
area, outturn, rent, cost of production of different
crops, and so on, for over 3500 holdings. He wrote after
the conclusion of his survey: 'One of the most remarkable
facts about cultivation in Gaya is that it does not, as
a rule, pay for its expenses.'[74] Having quoted the
relevant figures regarding size of holding and average
income and expenditure, he went on:

If we exclude other sources of income, 70 per cent

of the holdings of the district do not support
their cultivators. Those of them who have sufficient clothing and two meals a day must, in
addition to cultivation, have other sources of
livelihood.[75]

As regards the sources of supplementary income,
Grierson collected information from 163 families, comprising 1210 persons, in four villages. Their net income from agriculture, he found, was Rs.9,298, from
other sources another Rs.5,810. Of the latter, the
largest individual items were cattle-farming (Rs.1,027),
'service' (Rs.859) and artisanal work (Rs.814). It is
likely that the positions of 'service' and artisanal
work would earlier have been reversed. But now, about
Rs.600 was brought home as wages by men working as
chaukidars, peons, etc. within the district of Gaya,
whether in the village or elsewhere. The remaining Rs.
259 under 'service' was the amount remitted by men serving in Calcutta, Hooghly and other places outside the
district, as *darwans*, peons, domestic servants or weavers in jute mills. 'The Howrah mills', commented
Grierson, 'are full of Gaya Jolahas.'[76]

Conditions in Gaya were not markedly different from
those that obtained in the nearby districts of eastern U.P., and villagers here may be expected to have
relied in a similar way on a number of other occupations
to supplement their income from agriculture. The tract
as a whole was quite densely populated and, well before
the close of the nineteenth century, aided by the rigorous land revenue administration and legal system established by the British, the problems of sub-division and
fragmentation of holdings and rural indebtedness were
already becoming evident. In this situation large
numbers of the rural poor turned to the only avenue of
alternative employment open to them, migrating, with
their Gaya counterparts, to the industrial belt of
eastern India, the tea gardens of Assam and, as inden-
tured labourers, to plantations abroad. An official
report on Azamgarh noted that during the decade 1891-
1900 emigrants from the district had remitted an average
of Rs.1,300,000 per annum to their relatives at home:
it was probable, the report went on, that 'but for this
addition to their earnings, it would be impossible for
the people to support themselves by agriculture alone.'[77]

In 1881, the number of people living in the four
districts of the Calcutta metropolitan area who came
from outside Bengal was found to be 279,621 or seven per

cent of the total number of inhabitants. In the twenty
years, 1891 to 1911, the number of immigrants from
Bihar, Orissa and U.P. swelled by over 100 per cent, to
695,855. U.P. alone provided about a third of the total
number of migrants throughout this period: 95,346 in
1891, 188,543 in 1901, and 235,487 in 1911. Of the U.P.
migrants, by far the largest number came from a handful
of districts in the east of the province, notably Ghazipur which contributed nearly 29,000 migrants in 1901,
Azamgarh and Ballia (nearly 25,000 each in the same
year), Banaras (over 20,000) and Jaunpur (over 17,000).[78]

Nor may this be read as a simple case of changing
one occupation for another. The point has been argued
forcefully that the migrants from these areas had no
choice in the matter.[79] The nature of this migration
was quite without precedent in the history of the sub-
continent, and the personal crises that it created -
though we know precious little about all this yet -
were entirely new.

7

'The history of the weavers in the nineteenth century
is haunted by the legend of better days.'[80] E.P. Thompson's observation on English weavers is equally applicable to the weavers of eastern U.P. 'Fifty years ago
...': Raza's statement echoes a nostalgia found in many
of the reports coming in from northern and central
India in the later nineteenth century.[81] We know that
Raza's comment was accurate in a quite specific sense:
the conditions of trade in handloom products were distinctly more favourable in the 1830s than half a century
later. Yet Raza's lament was the result not only of the
decline of his particular craft, but of a more extensive
dislocation that affected all sections of the society
in which he lived. The growing trend of migration was
one indication of this barely comprehended change all
around.

Migration had in earlier times been an emergency
remedy during famines and other situations of crisis.
Frequently, it had been used by weaving communities and
other oppressed classes as a weapon of protest. As Rana-
jit Guha says of eighteenth-century Bengal, 'The primitive or one might say natural method - the only method
in fact - yet known to the ryot for enforcing [a] bargain
was migration'.[82] It had been a collective action that
not only succeeded occasionally in winning for peasants

and artisans the concessions that they sought, but also
emphasized their identity of interests and sense of
community. By the latter decades of the nineteenth
century, much of this was being eroded, the wholesale
migration of a community either to escape from oppression
or to look for greener pastures was no longer possible,[83]
and a collective act of protest had been transformed into
an individual act of desperation. The folklore of the
Bhojpuri region (eastern U.P. and western Bihar) cap-
tures some of the hopes and travails that arose out of
this transformation:

> *Poorab ke deshwa men kailee nokaria*
> *Te karee sonwan ke rojigar jania ho.*
>
> [One who gets a job in the East
>   can fill his house with gold.]

But also:

> *Railia na bairee*
> *Jahajia na bairee*
> *Nokaria bairee na.*[84]
>
> [Railways are not our enemy,
>   Nor are the steamships:
>   Our real enemy is *naukri* [service]).

At the same time, the resistance of the lower
classes in the region tended towards a new extremism
and violence. The history of the weavers illustrates
the point well. The Julahas (or Muslim weavers) were
described repeatedly in the nineteenth century as a
particularly 'bigoted' and 'fanatical' community who
time and again took the lead in communal rioting. Weavers were singled out in contemporary reports from
various parts of northern India as being among the most
militant elements in the rising of 1857-59. They were
prominent in other kinds of mass violence too - such as
grain riots. An observer in central India wrote:

> It is significant of the hand-to-mouth existence
> of the weaving community, that at the time of the
> riots which in September 1896 followed in the Nag-
> pur Division close on the sudden rise in prices
> that heralded the famine, the weavers were promin-
> ent among the ringleaders.[85]

The new elements in these outbursts perhaps need

emphasis: 'bigotry' and 'fanaticism', sectarian strife
and (here, as in grain riots) hatred of the bania and
the moneylender. This last appears, contrary to one's
expectations, to have been a quite novel phenomenon.
In medieval north India, the bhakti saints had extolled
the services of the moneylender, and even likened the
relationship between peasant and moneylender to that
between a *bhakt* (devotee) and *bhagwan* (object of worship,
god).[86] By the latter half of the eighteenth century,
and more clearly in the century that followed, the popular perception of this relationship changed radically.
Thus the term *mahajan* (substantial trader, moneylender)
had come to be used in U.P. in the later nineteenth
century as the Kahars' slang for human excrement. And
a folk-ditty recorded in the region at the time, ran as
follows:

> *Sāt sunārā nau thaggā;*
> *Sau that Baniya ēk;*
> *Sau baniye ko mārke,*
> *Garho mahajan ēk.*

> [Seven Sunars, goldsmiths, equal nine thugs,
> a hundred thus one Bania. But you need to kill
> one hundred Banias to create one Mahajan.] [87]

The fact that the bigger traders and moneylenders
in the weaving centres of eastern U.P. tended to be
Hindus, and that members of the hard-pressed communities
of Muslim weavers were among their chief clients, certainly contributed to the atmosphere of communal animo-
sity. It comes as small surprise to find, for instance,
in the weaving town of Mubarakpur, which was the scene
of extended friction between Hindus and Muslims in the
earlier decades of the nineteenth century and of two
major outbursts of rioting in 1813 and 1842, that Julahas were among the chief protagonists and Hindu money-
lenders among their primary targets: in 1813 the houses
of two moneylenders were attacked and a merchant money-
lender called Rikhei Sahu killed; in 1842 some five
moneylenders' households were plundered and relatives
and servants found inside two of these houses were
killed. [88] But growing communal feelings were probably
as much a reflection of the loss of earlier community,
of a search for identity in a world that appeared to
be crumbling. The community of groups like the Julahas,
grounded in a common heritage, in common occupations
and actions in the past, was now severely threatened.

Many individuals broke away in order to seek a better fortune for themselves and their families. But there is evidence, from the same period, of a community struggle to prevent the obliteration of their culture and way of life. One aspect of this struggle was the Julahas' underlining of their Islamic identity. Another, about which we know less, was an extended battle against the factory system.

8

At the turn of the present century a Kayasth entrepreneur set up a factory for the production of cloth in Mau. Immediately, however, he came up against a serious obstacle. The Mau Julaha refused to take up employment in his factory 'even for double the wage that he earns outside'.[89] Rai Bahadur Goshain Bhawanipuri had encountered exactly the same difficulty a little earlier in Banaras.[90]

Behind this resistance, and their sense of isolation and loss, lay not only the straitened material circumstances of the weavers and spinners but also the memories and self-consciousness and pride of living people. The cloth-manufacturers of Azamgarh district serve as a good example.

The handicraftsmen of Mau could trace the beginnings of their position as an important manufacturing class back to the reign of Shah Jahan. The pargana of Maunath Bhanjan was at the time assigned to the Emperor's daughters, Jahanara and Chimunee Begum, 'for their supply with cloth and sugar, the two great staples of the place', and its chief town (Mau) appears to have been named Jahanabad. Under the patronage of the two princesses, the town flourished.

> Substantial buildings were erected, a large market place built, and every means employed to induce persons to resort to the town and take up their abode there.

The town quickly grew to have 84 mohallas (residential areas) and 360 mosques. Julahas (Muslim weavers), Katuas (Hindu spinners) and traders constituted a large proportion of its population. An important cotton-cloth manufacturing industry developed, and the subsequent establishment of an imperial customs post at Mau indicates the volume of traffic that passed through it.[91]

It is scarcely surprising that Mau's skilled cloth-producers, thus promoted to a place of honour by the orders of the Imperial Court, should display deep pride and a strong sense of brotherhood. Communities of skilled artisans have everywhere tended to be proud of their independence and their skills. The Julahas of northern India have made a determined effort, over a long period, to overthrow the derisive, even contemptuous, view that other sections of the society seem to have had of them. To others' derivation of the name Julaha from the Arabic *juhala* (meaning 'the ignorant class'), for instance, they responded with the suggestion that it was derived from *jils* (decorated), *jal* (net) or *ujla* (lighted up, or white) – from which last perhaps came one of the other names that the Julahas used for themselves in the nineteenth century, *nurbaf* or 'weavers of light'.[92] Already in the later nineteenth century (and more aggressively since then) Muslim weavers in many parts of northern India had come to reject the name Julaha altogether, and insisted that they be called Ansaris (after a claimed Arabic ancestor who practised the art of weaving) or Momins, that is, the faithful, or people of honour.[93]

Of the Ansaris, or Julahas, of U.P. it was said at the end of the last century not only that they were generally 'inclined to fanaticism', but that they displayed 'a strong clannish feeling, helping one another, and to a great extent settling disputes between members of their own caste among themselves'.[94] Those of Mau, Mubarakpur and Kopaganj in Azamgarh district would seem to have been among the leaders in this regard. J.R. Reid, writing in the 1870s, reported the existence of an interesting social custom that was peculiar to them. All marriages in the community took place together on one day fixed for the purpose every year.[95] The object was to reduce wasteful expenditure. The custom showed the solidarity and the single-mindedness of the Azamgarh Ansaris, factors whose influence persisted well into the twentieth century.

Over time the weavers of Mau appear to have attained a special status and a position of leadership relative to other, nearby weaving communities. In the 1880s, the Settlement Officer of Ghazipur (the district adjoining Azamgarh on the south-east) reported that the district had 'no counterparts to Mau and Mubarikpur', and that the district's major weaving centre – Banka, near Bahadurganj in pargana Zahurabad – was simply 'an offshoot from Mau'.[96] The Katuas of Mau were similarly

said to be connected with those of Banaras, Bahadurganj (in Ghazipur) and Tanda (in Faizabad), apart from
Kopaganj and Ghosi in Azamgarh district. They, too,
claimed a distinguished ancestry. They were Bais Raj-
puts, according to their story, who had once been
imprisoned for resistance to authority and released on
the condition that they followed the woman's pursuit of
spinning. They had then moved from Bheri Tal in Gorakhpur, first settling at Ghosi, then moving on to Mau and
from there, at a later stage, spreading out to the
various places mentioned above. In the latter half of
the nineteenth century, they maintained their status as
a distinct caste whose members wore the sacred thread -
traditionally a privilege of the twice-born.[97]

The weavers and spinners of Mau, Mubarakpur and
Kopaganj may have been a special case. But they were
far from being unique in their self-image or their
pride. The weavers of Tanda in Faizabad district, Jais
in Rae Bareli district and other such centres traced
back the origins of their privileged status to the days
of the early Nawabs of Awadh and of their skilled production to a time much earlier. Thus the ancestors of
Madar Baksh, whose figured muslin fabrics were said to
be 'the finest specimens of this work', had been resident in Jais, Rae Bareli district, for eight centuries
(as the family account had it).[98] Towards the end of
the eighteenth century, a member of the family, Bhika,
evolved a style of inter-weaving words, flowers and so
on into patterns on fine muslins. He then devoted himself to the preparation of a kurta and pagri of the
finest materials, elaborately interwoven with the names
and praises of the Nawab of Awadh, Asaf-ud-daulah. The
Nawab, greatly pleased with Bhika's effort, made to him
a large grant of land in perpetuity. Later, Bhika made
a similar kurta and pagri for Sikandar Jah, the Nizam
of Hyderabad, and received for it a gift of Rs.5,000 -
for which he was waylaid, plundered and killed by highway robbers while on his way home.

At the end of the nineteenth century, Bhika's
direct descendants still held the land granted by Asaf-
ud-daulah. They had abandoned their original craft,
which passed to a younger branch of the family into
which Madar Baksh was born. Madar Baksh specialized in
the manufacture of caps and handkerchiefs (*rumals*) with
words in Arabic or other languages interwoven into
them. In the 1890s, some of his caps fetched as much
as Rs.10, some of his rumals up to Rs.100. He took $3\frac{1}{2}$
to 4 months to weave a rumal that sold for Rs.50.

As the only working member of his family, Madar Baksh will certainly have been under pressure to weave more, and if necessary slightly less 'superior' goods. As far as is known, it was not a pressure to which he succumbed.

Whereas the line of Madar Baksh died out after him, the weaving industry of Mau and numerous other centres survived, as we know, in altered circumstances. How the developments of the nineteenth century, and the far more intrusive presence of usurious capital at every stage of the manufacturing process from the procurement of cotton to the sale of cloth, were viewed by the weaving communities of U.P. was noticed by some observers even at the time. We have earlier quoted from H.D. Robertson's comments on the loss of their independent position by the weavers of Saharanpur district at the time of the cotton famine in the early 1860s. Robertson concluded his remarks on the weavers' loss of independence with the following observation: 'I generally found that *they viewed this as more serious than the loss of income*, which has undoubtedly been considerable.'[99]

The vigorous and extended resistance offered to the factory system of production by weavers in many different parts of India (as elsewhere) is in line with this response. When weavers in Mau expressed their willingness to make the finest cloth 'cheaper than the coarser' during the American Civil War, they testified to the unprecedented reversal that had taken place: their labour and skills had become an entirely subsidiary consideration compared to the cost of the raw material. In some senses the plight of the men captured the tendency of the age as a whole - which was to reduce the man behind the loom to practical insignificance. What the Kayasth entrepreneur of Mau wanted at the turn of the century, and Rai Bahadur Goshain Bhawanipuri in Banaras a little earlier, was not craftsmen working on their own to produce articles of beauty, but more or less intelligent employees who could be told how to watch over a powerloom functioning at speed and producing cloth of a uniform quality on a larger and larger scale for distribution in farflung markets. The weavers' reaction, as we know, was a general refusal to take up employment in their factories.

There can be no explanation of this in simple economic terms. The Indian Industrial Commission's later strictures against the Indian artisan's 'conservatism, lack of ambition and present inability to appreciate a

higher standard of living',[100] missed the point in this
regard. The resistance of the artisans was a struggle
for an autonomous culture as much as, if not more than,
a protest against material deprivation. What the weavers of eastern U.P. appear to have feared above all
was an alienation from their means of production,[101]
and a fall from the position of proud independent producers to that of working dependants or mere wage
earners. What they resented most was the indignity of
being ordered about.[102]

9

It has been one aim of this paper to suggest that the
decline of an artisanal industry in northern India in
the nineteenth century cannot be measured merely in
terms of the numbers employed in the craft: it must be
viewed, too, in the light of their displacement from
the position of manufacturing quality goods to one of
producing inferior ones. It has been argued also that
the process that has been designated the 'de-industrialization' of India, which we may never be able to
quantify satisfactorily, was part of a broader economic
dislocation that came about as a result of the progressive integration of the local economy with the economy
of a commercially and, then, industrially powerful
metropolis. Closely related to this is another point.
While there were, without doubt, fluctuations in the
standing of traditional crafts in one region and another
long before the period here under study, the decline of
the colonial era was of a rather different quality. For
it occurred, as the U.P. example amply demonstrates, at
a time when the buying up of property and other rights
in land (both cultivated and waste), combined with a
rigorous legal system and (though this is a relatively
late problem) the growth of the population which altered
the man:land ratio, had made a move to other areas or
alternative employment far from easy.

The common objection that all this was inevitable,
that older, less efficient modes of production must
necessarily give way to more rational and modern ones,
is deficient on two counts. The first, put simply, is
that it overlooks the history of the generations who
lived through the alleged 'period of transition': it
is as though Raza and his untraced son might never have
been. Secondly, it fails to take account of the parti-
cularities of the colonial experience. This is where

the very slow growth of modern industry created special problems, in India as in so many other Asian and African countries. There was a large-scale disruption of old forms, without a real transformation. The handicraftsmen of old, like vast numbers of the poorer peasants and agricultural labourers, found their means of livelihood in jeopardy: but their links with their rural homes were not completely severed. What was in western Europe a relatively short-lived if traumatic period of change became in the sub-continent and elsewhere a chronic condition.[103]

In eastern U.P. the reduced state of the artisanal classes, the survival of the weavers on sufferance, at the mercy of the moneylender and in pitiable conditions,[104] the effort to eke out a living from minute plots of land, and the necessity of 'semi-permanent' migration: all this continued. In 1941 emigrants from the tahsil of Phulpur in Azamgarh district alone remitted a sum of over Rs.60 lakhs to their relatives and dependants at home.[105] In 1942 the Magistrate of the district recorded that the Julahas of Mau could still think of nothing but 'their looms and their religion'.[106]

Pandey, 'Economic dislocation in nineteenth-century eastern Uttar Pradesh: some implications of the decline of artisanal industry in colonial India'

In this paper 'U.P.' refers to present-day Uttar Pradesh, or, earlier, the United Provinces of Agra and Awadh. I owe thanks to the participants in the 'External Dimension' seminar held at SOAS, London, in December 1980; also to Shahid Amin, Amiya Bagchi, Barun De, Indrani Ray, Sumit Sarkar and, especially, Gautam Bhadra for their comments on an earlier draft.

Abbreviations

BTC   Board of Trade (Commercial) Proceedings, West Bengal Archives, Calcutta

IESHR   *Indian Economic and Social History Review*

SR   Settlement Report

     1. Among the recent contributions are D. Thorner, 'De-industrialisation in India' in D. and A. Thorner, *Land and Labour in India* (Bombay 1962); J. Krishnamurthy, 'Changes in the Composition of the Working Force in Manufacturing, 1901-51', *IESHR* VI, 1 (1967); A.K. Bagchi, 'De-industrialisation in Gangetic Bihar, 1809-1901' in *Essays in Honour of Prof. S.C. Sarkar* (Delhi 1978), and 'De-industrialisation in India in the Nineteenth Century. Some Theoretical Implications', *Journal of Development Studies*, 12, 2 (1976) - see also M. Vicziany 'The De-industrialisation of India in the Nineteenth Century: A methodological critique of A.K. Bagchi', *IESHR* XVI, 2 (1979), and Bagchi's 'Reply', loc.cit. -; and R. Chattopadhyaya, 'De-industrialisation in India Reconsidered', *Economic and Political Weekly* X, 12 (22 March 1975).
     2. There is a considerable and growing body of literature on the textile industry in this period. See, e.g. Irfan Habib, 'Indian Textile Industry in the 17th Century' in *Essays in Honour of S.C. Sarkar*, and K.N. Chaudhuri, 'The Structure of Indian Textile Industry in the 17th and 18th Centuries', *IESHR* XI, 2-3 (1974). For the different levels of production and the role of intermediaries, see especially Hamida Hossein, 'The Structure of Cotton Textile Production for the East

India Company, 1750-1800', *IESHR* XVI, 3 (1979); S. Ara-saratnam, 'Weavers, Merchants and Company: the handloom industry in south-eastern India 1750-1790', *IESHR* XVII, 3 (1980); G. Bhadra, 'The Role of Pykars in the Silk Industry of Bengal, c.1765-1830' (revised and expanded version of paper presented at the Indian History Congress, Aligarh 1975); and S. Bhattacharya, 'Industrial Production, Technology and Market Structure in Eastern India, 1757-1857' (*Cambridge Economic History of India*, vol.II, forthcoming).

3. Bhadra, Bhattacharya and Hossein,opp.cit.; also M.M. Martin, ed., *The History, Antiquities, Topography and Statistics of Eastern India, Vol.III* (1838, reprint New Delhi 1976), pp.971-8.

4. Bhattacharya, 'Industrial Production 1757-1857'; for the silk industry, also R.K. Gupta, 'Birbhum Silk Industry: A Study of its Growth and Decline', *IESHR* XVII (1980).

5. See Hossein, 'The Alienation of Weavers', p.324. As against this, it is necessary to note K.N. Chaudhuri's evidence regarding the strength of the specialised weavers' bargaining position; 'The Structure of Indian Textile Industry', p.155.

6. *Babarnamah*, tr. A.S. Beveridge (1970 reprint), p.487.

7. See A. Siddiqi, *Agrarian Change in a Northern Indian State 1819-33* (Oxford 1973); E. Whitcombe, *Agrarian Conditions in Northern India* vol. I (Berkeley and Los Angeles 1971); C.A. Bayly, 'The Age of Hiatus, the North Indian Economy and Society, 1830-1850' in C.H. Philips and M.D. Wainwright, eds., *Indian Society and the Beginnings of Modernisation* (London 1976); Bayly, 'Town Building in North India, 1790-1830', *Modern Asian Studies* 9, 4 (1975).

8. BTC vol.172, No.33, Letter from Resident, 'Gorruckpore', 26 March 1804, and 'Report on Commerce and Customs of Ceded Provinces' enclosed with Letter from Reporter-General of External Commerce, Patna, 20 October 1803.

9. Ibid., para 115.

10. J.R. Reid, *Report on the Settlement of the Temporarily Settled Parganas of Azamgarh District 1877* (Allahabad 1881), p.14; see also E.T. Stokes, *The Peasant and the Raj* (Cambridge 1978), p.67.

11. BTC, vol.172, No.33, Reporter-General's Letter, 20 October 1803, para.123.

12. Ibid., Report from Board of Trade-Governor General in Council, 17 December 1803, para.79.

13. Ibid., para.51; also 'Account of Goods Received from the Ceded Provinces up to the present time' (from Export Warehouse Keeper, 29 March 1804).

14. BTC, vol.166, Pt.II, No.66, Resident, Mow and Azimgurh to President and Members of Board of Trade, 16 August 1803, paras.8 and 20.

15. BTC, vol.172, No.33, 'Report on Commerce and Customs of Ceded Provinces', para.77.

16. Ibid., Report from Board of Trade, 17 December 1803, paras.55 and 92.

17. By 1806, the 'investment' in Mau-Azamgarh piece-goods was already down to s.Rs.135,000; in 1818 it was a little over s.Rs.117,000 for the combined *aurungs* of Banaras, Mau and Azamgarh; BTC, vol.196, no.19 of 1 April 1806, and no.70 of 13 February 1818. For the experience of the sugar trade, which took a far larger share of the Company's investments for most of this period, see Shahid Amin, 'Sugarcane Cultivation in Gorakhpur, U.P., c.1890-1940' (Oxford University D.Phil. thesis, 1979), pp.13 ff.

18. Figures quoted in J. Thomason, *Report on the Settlement of Chuklah Azimgurh* dated Agra, 16 December 1837 (Art.XV of *Selections from the Records of Government, North-Western Provinces*, Pt.XII-XXI, Agra 1855) p.131.

19. Ibid., pp.131-2.

20. Ibid., p.128. Emphasis added.

21. Reid, Azamgarh SR, p.59.

22. Ibid., 159, 169 and also 144. See also Whitcombe, op.cit. pp.252-70; Vicziany, op.cit., and Bagchi 'Reply'.

23. Thomason, Azimgurh SR, pp.130-1; Reid, Azamgarh SR, p.170.

24. Ibid., p.147.

25. W. Hoey, *A Monograph on Trade and Manufactures in Northern India* (Lucknow 1880), p.28. See also Report of the Indian Industrial Commission, 1916-18 (Calcutta 1918), para.225.

26. C.A. Silberrad, *A Monograph on Cotton Fabrics produced in North-Western Provinces and Oudh* (Allahabad 1898), pp.45-6. See also A. Blennerhassett, *Monograph on the Cotton Fabrics of the Central Provinces* (Allahabad 1898), p.3.

27. Reid, Azamgarh SR, p.169.

28. Ibid., p.170.

29. Papers Connected with the Industrial Conference held at Naini Tal, 1907. 'Note by the Honourable Rai Sri Ram Bahadur, C.I.E. on the Handloom Industry', p.44;

A.C. Chatterji, Notes on the Industries of the United Provinces (1908), pp.10-11. For India as a whole, during the five years 1924-25 to 1928-29, handlooms still provided some 25 per cent of the total consumption of about 5000 million yards of cloth, while 40 per cent was supplied by Indian mills and about 35 per cent was imported. Report of the U.P. Provincial Banking Enquiry Committee 1929-30, vol.III (Allahabad 1930), pp.386-7.

30. This argument was put forward by M.D. Morris, 'Towards a Reinterpretation of Nineteenth Century Indian Economic History', *IESHR* V, 1 (1968). It has been re-asserted by Vicziany, op.cit., p.158.

31. Hoey, *Monograph*, p.28. A.F. Millett, *Report on the Settlement of the Land Revenue of the Fyzabad District* (Allahabad 1880); Silberrad, *Monograph*, pp.32,46. For the same in central India, see Blennerhassett, *Monograph*, p.2.

32. A.C. Turner, *Census of India, 1931, United Provinces of Agra and Oudh. Vol.XVIII, Pt.1 - Report* (Allahabad 1933), p.426.

33. See Blennerhassett, *Monograph*, p.2.

34. BTC, vol.166, Pt.II, No.66, Resident Mow and Azimgurh to Board of Trade, 16 August 1803, para.14.

35. Ibid., para.16.

36. Thomason, Azimgurh SR, pp.136-7.

37. J. Deloch, ed., *Voyage en Inde du Comte de Modave, 1773-76* (Paris 1971), pp.140-1 (I am indebted to Aniruddha Ray for this reference); Reid, Azamgarh SR, p.150.

38. Ibid., 15.

39. BTC, vol.166, Pt.II, No.66, Letter of Resident Mow and Azimgurh, 16 August 1803, paras.13-20. For Mubarakpur, see Reid, Azamgarh SR, p.148.

40. The quotations are from Thomason, Azimgurh SR, p.130; Reid, Azamgarh SR, pp.147 and 170.

41. *Selections from the Records of Government, North-Western Provinces, Part XL* (Allahabad 1864), Art. IV - 'Information Regarding the Slackness of Demand for European Cotton Goods', p.149. For the adjoining district of Ghazipur, e.g., where the number of looms at work fell by half from 7,000, see ibid., p.152.

42. Reid, Azamgarh SR, pp.168-9.

43. Silberrad, *Monograph*, p.46. The exports went chiefly to neighbouring areas in U.P., Bihar and Central India, and a little also northwards to Nepal.

44. C.E. Crawford, *Final Report on the 7th Settlement of the Azamgarh District of the United Provinces* (Allahabad 1908), p.8; D.L.Drake-Brockman, *Azamgarh: A Gazetteer*, vol. XXXIII of U.P. Gazetteers (Allahabad 1911), p.62. H.R.Nevill,

Allahabad Gazetteer, vol.XXIII of ibid, p.273; H.R.
Nevill, *Benares Gazetteer*, vol.XXVI of ibid. (1909),
p.27.

45. Drake-Brockman, Azamgarh District Gazetteer,
p.255. Sharp fluctuations have occurred since then as
well. The national movement gave a considerable fillip
to the indigenous handloom industry, especially in the
1920s and 1930s. Then the introduction of the powerloom in the 1960s restored the fortunes of the local
cloth industry. Mau and Mubarakpur are probably bigger
centres of weaving today than they were before; but the
conditions of the trade now are very different.

46. Drake-Brockman, Azamgarh District Gazetteer,
p.255.

47. Crommelin, the Commercial Resident for Mau and
Azamgarh, was given a figure of about 10,000 as the
population of Mau in 1803, which he considered exaggerated, however. But Reid in his report on the district
in 1877 clearly declared his opinion that, in the 1780s,
the town of Mau was 'larger than now', Azamgarh SR,
p.15.

48. Such an equation is often made: see C.E. Crawford, Azamgarh SR (1908) p.9.

49. Judgement in Trial no.13 of 1863, Court of A.
Ross, Sub-Judge: Government v Sheonarian Rai and others,
Appendix D to 'Petition of Hindu Inhabitants of Mhow,
to Secretary of State for India in Council' (1893?).
(I am grateful to Shri D.N. Pandey of Mau, Azamgarh,
for allowing me to consult this document which is pre-
served in the library of his late father, a prominent
Hindu of the town.) Drake-Brockman, Azamgarh District
Gazetteer, p.62. It speaks of the transitory nature
of the local weavers' trade in the nineteenth century
that no-one in Mau appears to be able to recall what
exactly the *dakhini pagri* was and for what market it
was produced.

50. *Census of India, 1961, Vol.XV. U.P. Pt.VII.
Handicrafts Survey Monograph No.6*, R.I. Verma, 'Cotton
Textiles Industry in U.P. with special reference to
Maunath Bhanjan, Azamgarh'. Mubarakpur suffered a
similar dislocation. Famous for a silk-and-cotton
mixture like satin, woven into fabrics known as *sangi*
and *ghalta*, the weavers of Mubarakpur, it was said, at
the turn of the century, had 'owing to the trade
depression ... been compelled to resort to the weaving
of cotton handkerchiefs and *pagris*, which are now more
in demand than satins'; Drake-Brockman, Azamgarh District Gazetteer, p.62. Such dislocation was in fact a

very widespread phenomenon. Hites Sanyal gives me the
following example regarding Ramjiwanpur (Midnapur district) from his researches on West Bengal. Ramjiwanpur,
situated near the junction of the old Burdwan-Puri main
road and the chief trading road from Midnapur towards
the north-west, and surrounded by a number of smaller
cloth-manufacturing villages, was the nodal point of a
thriving inter-district and also longer-distance trade
in textiles at the beginning of the nineteenth century.
At this time, the cloths produced in the region were
chiefly *garah*, fine cotton cloth, silks and some *tassar*.
For several decades from the early nineteenth century,
local manufacturers were able to concentrate their
attention on silks and fine cotton cloths, for which
there was considerable demand. Sometime around the
middle of the century, silks began to lose their importance, and coarser cotton dhotis and saris joined the
finer cotton cloths as the chief products of the region.
By the end of the century, the market for the fine
cottons had also collapsed, and the weavers were occupied in the production only of coarse cotton cloths for
a local market.

 51. Blennerhassett, *Monograph*, p.5.

 52. A. Yusuf Ali (comp.), *A Monograph on Silk
Fabrics Produced in the North-Western Provinces and
Oudh* (Allahabad 1900), p.103, writes of Azamgarh: 'In
silk fabrics, especially of the mixed kind manufactured
in this district, there is a peculiar adaptation to
local conditions and prejudices, which enables the
industry to hold its own, or at least to decline less
slowly than it would otherwise have done'. For a
different view of the significance of old tastes, see
Silberrad, *Monograph*, p.46.

 53. 'Slackness of Demand for European Cotton
Goods', p.116.

 54. Ibid., p.119.

 55. Silberrad, writing in 1898, accounted it as a
specially powerful argument in favour of handmade cloth
in the cotton-growing districts: the women of the
cultivator's household spin some of their home-grown
cotton into yarn, which the Kori then weaves for them;
Monograph, p.46.

 56. See, for the example of sugar-cane cultivators
in an era of considerable expansion of the area under
the crop and, indeed, of the establishment of modern
factories for the refining of sugar, Shahid Amin,,
'Sugar-cane Cultivation in Gorakhpur, c.1890-1940', passim.

 57. 'Slackness of Demand', p.119.

58. Ibid., p.118.
59. Ibid., p.148.
60. Ibid., p.121.
61. Siddiqi, *Agrarian Change*, p.155.
62. *The Imperial Gazetteer of India. The Indian Empire.* III (Oxford 1908), p.465. See D.R. Gadgil, *The Industrial Evolution of India in Recent Times, 1860-1939* (Delhi 1972), pp.21-2, 65; and Whitcombe, op.cit., pp.102-3, 178-9 and Fig.3 at end of book. These present some of the evidence regarding general price movements during the period.
63. See M. Vicziany, 'Bombay Merchants and Structural Changes in the Export Community, 1850-80', in K.N. Chaudhuri and C.J. Dewey, eds., *Economy and Society. Essays in Indian Economic and Social History* (Delhi 1979).
64. Naini Tal Industrial Conference Papers 1907, p.44. See also Indian Industrial Commission Report, p.7.
65. Drake-Brockman, Azamgarh District Gazetteer, p.118.
66. Naini Tal Industrial Conference Papers 1907, p.44; R. Baird-Smith, *Report on the Famine of 1860-61* (Roorkee, May 1861), p.31; F. Henvey (comp.), *A Narrative of the Drought and Famine which prevailed in the North-Western Provinces during 1868, 1869 and 1870* (Allahabad 1871), p.2; Gorakhpur Commissioner's Record Room, Dept.XIII, File 40/1905-9, 'Rules for the Relief of Distressed Weavers'.
67. 'Slackness of Demand for European Cotton Goods', p.146.
68. Government of India, Revenue and Agriculture Dept., Famine. Progs.1-24, December 1888, 'Reports on the Condition of the Lower Classes of the Population of India', Report from Banaras Division, para.17. Blenner-hassett, *Monograph*, p.3, writes of how thirty years ago, the weavers were 'a prosperous community', common weavers, let alone those of special skill, earning Rs.50 per month, whereas now the average income was probably as low as Rs.3 to Rs.5 a month.
69. Silberrad, *Monograph*, p.49.
70. 'Condition of the Lower Classes', Banaras Division Report, para.17.
71. Silberrad, *Monograph*, p.46.
72. Reid, Azamgarh SR, p.129; A.K. Bagchi, *Private Investment in India 1900-39* (Cambridge 1972), p.221, n.8.
73. 'Slackness of Demand for European Cotton Goods', p.91.

74. G.A. Grierson, *Notes on the District of Gaya* (Calcutta 1893), p.91.

75. Ibid., p.95. Emphasis in the original.

76. Ibid., p.107.

77. Drake-Brockman, Azamgarh District Gazetteer, p.118. J.R. Reid noted in 1877 that employment on public works in the Azamgarh district did not compensate for the loss of service 'in the Native Army and with Native Princes' from which 'extraneous source of a good deal of money used to come into this part of the country', cited in Whitcombe, op.cit., p.140.

78. R. Das Gupta, 'Factory Labour in Eastern India: Sources of Supply, 1855-1946', *IESHR*,XIII, 3 (1976), pp.289-91, 310, 312.

79. L. Chakravarty, 'Emergence of an Industrial Labour Force in a Dual Economy - British India, 1880-1920', *IESHR*, XV, 3 (1978).

80. E.P. Thompson, *The Making of the English Working Class* (Harmondsworth 1968), p.297.

81. See Blennerhassett, *Monograph*, p.1.

82. R. Guha, *Report on an Investigation of the Gauripur Raj Estate Archives* (Annual Report, Regional Record Survey Committee, West Bengal, 1955-56), p.29. I am grateful to Gautam Bhadra for drawing my attention to this report.

83. There were a few exceptions in special circumstances, such as migration in times of famine, or the hijrat of Patidar peasants from Kheda and Surat districts during the Civil Disobedience Movement of 1930-31 which was made possible by 'the jigsaw-like juxtaposition of British and Baroda territory in the area'; D. Hardiman, 'The Crisis of the Lesser Patidars: Peasant Agitations in Kheda, Gujarat, 1917-34', in D.A. Low, ed., *Congress and the Raj* (London and Delhi 1977), p.63.

84. Quoted in D.P. Saxena, *Rururban Migration in India. Causes and Consequences* (Bombay 1977), pp.175, 178.

85. Blennerhassett, *Monograph*, p.4.

86. I owe this point to Gautam Bhadra. For an elaboration, see his *'Mughal Juge Bhartiya Krishi Arthaniti te Sreni Vinyas O Sreni Dwanda'*, *Anya Artha*, 7 (January-February 1975).

87. Both these examples are from W. Crooke, *A Rural and Agricultural Glossary for the North-Western Provinces and Oudh* (Calcutta 1888), p.181.

88. U.P. Regional Archives, Allahabad, COG (Gorakhpur), Judicial (Azamgarh), vol.68, File 47, 'Outbreak

in the Town of Mubarikpur, Azamgarh 1845'. Drake-
Brockman, Azamgarh District Gazetteer, pp.261-1. For
a fuller discussion of this subject, see my 'Sectarian
Strife in the Bhojpuri Region, c.1806-1917' (forthcoming).

89. Naini Tal Industrial Conference Papers (1907),
p.40.

90. Ibid.

91. U.P. Regional Archives, Allahabad, COG (Gorakhpur), Revenue (Azamgarh), vol.27f, File 331, J. Thomason, Collector Azimgurh to F. Currie, Commissioner
Revenue 5th Division, 22 June 1836, para.22; Reid;
Azamgarh SR, pp.146-7.

92. Silberrad, *Monograph*, p.1; W. Crooke, *The
Tribes and Castes of the North-Western Provinces and
Oudh* III (Calcutta 1896), pp.69-70.

93. Ibid.; also interviews with Maulvi Kamruzzaman,
Mubarakpur, Azamgarh.

94. Silberrad, *Monograph*, p.1.

95. Reid, Azamgarh SR, p.147n.

96. W. Irvine, *Report on Revision of Records and
Settlement Operations in the Ghazipur District, 1880-
85* (Allahabad 1886), p.127. See also Collector of
Mirzapur's report, in 'Slackness of Demand for European
Cotton Goods', p.149.

97. Reid, Azamgarh SR, p.147.

98. The following account is based on Silberrad,
Monograph, pp.32-3.

99. 'Slackness of Demand', p.148.

100. Indian Industrial Commission Report, p.195.

101. The point is made by S. Bhattacharya, 'Cultural and Social Constraints in Technological Innovation', *IESHR* III, 3 (1966).

102. See Thompson, op.cit., p.338.

103. See Bagchi, 'De-industrialisation in Gangetic
Bihar', pp.500-1, and 'De-industrialisation in India',
pp.136-7.

104. See, for example, K. Nair, *Blossoms in the
Dust* (London 1961), pp.35-6.

105. Ram Rup Singh, *Assessment Report of Tahsil
Phulpur, District Azamgarh* (Allahabad 1944),p.4.

106. U.P. Regional Archives, Allahabad: List 35,
R.H. Niblett, District Officer (1 December 1939 to 22
August 1942), 'Who's Who in Azamgarh District', entry
no.86.

RURAL LABOUR IN THE BOMBAY TEXTILE INDUSTRY AND THE ARTICULATION OF MODES OF ORGANIZATION

Dick Kooiman

Introduction

One of the most fundamental problems of historical
analysis is the specification of particular modes of
production within a given social formation and the way
in which one mode requires for its own reproduction
dominance over the other. Recently, this claim has
been put forward most emphatically and persistently by
adherents of the so-called mode of production school of
thought. And it must be conceded that this approach
has proved its worth and has yielded interesting
results as far as African and Latin American studies are
concerned. Asian studies, however, seem to be lagging
behind in this field of research. It may be that the
lack of written sources, especially for Africa, has
prompted historians to investigate the past by extra-
polating from the present with the help of comprehensive
theories, whereas in the field of South Asian studies
historians, worming their way through huge piles of
documentary evidence, are more inclined to cling to
the established practices of their profession. Nevertheless, mode of production studies on South Asia do
appear occasionally and in all probability have come
to stay.[1]
  Most studies made from this perspective agree that
imperialism, by imposing private property and establishing large scale commodity production, subordinated
indigenous agriculture to the exigencies of the world
market. But although imperial power drastically
changed the existing relations of production in agriculture, it prevented native societies from fully
industrializing. Consequently, the majority of the uprooted peasants could not be absorbed by industrial
growth but had to fall back upon village society and
thus the essential backwardness of agriculture was maintained.
  As a matter of course, this quite general picture
needs further elaboration to fit specific situations.
But the filling in of more details generates a lot of
discussion about the extent to which capitalism succeeded in transforming indigenous society, the exact
definition of the agrarian, non-capitalist sector

and the existence or non-existence of free wage-labour
in agriculture.[2]

It is not the purpose of this paper to bother
about the many niceties of this ongoing debate. Rather,
it focuses on one central notion, the articulation of
two different modes of production. This articulation
can be conceptualized as the co-existence of a non-
capitalist (agrarian) mode of production and a capitalist (industrial) one within a given social formation.
But this dualism does not imply a complete separation
or lack of communication between the two modes of production. Peasant social formations in the Third World
have been penetrated by foreign as well as indigenous
industrial capital, which drew its labour from the
agrarian sector. But as Meillassoux has pointed out
for Africa, industrial capitalism became interested in
the maintenance of that agrarian society (the 'commu-
nauté-domestique'), as it represented a source for the
reproduction of labour, that is the provision of social
services, care of the sick and aged, child-rearing and
so on. For the wage-earners also, the preservation of
village and family ties was of utmost importance, as
the agricultural self-sustaining community fulfilled
the vital functions of social security that industrial
capitalism refused to assume. Whereas in Europe capitalism arose by destroying feudalism, in the Third
World it developed by maintaining previous modes of
production and Meillassoux concludes that 'the agricultural communities ... are being both undermined and
perpetuated at the same time, undergoing a prolongated
crisis and not a smooth transition to capitalism'.[3]

An attempt to apply this frame of analysis to
colonial India has recently been made by Gail Omvedt.
She emphasizes the lack of a family wage as the main
mechanism through which cheap labour could be employed
and manufacturing costs reduced. By leaving the costs
of reproduction of labour power to the non-capitalist
agrarian sector, capitalism also forced a sexual division between the villages, where most women and family
members remained, and the new centres of employment to
which the male workers migrated in large numbers. Although Omvedt is laying more stress on the crucial role
of the colonial state, she reaches the same conclusion
as Meillassoux in the sense that the development of the
capitalist mode of production is furthered simultane-
ously with the maintenance of feudal relations in agriculture.[4]

In this paper, I want to carry the argument of

131

Gail Omvedt a bit further. First of all the concept
of a dominant capitalist and subordinated feudal mode
of production will be narrowed down and its applicabil-
ity tested by focusing on the city of Bombay and its
surrounding hinterland before World War II. The textile industry of this city represented one of the most
developed sectors of the British-Indian economy, while
the surrounding village societies may be called non-
capitalist or even feudal in the sense that their economy was characterized by personal relationships of
dependence based on the differential access to land and
(mainly agrarian) employment opportunities. Next,
attention will be paid to the so-called jobber, who as
a recruiter of labour served as a linkage between these
rural localities and the wider world of urban industry.
Finally, the most important question will be, to what
extent the articulation of two different modes of production determined the character of the emerging trade
unions in the Bombay textile industry and how far our
analysis may benefit from the introduction of the concept of articulation of modes of labour organization.

Bombay and the Textile Industry: Migration of Labour

The Bombay textile industry was started in the mid-
nineteenth century by native enterprise. It combined
indigenous capital with European management and technical equipment. After a period of extensive growth
it very soon came to dominate the city's economic life.
By World War I the industry numbered more than eighty
mills and employed one quarter of the total working
population. Except for its textile mills Bombay had
little claim to be called an industrial city and economically it may be characterized as a city which combined the textile specialization of Manchester with
the trade and shipping of London.
     The labour needed by the growing number of mills
was mainly drawn from the surrounding districts, and,
of course, this labour drain had far-reaching consequences both for city and countryside. The peculiar
composition of Bombay's urban population in terms of
sex and age bore testimony to this and may be seen as
a clear example of the way in which industrial capitalism made use of labour from the non-capitalist
sector.
     First of all, Bombay was primarily a city of immi-
grants. According to the census, the percentage of

the urban population born outside Bombay was 69 per cent in 1872 and never fell below the 70 per cent level in any subsequent census. There is, however, some inflation in this figure, owing to a widespread female custom of returning for confinement to the village of origin.[5]

Most migrants went to Bombay alone in search of employment. A married man would leave his family behind until such time as he might decide to make a home for them in the city. In most cases, however, that time never came and thus the worker had to pay periodical visits to his village to fulfil the necessary family obligations. Therefore, the proportion of females was very low among the immigrant groups and in 1931, for example, amounted to only 541 females for every thousand males coming from Ratnagiri, the main labour-supplying area. This figure does not distinguish between textile workers and other types of migrants. On the basis of census data, however, the sex-ratio of immigrant textile workers from the main labour catchment areas can be calculated at least approximately (as in table 1).[6]

Table 1: Sex-Ratio among Immigrants in Bombay (1931) · Females per 1,000 Males

Place of Origin:	Sex-Ratio (General)	Sex-Ratio (Textile Labour Only)
Poona	661	599
Kolaba	619	375
Satara	545	274
Ratnagiri	541	459
United Provinces	211	38
Total	489	323

As might be expected, the sex-ratio of textile workers turns out to be considerably lower than that of the whole migrant group from the corresponding region, and the far-away districts of U.P. were represented by a low of 38. The number of females per 1,000 males for Bombay as a whole was 554 and the general census report mentioned that the sex-ratios of Bombay City and Ratnagiri district offered interesting complements to each other.

Not only was the sex-ratio in Bombay exeptional, but the age composition of the urban population also differed markedly from the rural hinterland. The

censuses show a great preponderance of adults in the
active wage-earning periods of life. Whereas in the
Presidency as a whole the 15-40 age-group year numbered
41.8 per cent of the total population, in Bombay City
its proportional representation was no less than 61.3
per cent. Especially in this age-group there was a
marked deficiency of females (248 per 1,000 males) and
only in the lower and higher age-groups did the female
ratio approach a more even distribution. This very
particular demographic structure clearly reflects the
special economic needs and labour recruitment in Bombay's capitalist mode of production. It proves that
the greater number of workers born outside Bombay did
not reside in the city permanently. They spent the
most productive period of their lives there, then left
the city when they ceased working.

In 1931 the census concluded that Bombay 'has become less and less a place for children and old people'.
It even discerned a tendency for workers to retire from
factory work at an earlier age than formerly, suggesting that Bombay was also becoming 'progressively a
place for younger and younger workers'.[7] The average
age of the male operatives was computed at 26 years.[8]

The 1908 Labour Commission reported that the migrant worker could return to his village the moment he
came to dislike factory labour. Back home he could
always find some work to do, while the joint family
system secured him against want.[9] But that is a much
too rosy picture of the situation. From an interview
with returned workers, a *mamlatdar* in one of the main
labour supplying areas concluded 'that the lot of these
persons is a hard one and that if they take to mill
life it is not so much out of love as out of necessity'.[10] As their villages did not offer sufficient
work they had to seek employment elsewhere. Or, as
the Whitley Commission had it, in its classical phrase,
the migrant workers 'are pushed not pulled'.[11] The
areas they came from suffered from a poor agriculture
hampered by too heavy or scanty rains, an increasing
population pressure and the dwindling importance of
local handicrafts.[12]

A frequently observed and much discussed aspect
of this labour migration was the workers' habit of
returning to their villages quite regularly. Apart
from family obligations, considerations of health and
climate also afforded strong motives for temporary
retirement. The modern factory with its deafening
noise, lack of ventilation and artificial humidity

tested the villagers' staying capacities to the utmost,
let alone their working capacities. Especially during
the summer with its suffocating heat were they exhausted. A periodical return home, it may be presumed,
was absolutely necessary to recover from the fatigue
caused by continually working under these circumstances
ten hours a day, twenty-six days a month.

There are also some indirect indications of a continuing influence of the agrarian cycle on the movements of labour. Although in the twentieth century the
Bombay mills had generally passed the stage of being
compelled to adjust their production to the agrarian
season, government officals kept reporting on a largely
seasonal migration of labour from their districts. In
May, as the flow-back to the countryside began, some
mills increased their piece-rates and those in charge
of recruitment had to make more efforts to enlist the
normal complements. And big textile strikes, like
those in 1928, 1929 and 1934, invariably began in the
month of April. On the eve of the summer rains, the
call to stop work with the implicit consequence of
returning to the village was sure to fall on fertile
soil.[13]

According to all descriptions, the workers' dwell-
ings were distinctly dark, damp and ill-ventilated.
They were surrounded by narrow gullies for carrying off
waste and sewage, which permeated the whole of the
surrounding atmosphere with an offensive odour. Moreover, they were terribly overcrowded. The very great
majority of the working-class population lived in single
room tenements and a single room was very often shared
by several groups or families. The miserable housing
conditions and bad sanitary arrangements had a most
disastrous effect upon the health of the workers, and
a contemporary observer called these *chawls* 'pestilen-
tial plague spots'.[14] Death-rates were very high and
during the 1918-1922 period the average infant mortality in these chawls amounted to 572 deaths per 1,000
births.[15]

The working-class population was also frequently
harassed by epidemics and plague. But respiratory
diseases, caused by the breathing of foul or dust and
fibre-laden air constituted the determining factor in
the high death rate in the workers' chawls. Malaria
was also a standing menace and health officers pointed
to the striking correlation between the intensity of
malaria and the proximity of the mills.[16] These highly
unsatisfactory conditions of health are also clear from

another expert's statement that the average of 99
pounds in weight for all mill operatives was below the
minimum weight for police recruits of the same average
height.[17]
There was no sustained and convincing effort on
the part of the employers to create a more settled
labour force and to incorporate the workers more permanently into the capitalist sector. Some mills boasted
of their dispensaries for medicines and of their attendance by qualified medical practitioners. But in fact
these were mere first-aid centres. So, if in case of
illness the house remedies failed, the worker went to
see a country *vaidya* (practitioner) and returned home to
be nursed by his family. The mills profited from his
improvement in health, although they frequently complained of absenteeism.
Apart from the lack of medical attendance there
was also a marked neglect of the workers' housing.
Employers and government had both started housing
schemes to provide accommodation to at least a small
section of the labouring poor. But a considerable
number of these one-room tenements remained unoccupied
or were sublet to outsiders. In 1925 76 per cent of
the chawls built by the government Development Department stood empty and a representative of the Bombay
Millowners' Association (B.M.O.A.) wondered with
slightly concealed annoyance, why the Bombay mill-
hand 'should prefer to live in horrible slums to the
sanitary and up-to-date chawls which had been built
for him'.[18] But he glossed over several important
objections. The workers were reluctant to take advantage of the employers' chawls, as experience had shown
that their independence was severely curtailed by living
there and they might instantly be evicted in case of
strike. As for the Development Department chawls, the
rent was prohibitive and their concrete construction
made them too hot in summer and too cold in winter.
These and other disadvantages made the workers prefer
to stay in their comparatively cheap but unhealthy
environments, where the traditional relationships with
their co-villagers could be maintained.[19]
To the children and the aged the mill industry had
nothing to offer to make life in the city an attractive
proposition. Since successive Factory Acts had rigor-
ously reduced the maximum working-day for children,
primary schools had been established in some mill com-
pounds. But in the majority of cases mill managements
used these schools for the sole purpose of having a

hidden reserve pool of labour at hand. And workers
who had spent their productive years in the mills had
no source whatsoever to depend upon after retirement,
as pensions and provident funds were lacking. They
had to return to their village to eke out a meagre
existence among their family members.

Now it is remarkable that the very mill-owners,
who were primarily responsible for this state of
affairs, consistently complained of the migratory
habits and unsettled character of their work force.
Their reading of the facts was bitterly disputed by
welfare workers and trade unions, who claimed that
workers generally stuck to their mills, often serving
ten or twenty years or even more. In the absence of
reliable and accurate data, however, the least that can
be said is that the employers are under the strong sus-
picion of exaggerating the migratory charactor of their
labour in order to shirk their duties in the field of
personnel management. And the Bombay Textile Labour
Union was very much to the point in remarking that the
mill-owners' inability to build up a permanent industrial workforce reflected little credit on their reputation as efficient managers (as they claimed to be).[20]

As has been postulated by the mode-of-production
theorists, the crucial characteristic of colonial labour
was that it was paid no family wage. The capitalist
sector paid the worker just enough to maintain himself
but relegated him to village society for the maintenance of his family. Remittances sent home or savings
brought back are not supposed to have been substantial.[21]

As was the case with migration, a discussion of
wages and costs of living has to cope with the problem
of lacking or unsatisfactorily based statistics. Therefore, one has to find one's way through a jungle of
contradictory statements and impressionistic views.

Before World War I, the employers, in defence of
their wage policy, emphasized the workers' 'extravagent
habits' like drinking, gambling and other vices, whereas government reports tended to express the opinion that
the mill-workers as a thriving community yearly sent
large sums home, which were partly invested in buying
land.[22] A third viewpoint was put forward by N.M. Lokhande, renowned as Bombay's first labour organizer and
himself employed in several mills as storekeeper. In
1884 he petitioned government on behalf of the operatives 'who as a rule save nothing and are mostly involved in debt'.[23]

After the war the Bombay Labour Office was

inaugurated by the government to examine in a scientific and exact manner the real conditions of work and wages. In 1922-23 it conducted one of its first and most frequently quoted reports on working-class budgets in Bombay.[24] This inquiry, based on about 3,000 budgets of families and single men, nearly 50 per cent of which were mill-workers' budgets, disclosed the monthly remittance of considerable sums of money, from Rs.1/11/1 in the case of families to Rs.11/7/1 in the case of single men. But at the same time it concluded that half the mill population was in debt and that every worker earning less than Rs.30 per month added one rupee to his burden every month. As might have been expected, this report in no way solved the dispute. The mill-owners missed no opportunity to quote the remittances, whereas labour sympathizers kept referring to the existence of mass indebtedness.

There were, however, some fundamental weaknesses in the report as has been shown very competently by the Bombay Textile Labour Union.[25] First of all, the finding that the textile worker's average earnings were Rs.30/10/1 per month was greatly misleading, as the salaries of highly paid mill officials (masters, storekeepers, jobbers) were included in the calculations made. Equally erroneous was the report's failure to take account of the many deductions from the wages in the form of fines, interest or partial withholdings. Also, it was unmistakably clear from the report's own pages that remittances were sent in spite of the excess of expenditure over income, resulting in increasing indebtedness. Therefore, it is very difficult to accept remittances as an accurate index of the economic position of the worker.[26]

For our purpose the main point to note is that, if remittances were sent home, in most cases it was to the detriment of the workers' health, the recovery of which had to be paid by the same village society. And the most significant finding by the report might well be that industrial workers consumed less cereals than the diet prescribed by the Bombay Jail Manual, although 57 per cent of their income was spent on food.

In the introduction of this article we have outlined the model of a dominant capitalist mode of production that maintained and exploited the old village economy for the (re-) production of its labour. The discussion that followed tends to qualify but in the main to confirm that model as applicable to the situation in Bombay. But a comparison of Bombay with

Ahmedabad, the Gujarat centre of the textile industry, creates new problems that possibly contradict our analysis.

In 1929 the Ahmedabad mill-owners told the Whitley Commission that 80 per cent of their work-force was permanent, that only 10 or 20 per cent of workers went to the villages for about a week during festive seasons and that most of the workers brought their families with them to the city.[27] This more settled character of Ahmedabad labour can clearly be seen from the sex-ratio, that stood at 765 to 1,000 in 1921 (Bombay 525). But although most workers lived by wage labour alone and presumably did not fall back on village society, mills in Ahmedabad paid wages that were not higher, but even a bit lower than those in Bombay: the average monthly earnings of all workers in Bombay were Rs.16/6/3 in 1914 and Rs.30/10/1 in 1923 as against Ahmedabad Rs.13/9/9 and Rs.29/7/0 respectively.[28]

Some authors have attributed this wage difference to the many alternative jobs that were available in Bombay as a seaport. Migrant workers going to East Africa, for instance, were said to receive wages considerably higher than those paid by the Bombay mills.[29] This line of reasoning seems to imply that on the Bombay labour market the competition was for workers rather than for jobs, which contradicts the widely accepted view that generally Bombay enjoyed a more than adequate labour supply.[30] But for our argument the main point to note is that if Bombay's alternative employment opportunities did exert an upward pressure on wages, the mills must have paid their workers rates that were higher than the mere subsistence level.

Several contemporary witnesses advanced the view that the Bombay wage level was nothing but a reflection of the higher costs of living in this city. These costs were alleged to be very high and it was argued that after World War I it was absolutely impossible to live on wages less than Rs.30 p.m.[31] Now, unfortunately, there is no comparative cost-of-living index available for Bombay and Ahmedabad covering all the items of food, fuel, cloth and house-rent. But at least a comparative index for food prices has been computed every month since July 1921. Figures from this index show marked differences and fluctuations in food prices, but do not unequivocally suggest that in Bombay they were so much higher than in Ahmedabad.[32] And even if it could be shown that Bombay's slightly higher wages did indeed keep pace with its slightly

higher costs of living, the point still remains that
in Ahmedabad more people had to live on more or less
the same real wages. However, as the extant figures
and statistics are far from reliable, they have to be
treated with considerable reservation. And further
research will be needed into the position of the mill-
workers' women, who in Ahmedabad may have contributed
to the family's income with earnings from the informal
sector. So, we come back again to the problem of
sources, because what we urgently need, like Thomas
Gradgrind, is 'facts, nothing but facts'.[33]

The Textile Industry and the Jobber System:
Recruitment of Labour

It was the recruiters of labour who performed the vital
function of linking village society with the urban
capitalist mode of production. From the inception of
the Bombay textile industry this task of recruitment
was entrusted to so-called jobbers. Coming from the
rank and file, these jobbers were empowered to engage,
to discipline and to dismiss workers and to give what
elementary training was required. Unfortunately, as
most jobber dealings were off the historical record,
information is scarce and little research has been
done in this field.[34]

In the early days of the industry the rural population had not yet found its way to the factory gate.
Therefore, the mill management itself had to go on the
road to supplement the shortage of labour in the city.
For that purpose, the first jobbers went up country
and lured the economically affected villagers by pic-
turing urban factory life in bright colours and offering them travel expenses as an additional inducement.
By this personal approach special ties which lasted
for years were established between certain mills and
villages.

In the course of time, it was no longer necessary
- apart from exceptional circumstances - to recruit
labour in the countryside. Population pressure had
increased, the employment opportunities in the textile
mills had become sufficiently well known and migration
had considerably swelled the number of willing recruits
in the city. The itinerant jobber became a thing of
the past, as well as the migrant labourers came more
and more to the factory gates on their own. In spite
of these changes on the labour market, the jobber

remained in charge of the recruitment of labour for
his department. His recruiting activities, however,
became progressively more than an aspect of his role
as foreman and supervisor.

The main qualification of a jobber was his ability
to control a number of men. Most probably, in the
initial period, when industrial experience was still
largely lacking, the wielding of some influence over
labour was the sole criterion for appointment as a
jobber. More often than not physical force constituted an important element of that influence and probably
in the beginning the most aggressive mill-workers were
designated as jobbers.[35] In any case, it remained
usual to speak of the jobber as the *dada* or 'the strong
tough guy, who can terrorize the people'.[36] The frequent association of jobbers with *akhadas* or wrestling-
schools also points to the use of violent mechanisms
of control.

The oldest historical documentation on jobbers
can be found in the Factory Commission Report of 1875.
Of the two jobbers heard by the Commission - a Muslim
weaver and a Koli spinner - the former had been a
resident of Bombay for more than twenty years and the
latter had been born there.[37] This leads to another,
more or less obvious conclusion, namely that the first
jobbers were drawn from the more urbanized groups.
The textile mill was only one, although the most obvious sector of the jobber's activities. Apart from
that, he might run a shop, let rooms, head an akhada
or pursue other interests that tied him to the city.

A second generation of jobbers could be expected
to have at least some technical knowledge and experience. According to some observers that was indeed the
case,[38] but even in the 1920s complaints persisted of
jobbers who could never tackle a loom or make a
repair.[39] In the latter case, a jobber's lack of
technical skill was tolerated, simply because some
managers or department heads were not completely
indifferent to the possibility of material gain. They
expected financial compensation for the grant of
appointment and first of all weighed a prospective
jobber's ability to pay, a burden that the jobber
passed on to his gang of labourers (as discussed below). In many mills a community of interest developed
between management and jobbers, based on a joint
exploitation of labour.[40]

In reeling and winding departments, where mainly
women were employed, labour was recruited and

supervised by *naikins*, the jobbers' female counterparts. What has been said of the jobber also applied
to her. But according to some, an additional requirement pertaining to the naikens was the possession of
an attractive appearance and a willingness to please
the manager or department head in all respects. Therefore, mills sometimes found difficulty in getting naikins, as this position was not considered to be respectable and many women refused the job in spite of
its remunerative prospects.[41]

Since management had delegated the distribution
of eagerly-sought employment opportunities to him, the
jobber could build up a position of considerable
strength. As a result, the jobber and his men maintained a relationship of mutual but unequal interde-
pendence, that can most aptly be described as a form
of patronage.

Although formally the authority to hire and to
fire rested with the management, in actual practice it
was the jobber who assigned vacant places. Therefore,
the employment relationship may be said to have been
set up primarily between the jobber and his labourers,
even though the jobber was not in charge of wage payment as was the *maistry* on South Indian plantations.[42]
Kinship or common origin usually served as the main
basis for this employment relationship. But if the
immigrant labourer did not belong to the jobber's
personal acquaintances, he could be introduced to him
by co-villagers or family members, who had already
found their way in the urban industry.

Protection of his labourers' interests - which
were partly his own - was another aspect of the jobber's patronage. Labourers used to address their
complaints not to the mill officers but to the jobber,
who was expected to act as their spokesman. To keep
their confidence the jobber had to use his contacts
with management to get the grievances of his men
redressed or their conditions of work improved. In
that way, the jobber represented an important, if not
the sole channel of communication through which managers or department heads could remain informed as to
their employees' opinions and well-being. In the
majority of cases, however, this channel was used for
information in the oppositie direction and instructions to the men were issued not directly to them, but
via their jobbers. As a matter of course, there was
a strong tendency for these intermediaries to colour
this information in the process of transmission in

accordance with their own particular interests.

Immigrant labourers arriving in Bombay generally possessed little hard cash. In addition, they generally did not find work overnight and mills used to keep wages in arrears. Therefore, most newcomers soon ran into debt. Fines, illness or marriage sometimes increased their indebtedness beyond redemption. In contracting loans the jobber played an important part. Sometimes, he acted as a moneylender himself. But as his means were limited, the jobber usually introduced his men to other moneylenders, like mill officers, grain-dealers or Marwari merchants,and stood security for them. By providing or mediating the necessary loans the jobber not only profited financially, but also considerably strengthened his control over the men. But the dependence was mutual and so was the risk. If a labourer left before the debt was cleared, the jobber had to bear the loss. His risk, however, was small, as he maintained a wide set of personal relations with the labourers of his gang. He guided fresh recruits in the difficult process of urban adjustment, advised them in accommodation and family affairs and provided many services, which the industry and the government were unable or unwilling to provide. His strategic position in a network of social relations enabled him to act as a professional mediator in communication and distribution, strongly resembling the culture broker as described by Neale.[43] The preservation of customary social relationships in a new urban context made him also very much look like 'a city equivalent of the village headman' and the jobber was very commonly referred to as *mukadam* or traditional leader.[44]

The emergence of the jobber system may be attributed to the social and linguistic differences between the mill-owners and their management cadre on the one hand and the labourers on the other. The mill-owners came from prominent merchant communities like Parsis, Gujaratis and Iraqi Jews, and the management functions in their mills were filled by Europeans or Indians with an educated middle-class background, whereas the immigrant rural labour force was of Marathi-speaking peasant origin. Therefore, a system of intermediaries, like jobbers, would seem to be an obvious solution. To take personnel management in their own hands, the mill officers had to devise recruitment strategies for a culture they found difficult to understand and to communicate through interpreters with all the

concomitant frustrations and waste of time. And as
available labour was largely unskilled, no further
selection was required than a cursory examination of
the candidate's physical fitness. When later on management became more Indianized, the established practice was left untouched. [45]

Another, partly complementary explanation suggests
that from the beginning the jobbers were intended to
play the role of a middle management cadre. Primarily
interested in the making of quick profits, the mill-
owners were reluctant to invest in an expensive and
perhaps no more efficient personnel office to recruit
and discipline the work-force. Apart from that, the
Indian entrepreneurs had little personal experience
in labour administration, as their previous activities
were mainly in trading, banking and brokerage. Therefore, as long as the level of technology was very low
and the necessary skills could easily be acquired, no
one more sophisticated than a jobber was needed.
Exactly this lack of a well-organized personnel office
enabled the jobber to emerge as the key-figure in
labour relations and to assume the wide responsibili-
ties of hiring and disciplining the workforce. [46]

Whatever explanation we prefer, for the purpose
of our paper they amount to the same, namely the basic
non-interference by the industry in the nature of
village society with which it was linked and in the
social relationships that were prevalent there. As
long as the machines were properly manned and industrial peace was maintained, managements would not
bother their jobbers with irksome questions about how
exactly they dealt with their men. Therefore, one may
say, the capitalist mode of production not only pre-
served village society for the reproduction of its
labour, but also by its adoption of the jobber system
perpetuated social relations of a feudal kind within
the industrial framework itself.

The mill-owners readily used every opportunity to
stress the essentially alien character of their
workers' social background. When after the first world
war enquiries by government and labour sympathizers
brought to light the manifold malpractices connected
with the jobber system, the employers in defence
referred to the existence of vital differences in
social position, caste and language. For recruiting
to be successful, the Bombay Millowners' Association
(B.M.O.A.) declared in 1926, the recruiting officer
needs some point of contact with the men. The jobber,

coming from practically the same class as the worker,
is 'naturally in touch', but the mill officers above
him belong to very different strata of life. Therefore, a jobber was indispensable in the recruitment
of labour, as 'you cannot easily get at them unless
you have some point of contact with them, ...'[47] One
may add that stressing the social distance had the
additional advantage of exempting the mill-owners from
all further obligations they might have in regard to
their labour. In the Sinhalese plantations described
by Meyer the planters even deliberately fostered the
alien character of their Tamil workers to create a
submissive labour force and to prevent its integration
into Sinhalese society.[48]

The malpractices, mentioned in the preceding
paragraph, were mostly of a financial nature. The
jobber used to demand *dasturi* (fee or commission) as
the price of engagement or of re-employment after a
period of absence. Tha amount of dasturi could range
from some annas to a full month's wages and varied
according to time, place and the closeness of the
jobber's relations with his men. The Factory Commission of 1875 already felt obliged to make investigations into this matter and the B.M.O.A. included a
prohibition of taking or paying bribes (meaning dasturi) in its 1891 draft work regulations. Nevertheless, in the first quarter of this century the payment
of dasturi to the jobber was a fairly general condition for getting a job.

Summarizing, this meant that as long as the jobber
was considered to be an indispensable benefit or at
least an equally indispensable evil, he could reap
financial benefits from two different structural contexts. First of all, he received from the mill management his normal monthly wages that were paid on time-
rates or on piece-rates and exceeded the average
worker's earning twice or thrice. But apart from that,
he enjoyed an additional income, derived from sources
outside the capitalist industrial framework and based
on his informal position of labour recruiter.

The connection between the jobber's regular wages
and the capitalist mode of production is obvious. It
is less clear how far dasturi has to be seen as a form
of payment originating from Indian village society.
One may argue that it was a well-established custom to
offer gifts or render services to landlords in return
for their grant of protection or lease of land. Familiar with this custom in the countryside, the migrant

worker could not regard the gift of dasturi, after its
transplantation to an urban industrial soil, as unusual
or unreasonable. The workers' lack of opposition to
the payment of dasturi as such may also be put forward
to strengthen this interpretation. However, no dasturi
was paid in critical periods of labour scarcity, as
during the plague of 1897. This suggests that dasturi
was also closely linked with the economic law of supply
and demand and that capitalist mechanisms were operating within forms which appear on the surface to be
traditional institutions of peasant society.[49]

It was well-meaning outsiders, government officials and trade-union leaders, who in the 1920s began
to challenge this custom, which they branded as 'sheer
corruption' and 'actual extortion'.[50] But also, no
sharp distinction can be drawn between dasturi as
attribute of patronage and as form of corruption. The
only thing that can be said is that patronage always
bears an element of exploitation, as it is based on a
difference in power that can be used by the patron -
as the stronger partner in the relationship - in his
own favour. It might very well be that interpretations
of dasturi, stressing the corruptive and exploitative
element in it, are strongly coloured by value-judgements
derived from a capitalistic rationalism. This suggestion does not imply that ethical judgements are completely ruled out. It does mean, however, that dasturi
has to be understood first and foremost as part and
parcel of its specific socio-economic context.

Finally, the payment of dasturi also throws new
light on the absence of a well-organized personnel
office. For, entrusting the jobber with the recruitment, instruction and supervision of labour not only
meant that the employers shirked all their duties in
this field; it also implied that the costs that went
with these duties fell back upon labour itself in the
form of dasturi.

Jobbers and Labour Unions: Organization of Labour

Textile labour, far from being unorganized, was com-
posed of a multitude of particularistic jobber units.
This may explain much of Bombay's labour mobility.
The workers cnsidered their fortunes to be bound up
with their jobber, more than with the mill. Therefore,
when a jobber conflicted with his management or
received a more attractive offer elsewhere, he could

change mill and 'his' workers would follow him. Before World War I protracted strikes were very rare and
most conflicts remained confined to one mill, or more
often, to one department. Jobber moves were at the
centre of most of these early labour disputes and the
isolated and shortlived strikes before the 1920s coincided in their scope with the jobber's personal network. Sometimes it happened the other way round:
workers dissatisfied with their working conditions
left their mill, and the jobber, unable to control
labour unrest, preferred to become the leader of a
strike rather than lose his influence with the men.
But in all these cases vertical loyalties dominated
any sense of horizontal or collective solidarity.
Different jobber gangs competed for the same employment
opportunities, whereas conflicts with managements about
wages or work-rules were fought independently.[51]

The multicellular composition of the labour force
greatly influenced all attempts to organize the textile
workers into a larger whole. As long as the limitations of the small, particularistic groups could not
be overcome, gaining the jobber's support was the sole
way to mobilize labour on a wider scale. So, for
organizing purposes the combination of a number of
jobber units was an obvious starting-point.

According to Gail Omvedt in her recent contribution, labour recruitment through intermediaries began
to end when union organizing among the workers started
to develop. Workers organizing themselves into unions
fought the jobbers and she mentions the Bombay textile
mills as the first place where by 1930 their influence was on the decline as a result of militant labour
strikes.[52]

Personally, I do not find this view, quite current
among most labour historians, to be completely acceptable. Capitalism in the Third World did not completely
destroy previous modes of production. By the same
token, unionization did not rise from the ashes of
earlier organizations like the jobber unit. Therefore,
if modes of labour organization are also analysed in
terms of mutual penetration and articulation, a deeper
insight can be gained into the processes at work in
the emerging trade-union movement. I will briefly
present some empirical data to substantiate my point.

The first attempts to organize Bombay textile
labour were made as part of a wider non-Brahman movement, which worked for the general uplift of the lower
castes. In 1884 Lokhande, its most prominent leader

in Bombay, organized two mass meetings to petition
government on behalf of labour. For this purpose
Lokhande made use of an existing jobber association
that had been set up with the quite different intent
of collecting funds for the building of a *dharamshalla*.
Through this association other jobbers were summoned
to the meetings and five thousand workers attended as
a result. The Millhands' Association formed in its
wake also found its organizing basis in the jobbers,
but very soon disintegrated into its constituent
parts. [53]

From the same socio-political background, but
more important, was the Kamgar Hitwardhak Sabha (K.H.
S.), established in 1909. Founded by educated middle-
class non-Brahman leaders, the K.H.S. was essentially
a labour welfare association. Although it was not
exclusively meant to look after the interests of textile labour, its following was chiefly drawn from that
source. The membership was small, about two or three
hundred, but consisted of a great many jobbers and
other influential elements, so that its total support
may be reckoned at ten thousand workers. In spite of
their crucial position in the K.H.S.'s organization,
few jobbers served on its managing committee. This
was mainly because of the strong opposition exerted by
the employers against their workforce combining into
larger associations. [54]

The important point to make here is that the cases
of the Millhands' Association and the K.H.S. prove that
jobbers were not completely averse to concerted action.
They also prove that outsiders, to a certain extent,
could enrol the jobbers for joint action in accordance
with their own, that is non-Brahman, interests. Later
political movements did not fail to take this lesson
to heart.

After the first world war the nationalist movement
in India gathered momentum. The exigencies of the war,
the policy declarations by the British government and
the echo of the 1917 Revolution in Russia created a
suitable climate for political leaders to press their
demands. The Montford reform proposals fell far short
of the expectations raised. Therefore, the nationalist
leaders sought to strengthen their agitation for Home
Rule by broadening their political base and came to
appreciate support from an urban, concentrated labour
force as an invaluable asset to their political
struggle. In Bombay, Home Rulers of different shades
of opinion launched their own labour associations but

they did not strike root. Not until the Bombay Textile
Labour Union (B.T.L.U.) was formed (in 1925) did trade-
unionization really begin. This B.T.L.U. had grown
out of a Committee of Assistance which during the 1925
textile strike organized relief for those workers who
had remained in the city. After the strike this Committee was transformed into a permanent union, led by
labour politicians and social workers and presided over
by the well-known N.M. Joshi. In fact, the B.T.L.U.
represented a master union comprising several smaller
labour associations in a more centralized bureaucratic
framework.

After one year the B.T.L.U. numbered approximately
10,000 members. Most of these were employed in mills
on the southern fringe of the Bombay mill area and in
two northern mills in Kurla. This very uneven spread
of membership was partly a legacy of the smaller associations incorporated by the B.T.L.U. and partly a
result of the B.T.L.U.'s communal composition, its main
areas of strength being in Muslim-dominated wards. But
first and foremost this strongly localized membership
has to be seen as evidence that in fact the B.T.L.U.,
its formal bureaucratic structure notwithstanding, had
to rely on jobbers and other locally-influential
leaders among labour. This may be called the fundamental dilemma of the B.T.L.U. as it was of all labour
unions during the inter-war period.

For the enlistment of a membership or the setting-
up of mill committees, it was absolutely necessary for
the B.T.L.U. to gain the support of the jobbers or at
least to convince them that the union's intentions were
not detrimental to their position. In some mills the
B.T.L.U. proved successful in this endeavour and in
consequence it sometimes even came to champion specific
jobber interests. In many cases, however, this method
yielded no result. When the union arranged a meeting
with the jobbers and head jobbers of a mill in order
to persuade them to join the union along with their
men, it very often happened that the jobbers concluded
that a union did not suit their interests. They would
refuse to have any dealings with the union and their
labourers, if members, would withdraw. And if in case
of labour disputes the union could not reach a settlement that was favourable to its members, many jobbers
would back out again, as their B.T.L.U. connection had
not turned out to be a strengthening of their existing
powers. [55]

A completely different type of labour union had

been founded the year before, the Girni Kamgar Mahamandal (G.K.M.). Whereas the B.T.L.U. was primarily an outside initiative, the G.K.M. was formed by labourers themselves, at least by a more skilled and better paid section of them. Its leaders were mainly jobbers, who were joined by some clerks, shopkeepers and akhada-owners, D.R. Mayekar, A.A. Alve and G.R. Kasle being the most prominent among them. As their union was built on their respective client networks, it suffered basically from the same weaknesses as the B.T.L.U.: lack of centralization and a membership concentrated in some local bulwarks.

A special characteristic of the G.K.M. was its rejection of all outside interference. On several occasions the G.K.M. leaders declared the labour politicians from the middle class to be of no use, as they were completely unacquainted with the mill-workers' conditions. They even openly distrusted the outsiders' motives in trying to lead labour.[56]

Nevertheless, this attitude did not prevent out-siders, mainly of a communist persuasion, from taking increasingly more interest in the affairs of the G.K.M. Initially, the activities of the Bombay communists remained confined to the study of Marxism-Leninism and the dissemination of their newly-acquired views in English-language publications. However, they were unable to radicalize the Bombay Congress in labour matters or to make any inroads into the established nationalist trade-union movement controlled by N.M. Joshi. So, in 1927 they set up a Bombay Workers' and Peasants' Party (B.W.P.P.), which operating independently within the Congress aimed at the organization of workers and peasants and at the transformation of the parent body into a real mass party.[57] This was an enormous, if not impossible, undertaking, in view of the fact that the B.W.P.P. numbered about twenty members, mostly Brahman students, and had no connection with labour at all.[58]

In this situation, the jobber-led G.K.M. offered the communists an opportunity to establish the much-desired connection with the workers. But because of its special character, the G.K.M. had to be dealt with very carefully. Through a local Congress Committee K.N. Joglekar (B.W.P.P.) managed to develop a fragile relationship with Mayekar, the G.K.M.'s secretary. This was going to be the vital link. Joglekar spared no effort to introduce his friends into the G.K.M. as political advisers and - to use his own words - 'was doing consistently the boring work on behalf of the Party'.[59] This enabled the communists to pass themselves off as leaders of this textile union, a status that gained them important positions in the national trade-union federation. But in actual fact they were only marginally involved and were merely tolerated in their capacity as self-appointed advisers.

Economic developments, however, were to promote closer co-operation at least for the time being, between labour politicians and jobbers in general. After about 1924 Bombay suffered from an economic depression and to check this trend the mill-owners considered the introduction of rationalization schemes. Although these schemes generally implied increased efficiency, to the workers their implementation meant retrenchment, heavier workloads and, to some categories of labour, reduced earnings. In addition, the jobbers would have to face a drastic curtailment of their freedom of recruitment by increased demands for skill and efficiency. Introduction of these measures, therefore, provoked a wave of labour unrest, which provides the background to the 1928 and 1929 general strikes.

On the eve of this strike movement serious tensions arose in the G.K.M. Whereas Mayekar came to resist all further encroachments by the educated outsiders, Alve thought he could use them in the workers' fight against the new work schemes. Connected with this conflict was a dispute over the feasibility of organized opposition, Alve being more inclined to radical solutions. These tensions which divided the G.K.M. enabled the B.W.P.P. members to strengthen their influence, and in March 1928 the B.W.P.P. could report truthfully that 'at present Party members are more or less connected with the Textile Workers' Union'.[60] After a general strike had been called the B.W.P.P. influence grew further. When in May the Alve-led G.K.M. wing had itself formally registered as the Girni Kamgar Union (G.K.U.), jobbers and other labour leaders like Alve and Kasle sat on its managing committee alongside communist students like Joglekar and S.A. Dange. Again the co-operation of jobbers with politically-motivated outsiders proved to be the formula for trade-union formation.

The G.K.U. had its heyday during and immediately after the 1928 strike. The imminent rationalization of the industry had given rise to a broad resistance movement, which overstepped the limits of the small, particularistic group. This situation required a more

general leadership, able to negotiate with the employers concerning the little-articulated grievances
of labour and the economic problems of the industry
in a long-term perspective. As the jobbers could not
meet these requirements, the labour politicians of the
G.K.U. together with representatives of the more moderate unions filled in the gap and emerged as leaders by
acting as spokesmen. This was especially true of the
G.K.U. leaders, who formed the most energetic part of
the Joint Strike Committee and whose militant speeches
attracted large audiences.

During and after this strike jobbers co-operated
at two distinct levels. A small number of them co-
operated at the highest administrative level and made
the union more identifiable to labour by acting as its
president or sitting on its executive. A majority,
however, co-operated by supporting the strike on the
spot. They might have had private leanings toward the
union but primarily they fought the new work schemes
and did not mind that interested outsiders gave new
names to their traditional practices.[61] Alve and Dange
held special meetings with these jobbers to exchange
information, and thanks to their support the fight was
kept up for six months. After the strike the G.K.U.
sometimes effected the dismissal of hostile labourers,
revealing the active influence of jobbers who made use
of victimization to serve union purposes. Also, in as
far as the G.K.U. succeeded in enforcing some discipline, it was through the jobbers who by their personal
influence prevented the workers from using violence.[62]

The G.K.U. numbering about 60,000 members and 40
mill committees in the beginning of 1929, showed marked
progress over its various predecessors. But in the
last analysis it also had to keep a precarious balance
between using and losing the jobbers. At the end of
the same year, the G.K.U. membership had dwindled to
fewer than a thousand and it faded into insignificance.
To explain this spectacular decline much has been made
of the mill-owners' opposition and government intervention (the Meerut trial). But at the root of the
problem, again, we find the jobber.

The G.K.U. constitution permitted the mill committees to deal with grievances and to collect union fees,
but it did not authorize them to call a strike. Mill
committees, according to Dange, were meant 'to control
the workers' and the G.K.U. and its main enemy the
B.M.O.A. fully agreed on the need for control.[63]
Lightning strikes and irregular operation of the mill

committees, however, demonstrated that the workers could not be confined within the officially-prescribed rules as laid down by the communists in conjunction with the employers. In some places committee members claimed special privileges on the shop floor; elsewhere they agitated for the dismissal of jobbers who were disliked by their men.[64] In numerous ways the hierarchy of productive relations was disturbed and the resulting disorder made working impossible for mill and union alike.

Not only the mill managements, but also the jobbers began to resist the mill committees. That was a very critical development, as to a great extent the G.K.U.'s achievements had to be credited to the jobbers. From the fact that the mill committees were distributing jobs and material we may infer the jobbers' active participation. But slowly the jobbers began to change sides. After they had realized that some kind of rationalization had become inevitable, they came to discover the G.K.U. mill committees as a new and greater menace. These mill committees further reduced their freedom of action, and by dealing with grievances threatened to undermine their traditional mediation. These considerations made many jobbers decide to dissociate themselves from the union. During the 1929 strike they were conspicuous by their activities as strikebreakers and the G.K.U. lost the strike and its organizing base.

Following Joglekar's example, many labour politicians in Bombay associated themselves with rank-and-file labour leaders for the purpose of building new organizations by using traditional social networks. After 1929 leftists like B.T. Ranadive and S.V. Deshpande applied this formula by co-operating with the jobber G.L. Kandalkar and his group in the G.K.U. (Red Flag) and after 1934 the Royists conducted their Bombay G.K.U. in co-operation with the Muslim jobber Abdul Majid.[65] During the 1930s the jobber system came under heavy pressure from industrial reform and government legislation. But the jobbers remained active and proved influential enough to become towers of strength to the Rashtriya Mill Mazdoor Sangh, the nationalist textile union established in 1945.[66]

Conclusion

As has been said, the articulation of different modes

153

of production seems to be a useful concept to organize
and clarify most of the historical data concerning the
Bombay textile industry. The migration of mainly male
labour, their preservation of village ties for reasons
of social security and the apparent lack of substantial
remittances back home all clearly testify to the subordination of a weakened village economy to the needs
of the capitalist mode of production. This penetration
of peasant society by the capitalist mode created also
new phenomena, the most conspicuous being the jobber,
who transferred labour from the village to the urban
industry or recruited co-villagers at the factory-gate.
In fact, the jobber was the focal point in the whole
process of articulation, and around him the jobber-
unit was formed as an organization of labour that
adapted existing social relationships to new industrial needs.

We may discern the trade union and the jobber-
unit as two clearly distinct modes of labour organization. The trade union tended to treat the workers
as if they were a category and therefore to negotiate
for wages and employment in the industry as a whole.
The individual worker, however, remained personally
dependent on his jobber for a job or a loan and thus
a jobber-unit comprised a wide set of relations,
maintained even in situations of industrial peace or
temporary unemployment. Whereas the trade union's
approach was specific and bureaucratic, the jobber's
relations with his men were multi-purpose and face-
to-face. Therefore, the Bombay textile unions, their
ideological differences notwithstanding, had to build
on the jobbers as their main organizing base. Fundamentally, the modes of organization of trade union and
jobber may be opposed, but in actual fact they proved
to a large extent to be complementary. The jobber's
personal hold on the men was supplemented by the outsiders' administrative skills and their ability to
translate the workers' grievances into a political
idiom.

We may conclude from this case-study that the
articulation concept is fruitfully applicable to the
field of labour organization. Therefore, elabora-
ting the opening sentence of this article, one of the
fundamental problems of historical analysis may be
seen as the specification and articulation of particular modes of organization within a given association of labour.

As for Bombay, one may say that just as the

capitalist mode of production developed by the exploitation of village society for the cheap production of labour, in the same way trade unionism as a concomitant phenomenon could emerge by using the jobber-unit for the easy recruitment of a following. The high points of trade-union development in Bombay were reached when the union became the dominant mode of organization and succeeded in effectively subordinating these jobber-units. Thus, the decisive point in the development of the Bombay textile unions was not so much the mounting resistance of a class-conscious workforce against the jobber influence. Rather it was the relative success of the attempts to institutionalize informal, short-term interest organizations in bureaucratic frameworks.

There is yet another striking parallel. The millowners frequently complained of the migratory habits of their workers, but kept silent about the ways in which the maintenance of village ties contributed to the economic well-being of their industry. Likewise, trade-union leaders openly condemned the evils of the jobber-system, but were absolutely unwilling to acknowlege that the jobber represented an indispensable link in their organizational set-up. During my own interviews with pre-war union-leaders I found them rather tight-lipped as far as the jobbers were concerned and most of them contented themselves with classifying them as part of labour, if not as hand-in-glove with the employers.

Finally, village society also served union purposes by supporting workers in times of strike. So, in the 1920s strike committees actively furthered the workers' return to the countryside, even to the extent of dealing out steamer tickets, as strike funds in the city fell far short of wants.

However, there are also some differences which may prevent us from stretching the conceptual analogy too far. First of all, the political leaders of the trade union looked upon the jobber as a practical device which had to be used for a short time only but in the long run must be got rid of. Therefore, they were much more intent upon the final destruction of the jobber system than the capitalists were with regard to village society. Further, subordination to the trade union organization was not always as detrimental to the jobber as subordination to the urban industry was to village society. Many jobbers used the union in the struggle for their own immediate interests or as a

155

protective cover against threats like rationalization.
Some of them even rose to prominence as the union
offered an opportunity of upward mobility which they
lacked in the mill. But sooner or later most jobbers
became convinced that the outside union leaders only
seized upon the problems of labour to further vague
and distant political ends and they turned away in
bitterness. On trial in Meerut, Kasle lamented that
if the outsiders 'have made some secret plot behind
the backs of us workers ..., taking advantage of our
ignorance, ... only God knows it.'[67]

Finally, an increasing rationalization of production and personnel management (such as the introduction
of labour officers in the 1930s) was accompanied by a
further bureaucratizing of labour organization. There
was an ambivalent but undeniable trend discernible
towards a growing dominance of the union mode of
organization, especially after World War II. But for
the greater part of this period the most essential
characteristic of the Bombay textile unions was - to
use Meillassoux's phrase in a slightly different sense
- that traditional jobber-units 'were being both undermined and perpetuated at the same time, undergoing a
prolongated crisis and not a smooth transition to'
trade-unionism.[68]

Kooiman, 'Rural labour in the Bombay textile industry
and the articulation of modes of organization'

My thanks are due to Diane Papstein for help with the
English text.

1. Apart from contributions to the *Economic and
Political Weekly* (Bombay) by Ashok Rudra, Utsa Patnaik,
Paresh Chattopadhyay and Hamza Alavi, mention may be
made of Irfan Habib, 'Potentialities of Capitalistic
Development in the Economy of Mughal India', *Journal
of Economic History* XXIX (1969), pp.32 ff.; Brian
Davey, *The Economic Development of India - A Marxist
Analysis* (Bristol 1975); Kathleen Gough, 'Modes of Pro-
duction in Southern India', *Economic and Political
Weekly* Annual Number (February 1980), pp.337 ff.
2. D. McEachern, 'The Mode of Production in India',
Journal of Contemporary Asia VI, 4 (1976), pp.444 ff.
3. C. Meillassoux, 'From Reproduction to Production - A Marxist Approach to Economic Anthropology',
Economy and Society I, 1 (1972), p.103.
4. Gail Omvedt, 'Migration in Colonial India -
The Articulation of Feudalism and Capitalism by the
Colonial State', *Journal of Peasant Studies* VII, 2
(1980), pp.185 ff.
5. See Report of the Lady Doctor, Bombay, *Labour
Gazette* II, 1 (1922), pp.31 ff.
6. This table has to remain an approximation, as
the census succeeded in an occupational breakdown for
only some of the immigrants classified as actual
workers.
7. Census of India 1931, IX, I, pp.27-9.
8. Official Report on Mill Humidification (1923),
quoted in Royal Commission on Labour in India (Whitley
Commission), Calcutta 1931, Evidence I, 1, p.29.
9. Indian Factory Labour Commission, Simla 1908,
Report I, p.19.
10. Textile Factories Labour Committee, Bombay
1907, Evidence (in Proceedings of the Department of
Commerce and Industry), p.75.
11. Royal Commission on Labour 1931, Report, p.16.
12. Lalita Chakravarty has recently mapped out
these and other prominent labour catchment areas of
colonial India, laying great stress on the economic
factor in labour migration, L. Chakravarty, 'Emergence

of an Industrial Labour Force in a Dual Economy –
British India 1880-1920', *Indian Economic and Social
History Review* XV, 3 (1978), pp.249 ff.

13. A.R. Burnett-Hurst, *Labour and Housing in Bombay – A Study in the Economic Conditions of the Wage-
earning Classes in Bombay* (London 1925), p.51; Report
of the Indian Tariff Board (Calcutta 1927) III, pp.553
ff.; Indian Factory Labour Commission 1908, Evidence
II, p.84; R.G. Gokhale, *The Bombay Cotton Mill Worker*
(Bombay 1957), p.70.

14. Textile Factories Labour Committee 1907,
Report, pp.3 ff; Report of the Lady Doctor, Bombay,
op.cit.; A.R. Burnett-Hurst, op.cit., pp.30 ff.

15. Annual Reports of the Executive Health Officer
for the City of Bombay, quoted in A.R. Burnett-Hurst,
op.cit., p.35. One has to bear in mind, however, first
that these were the years of the influenza epidemic
and second that deaths were more accurately registered
than births (partly outside Bombay).

16. J. Sandilands, M.D., 'The Health of the Bombay
Worker', *Labour Gazette* I, 2 (1921), pp.14-16; Royal
Commission on Labour 1931, Report, p.24.

17. Quoted in the Royal Commission on Labour 1931,
Evidence I, 1, p.317.

18. *Times of India* 25 December 1925.

19. Indian Factory Labour Commission 1908, Evidence II, pp.72, 86; Report of the Indian Tariff
Board, Calcutta 1927, I, p.140; III, pp.449, 563;
Royal Commission on Labour 1931, Evidence I, 1, p.24;
I, 2, p.256; S.D. Mehta, *The Cotton Mills of India
1854-1954* (Bombay 1954), p.154; A.R. Burnett-Hurst,
op.cit., p.62.

20. Indian Tariff Board 1927, III, p.452; Royal
Commission on Labour 1931, Evidence I, 1, pp.296, 394.

21. For instance Gail Omvedt, op.cit., p.195.

22. Indian Factory Labour Commission 1908, Evidence II, pp.66, 85, 116; Royal Commission on Labour,
II, *The Colonies and the Indian Empire* 1892 (Parliamentary Papers XXXVI: 5 1892), p.174; Gazetteer of the
Bombay Presidency, X (Ratnagiri and Savantvadi) (Bombay
1880), p.143.

23. Petition in Factory Commission Report, Bombay
1885, pp.230-1.

24. Labour Office, Government of Bombay, Report
of an Enquiry into Working Class Budgets in Bombay
(Bombay 1923).

25. B.T.L.U. in Indian Tariff Board 1927, III,
pp.443-7 and in Royal Commission on Labour 1931,

Evidence I, 1, pp.344-5.

26. Harold Mann, who did research in what alleged-
ly was the receiving end of the remittances, a Deccani
village, estimated the amount of money brought or sent
back to be much smaller than was often supposed; H.H.
Mann and N.V. Kanitkar, *Land and Labour in a Deccan
Village* (Bombay 1921), pp.111 ff.

27. Royal Commission on Labour 1931, Evidence I,
1, pp.258-9.

28. Indian Tariff Board 1927, I, pp.111-13; Royal
Commission on Labour 1931, Evidence I, 1, pp.166-7.

29. K.L. Gillion, *Ahmedabad, A Study in Indian
Urban History* (Berkeley 1968), p.102; L. Chakravarty,
op.cit., pp.267, 284.

30. Morris D. Morris, *The Emergence of an Industrial Labor Force in India - A Study of the Bombay
Cotton Mills 1854-1947* (Berkeley 1965).

31. Indian Tariff Board 1927, III, p.472; Royal
Commission on Labour 1931, Evidence I, 1. p.300.

32. Comparative Retail Prices of Food for Bombay
and Ahmedabad, based on the prices for seventeen
commodities commonly consumed by the working classes
(cereals, pulses, sugar etc.), are given in every issue
of the Bombay *Labour Gazette* since 1921. The index for
Ahmedabad (Bombay prices = 100) was in July 1921:
101; 1922: 98; 1923 : 92; 1924 : 96.

33. Charles Dickens, *Hard Times* (London 1854), p.1.

34. Mention may be made of M.D. Morris, op.cit.;
R.K. Newman, 'Labour Organisation in the Bombay Cotton
Mills 1918-1929', Unpubl. Ph.D. Thesis, University of
Sussex 1970; D. Kooiman, *Koppelbazen, Kommunisten en
Ekonomische Krisis - Arbeidersorganisatie in de
Textielindustrie van Bombay 1917-1937* (Jobbers,
Communists and Economic Crisis - Labour Organization
in the Bombay Textile Industry 1917-1937) (Amsterdam
1978) (Dutch with English summary).

35. S.M. Rutnagur, *Bombay Industries, the Cotton
Mills* (Bombay 1927), p.326; M.D. Morris, op.cit., p.130.

36. H.S. Poredi, Labour Office Bombay Millowners'
Association, Bombay, 12 November 1974.

37. Report of the Factory Commission (Bombay 1875),
pp.88-90.

38. S.M. Rutnagur, op.cit., p.326; Royal Commission
on Labour 1931, Report, p.23; *Labour Gazette* XIII, 2
(1933), pp.111 ff.

39. Indian Tariff Board 1927, IV, pp.178, 193;
Royal Commission on Labour 1931, Evidence I, 1, p.296.

40. In 1929 the Millowners' Association drafted

new work-rules including 'that any heads of departments, assistants or jobbers accepting bribes from the
work-people would be instantly dismissed', *Report of
the Bombay Millowners' Association* (Bombay 1929), p.60.

41. J.H. Kelman, *Labour in India, A Study of the
Conditions of Indian Women in Modern Industry* (London
1923), pp.110-11; Maniben Kara and Ushabai Dange,
former trade-union leaders, Bombay, 9 and 23 November
1974.

42. See Nurit Bird in this volume, above.

43. Walter C. Neale in this volume, below.

44. Royal Commission on Labour 1931, Evidence I,
1, p.10; W.L. Rowe, 'Caste, Kinship and Association in
Urban India' in A. Southall, ed., *Urban Anthropology*
(New York 1973), p.231; the quotation is from Gail
Omvedt, *Cultural Revolt in a Colonial Society, the Non-
Brahman Movement in Western India 1873-1930* (Bombay
1976), p.252.

45. R.C. James, 'Labor Mobility, Unemployment and
Economic Change, an Indian Case', *The Journal of Political Economy* LXVII, 6 (1959), p.546; S.C. Jain,
*Personnel Management in India, its Evolution and Pre-
sent Status* (University of North Carolina, Chapel
Hill 1968); H. Crouch, *Trade Unions and Politics in
India* (Bombay 1966), pp.17-18; see also the Open Letter
from a mill-agent in *Indian Textile Journal* XX, 229
(1909).

46. M.D. Morris, op.cit., pp.131-2; R.K. Newman,
op.cit., p.22. A slightly different analysis of the
jobber system, stressing the concepts of risk and
uncertainty, has been offered by M.D. Morris, 'Modern
Business Organisation and Labour Administration',
Economic and Political Weekly XIV, 40 (1979), pp.1680
ff.

47. Indian Tariff Board 1927 II, pp.348, 350.

48. Eric Meyer in this volume, above.

49. D.B. Miller, ed., *Peasants and Politics, Grass
Roots Reaction to Change in Asia* (London 1979), pp.13,
106; for the 1897 plague and the labour market see
Annual Factory Report of the Presidency of Bombay (Bombay 1897, p.8.

50. See for instance Royal Commission on Labour
1931, Report, p.24.

51. Royal Commission on Labour 1892, pp.123-4,
174; Indian Industrial Commission 1916-1918, Evidence
IV, London 1919, p.341; Indian Tariff Board 1927, II,
p.224; III, p.542; IV, p.204; D.H. Buchanan, *The
Development of Capitalistic Enterprise in India*

(London 1966), p.124; R.C. James, op.cit., p.547.

52. Gail Omvedt, 'Migration', p.195.

53. Factory Commission 1885, pp.98-105, 230-321; *Times of India* 25 September 1884, 6/7 and 13 October 1884 and 26 November 1884.

54. B.G. Meher, 'Early Labour Movement in Bombay City 1875-1918', Unpubl. Master Thesis, Tata Institute of Social Sciences, Bombay 1965, Chapter VI.

55. Indian Tariff Board 1927, III, pp.455 ff., 460, 541, 552-3; P.S. Lokanathan, *Industrial Welfare in India* (Madras 1929), pp.172-3; R.K. Newman, op.cit., pp.201 ff.

56. *Times of India*, 23 February 1924, Indian Tariff Board 1927, III, p.567.

57. G. Adhikari, ed., *Documents of the History of the Communist Party of India* (New Delhi 1979), III B, Chapter IV; S. Choudhary, *Peasants' and Workers' Movement in India 1905-1929* (New Delhi 1971), p.238.

58. Later, the Bombay communist Dange admitted that the B.W.P.P. 'had never its roots in the masses'; S.A. Dange, 'The Situation in India', no date (1930) Meerut Exhibit p.2512, in S.A. Dange, *Selected Writings* (Bombay 1977) II, p.508.

59. *Meerut Judgment - Judgment delivered by R.L. Yorke, Esqr, I.C.S. Additional Sessions Judge, Meerut on 16 Jan. 1933 in the Meerut Communist Conspiracy Case* ... Simla 1932, I, p.251; II, pp.370, 415.

60. Ibid. I, pp.250-1; II, pp.414-16; the quotation is from p.415.

61. D. Kooiman, 'Jobbers and the Emergence of Trade Unions in Bombay City', *International Review of Social History* XXII, 3 (1977), pp.321 ff.

62. In *S.C. Ghate, Our First General-Secretary - A Memorial Volume* (New Delhi 1971), p.105, the communist M.B. Rao vividly describes how the *Lal Bavta* (G.K.U. Red Flag) prevented an angry crowd of Hindu and Muslim labourers from coming to blows at Byculla bridge during the communal riots of February 1929. But he does not mention that the leader whose words had so much influence on the men was Alve.

63. Dange in Report of the Court of Inquiry, Bombay 1929, summarized in *Indian Textile Journal* XXXIX; 468 (1929), p.432.

64. Ibid, in *Indian Textile Journal* XXXIX, 468 (1929), pp.433-4, and Evidence from the Court of Inquiry, quoted in R.K. Newman, op.cit., p.308.

65. D. Kooiman, *Koppelbazen*, Chapters VII and VIII.

66. P.N. Inamdar, Rashtriya Mill Mazdoor Sangh official, Bombay 22 November 1974.
67. Meerut Judgment II, p.428.
68. See above, note 3.

THE ROLE OF THE BROKER IN RURAL INDIA

Walter C. Neale

Money-lenders and money-lending merchants have long been villains in Indian oral tradition and in the literature about the economic problems of India's villages. One need only read Malcolm Darling's *The Punjab Peasant in Prosperity and Debt*[1] to get the flavour of the tradition, or consult the Reserve Bank of India's *All-India Rural Credit Survey*[2] to learn how money-lenders exacerbated the problems of rural credit. They were said to charge outrageous rates of interest; to charge unconscionably high prices; to falsify the books; to cheat on weights and measures; to absorb an undue portion of the peasantry's saleable crop and thereby reduce the peasants' investment in agricultural improvement and lower the peasants' standard of living; to thrive on the peasants' ignorance and to abuse a monopoly position.[3] They were exploiters without socially redeeming traits.

Such was and is a common view, and from this common view followed programmes varying from legislative requirements that written receipts be given; through the establishment of the Indian Co-operative Movement and the proposal that the peasantry should be taught to read, write, and figure in order to prevent money-lenders from cheating; to the employment of a variety of extension officers to deal directly with the villagers.

If one pauses, however, to consider the money-lender's history, one is struck by certain peculiarities. First, the money-lender not only exploited the lower orders of Indian rural society but also exploited the higher orders, members of dominant castes in the villages.[4] Second, the money-lender and money-lending merchant antedate the 'capitalist' or market system in India by many years.[5] Third, the money-lender and money-lending merchant survived the introduction of the co-operative movement and later survived the India-wide spread of community development. In fact, they more than survived, for they have been blamed for the failure of the co-operative movement and observers have noted that villagers often turned to the money-lender in preference to other sources of finance and goods.

The money-lender's first peculiarity, the length

of his history, indicates that he was not only a capitalistic or commercial exploiter - or at least that,
in his origin, he did have other functions. The
second peculiarity, that he exploited the powerful as
well as the weak, raises the question of why the powerful did not 'do away with him' - that is, simply drive
him out of the village or kill him, or perhaps just
beat him (procedures which have been used by the powerful against the lower orders often enough). Unlike
other exploiters of India's poor - landlords, landlord
money-lenders, village headmen - the small-scale money-
lender had no political base in the village. Unlike
other exploiters of India's village rich as well as
poor - absentee landlords, politicians, larger merchants, and corrupt police officials - he had no
political base outside the village. What protected
him? The money-lender's physical survival despite his
villainy implies that he was necessary to the village
and, curiously, that people saw reason not only for
tolerating him but also for tolerating the 'outrageous
profits' which he made. The third peculiarity, the
money-lender's survival in the face of 'low cost'
competition, implies that in some sense the money-
lender's prices were not outrageous, that he did give
something of value which others - the co-operative
movement, for instance - did not. How can one account
for the long-term survival of one regarded as a villain
when his victims had the opportunity and the power to
dispose of him - how, unless they needed him badly?
It is certainly true that the money-lender had money
to lend, and that people came to him to borrow; but
other people in the villages were wealthy and, for
productive purposes, the co-operative societies were
there to provide cash and the government was there to
provide takkavi loans in kind.

It is to the mystery, or at least the question,
of why the money-lender survived that this essay
addresses itself, and in the process presents the
hypothesis that many of the relationships between rural
and urban India depended upon and were conducted by a
variety of people in social roles to which the literature of anthropology has attached the rubric 'culture
broker';[6] that the culture-brokering characteristics
of these roles were often more important to the relationships existing between villagers and others than
were the specific functions implied by the administrative or occupational titles of the brokers; that some
of the developmentally ineffective responses to the

stimuli of British rule, with its commercial and con-
tractural outlook, were a result of the need for inter-
mediating culture brokers; and that some further understanding of the difficulties modern developmental services experienced in the rural areas is to be gained
by realizing that it was, among other things, as culture brokers that extension and development officials
failed.

Unlike the Indian marriage-broker, or other brokers found operating in both the Indian and western
economies, the culture broker's peculiar expertise is
not in supplying a particular item or service, although
he does that, but in being able to operate in two
different cultures or subcultures because he under-
stands the folkviews and cognitive maps of both. He
is thus able to give each culture *access* to the other.
He is a link between two cultural worlds and might
better be called a 'social translator' than a middleman or a broker.

Culture-broking roles have formal resemblances
and some matters of substance in common with western
middlemen and with some of our service industries and
financial institutions, but their primary function and
the source of their strength are different. Middlemen
and brokers exist in western societies because, in
varying proportions, they speed the flow and reduce
the costs of information; they perform a specific economic function more cheaply than their clients could
provide it for themselves; they possess an expertise
which most people cannot be expected to master; or
they fulfil a role given by the institutional structure of society. Real-estate brokers and estate
agents illustrate the first sort of function, as do
employment agencies. Stockbrokers, wholesalers, and
savings associations and building societies exist because they can perform more cheaply than those they
serve; and financial firms, such as stockbrokers or
building societies, provide a technical expertise
their clients lack - how to write a contract of sale
or a mortgage. Lawyers similarly provide a technical
expertise, but they also derive their role from the
presumed impartiality of our courts and consequently
institutionalized arm's-length relationship of suitors
to judges and juries. Banks, while performing the
same functions as savings associations and building
societies, also and importantly exist as middlemen
because our laws and institutions give them something
close to a monopoly of the power to create money. In

each case it is not that the two parties to a possible
transaction or relationship cannot understand each
other or deal with each other if they come face to
face. Sellers and buyers of houses or stocks, savers
and borrowers, and plaintiffs and defendants understand
each other's aims; and if by chance they come face to
face with each other, they are often capable of carrying through the transaction more cheaply than they
could by employing a broker. Even in the case of
plaintiffs and defendants, it is not lack of mutual
comprehension that requires the lawyers, but rather
the system of courts which requires the lawyers; and
the system of courts is required to prevent blood feuds
and to enforce decisions, not to introduce the parties
to a dispute to each other.

Perhaps the best example, in modern western history, of a broker *in cultures* - as opposed to the sorts
of brokers discussed above - is the ward or precinct
boss of American politics during the late nineteenth
and early twentieth centuries. The newly-arrived
immigrant had no idea of where to go to complain about
a landlord, no idea of how to get admitted to a city
hospital, no idea of how to deal with a desk sergeant
at a police station - and was often terribly afraid to
try. He faced a person with power who asked incomprehensible questions and gave incomprehensible directions. If one did not do as one was told, one failed;
and how could one follow directions if the directions
made no sense? Conversely, the confusions, ignorances,
and fears of the immigrant were often a mystery to
those born and bred in the U.S.A. Immigrants raised
in a society whose rules and perceptions were not
American appeared ignorant, stupid, incompetent, demanding, whining, violent, unco-operative - in fact,
different. The precinct boss understood the needs
and the fears of the immigrants and knew how to talk
with them to find out what they wanted. He also knew
how to get admitted to a hospital and how to soothe a
policeman. And he would lend five dollars in an emergency. In 'exchange', gratitude and the need to keep
such bosses and their superiors in office guaranteed
the votes of the newly naturalized. While language
could be a barrier, the important function of the boss
was to overcome the cultural barrier.

The importance of the culture broker has been
recognized in the literature of anthropology, where a
number of different kinds of such brokers has been
identified. For instance, Silverman's central Italian

brokers were (a) members of the village community, and
(b) from patron families of long standing in their
villages.[7] Wolf's Mexican brokers were from outside
the old communities and were members of the new group
of politician-entrepreneurs who ruled the country.[8]
According to Geertz, the Javanese kijaji who added
'political brokering' to their former religious brokering role were honoured members of the community
and commanded local support.[9] Among those in rural
India who could be described as culture brokers, only
the village headman and, more recently, the elected
members of the institutions of panchayati raj had political roles or could be likened to patrons. Certainly
the village money-lender lacked both characteristics
of the Italian and Javanese culture brokers: he was
far from being a member of the ruling group and he
certainly did not command a loyal local following,[10]
unless, of course, he was also a landowning member of
the dominant caste.[11]

Indian village money-lenders and the men who were
both money-lenders and merchants filled one of several
culture-brokering roles, albeit their primary function
may have been the economic one of providing credit and
goods from outside. Other brokerage roles included
village headmen, lawyers, and politicians.[12] All survived, although disliked and distrusted, because they
were necessary links between village and town, villager
and official, villager and court, villager and state.

The Indian economy was long 'segmented', meaning
that policies and procedures effective in the organized or modern sector had little effect upon the unorganized, largely rural sector. Thus interest rates
charged in the cities had virtually no effect on
interest rates charged in the countryside, while the
distribution of acreage among crops was only marginally
influenced by the relative crop prices existing in the
centres. There were linkages between village and town.
Of necessity there had to be linkages: because of marketing of commercial crops and some marketing of
staples; the payment of land revenue; and the enforce-
ment of laws about landed property and tenant rights.
After the turn of the twentieth century there were
increasing efforts to increase the number and improve
the effectiveness of the linkages, culminating in the
intensive efforts of community development and other
services after independence. But until the 1970s
these linkages remained weak. Partly they remained
weak because the rural economy could function with

little dependence on the urban economy, while the
urban economy could function with little dependence on
the rural economy so long as commercial crops and some
staples continued to flow from the rural areas. Tea,
coffee, and later rubber provided examples of the
urban, organized sector assuring the flow of commercial
crops quite independently of the village agriculture.
But partly the linkages remained weak because there
was a cultural barrier between the two segments. Culture brokers arose to provide links where there were
none, or only weak ones.

What did Indian culture brokers do? The money-
lender provided the wherewithal - money - essential to
transactions in the commercial sphere. The headmen
collected the revenue and turned it over to higher
authorities while enjoying the support of higher authorities in enforcing law and order and in pursuing his
own aims within the village. The rural lawyer - that
tout so looked down upon by British administrators as
well as so distrusted by villagers - took the villagers
into the courts to plead cases, explained (if not too
accurately) the rights, powers, and so on that the law
gave to plaintiffs and defendants, and got such documents drawn and registered as the villager might need
or want. The Congress Party 'constructive worker'
tried to organize the villagers to support the national
independence movement and then to mobilize votes for
Congress Party candidates. He was also supposed to be
- with what effectiveness opinions differ - the eyes
and ears of the Congress Party in the villages, and in
consequence it was through him that villagers dealt
with the Party and with legislators.

What each of these brokers had that other villagers did not have was *access*. In the case of the
money-lender, it was access to the urban money-lenders
and bankers and to the urban wholesale merchants. He
had access because he knew how to talk to bankers and
wholesale merchants, he knew what they could and could
not do, and he knew what they were willing to do under
various specified conditions. The villager also had
access in the physical sense. He could find the location of an urban establishment; he could walk in the
door and ask for what he wanted - but he did not know
how to ask for help or to argue over terms in a way
that was comprehensible, trustworthy, and persuasive
to the person he would then be addressing. Conversely,
the urban banker and merchant were unable to deal with
this strange peasant - although, of course, they did

not describe the peasant as 'strange' but rather as 'poor, simple, ignorant', and so on. What the urban commercial person and the peasant needed was a go-between and the money-lender fitted here between the town and the needy peasant. The needy peasant rarely went into the urban bank or wholesale establishment, while the urban banker and wholesaler seldom if ever went to the village. In a way the money-lender was a 'drummer' for the more organized (and, in our terms, more sophisticated) financial sector of the economy, but he differed from the 'drummer' in our society in that the problem was not finding potential borrowers in the villages. The problem was organizing and administering the borrowing and lending business in the village in terms, through procedures, and in a vocabulary of discourse and of obligation which the villager understood. To say here, 'the villager understood', does not mean that he understood the accounting system used by the money-lender, or that the money-lender taught him household and farm finance. What it means is that the procedures and proposals as put to the villager by the money-lender were ones which made sense to the villager and that the villager knew how to talk to the money-lender and what to expect of him - in short, how to do business with him. In F.G. Bailey's expressive way of describing how the political agent worked,[13] the money-lender was a man who knew how to wear a dhoti in the village and trousers in the town.

In effect, what is suggested here is that we look upon a 40 per cent rate of interest charged by a money-lender as consisting of 10 per cent for the money plus 10 per cent for the expenses of collecting debts plus 10 per cent for wearing a dhoti plus 10 per cent for wearing trousers. If one accepts this proposition, then one should not argue that 40 per cent was an outrageous rate of interest for money (that rate was a mere 10 per cent), but rather that 20 per cent was an outrageous wage for intercultural transvestism. It may have been outrageous; it may not have been outrageous - who knows the just price for simultaneous translation between cultures? - but the 40 per cent fee should not be compared with commercial rates of interest.

The major points of contact between the village and the larger world were the use of the monetary system and monetary devices by the villagers; the collection of land revenue by the government; the use of the

police and the courts by the state, the villagers, and
others; and the efforts of political parties to organize village support. The untrustworthy and, in academic and village folkview, even villainous headman,
zamindar, talukdar, jagirdar, money-lender or money-
lender-merchant, petty lawyer, and politician were the
inside-outsiders (or outside-insiders), each of whom
had a brokerage role corresponding to one of the points
of contact (kinds of events) which linked the villager
with the nation and the world. To convey attitude,
rather than information, one might assert that these
people 'did not exploit the villager' but that they
'exploited an opportunity provided by the differences
between the social systems and attitudes of the towns
and the social procedures and beliefs of villagers'.

It is peculiarly revealing that the degree of contempt, although perhaps not of dislike, in which the
linking brokers were held was, if only roughly, *inver-
sely proportional* to the degree to which the linking
brokers were participants in the events of village
life *independently* of their roles as linking brokers.
If it was true that the respect/contempt rankings here
suggested corresponded with that village hierarchy of
values which placed agriculture above all other activities (except, in principle, holy ones), it was also
true that the rankings correlated with the degree to
which the person's daily round of activities was integrated with the common daily round of village activities. Since the daily round was largely agricultural,
those engaged in agriculture were involved in many of
the 'multiplex' relationships of a 'simplex' village
society and hence villagers regarded them as village
agriculturists rather than as linking brokers.[14] Also,
as a consequence of this integration with the village,
the more 'inside' of the linking brokers - such as a
resident landlord-headman - spoke and acted in the
terms of the village folkview more fluently and completely than did the others. Their activities were
therefore more comprehensible to the villager and the
individuals themselves appeared to be more trustworthy.
The result was that, even though hatred for resident
landlords and money-lenders may have exceeded hatred
for lawyers and politicians, the latter two were held
in greater contempt. As between landlord and money-
lender, there is no doubt that the money-lender was
the more contemptible - no doubt that in fact the
landlord, whatever else he may have been, was not an
object of contempt. A wealthy landholding resident

of the village who was also a money-lender was held in
greater respect, and even disliked less, than the pure
money-lender or the money-lender who also engaged in
trade but not in agriculture. Similarly, members of
the new local legislative bodies under panchayati raj
were often given more respect than were the members
of the state legislative assemblies.[15] It was probably because they were drawn directly from the village
populations that those elected to these bodies were
held in greater esteem.

Much has been made of monetary profits gained in
brokering roles. Money was certainly one of the rewards for undertaking a brokering role, and for the
money-lender in particular the major reward; but it
was not the only reward, and for the headman-zamindar
money may well have been less important than the power
which came from contacts with the police and revenue
officers of the urban-based culture. By emphasizing
the monetary rewards of brokering roles observers and
reformers have perceived and therefore classified
problems and conflicts arising from the existence of
brokering roles as 'economic'. This has led to ex-
plaining the roles, the motives of the brokers, the
situations in which the brokers operated, and the consequences of brokering in economic terms. Because
economic analysts do not worry about subcultural differences in perceptions (and are strongly inclined to regard institutional variations as 'non-economic', if not
downright idiosyncratic), the possibility that brokers
survived and even throve to serve other ends than profit and the supply of goods or money has been overlooked. The situation misclassified, the problems have
been misunderstood. A narrowly economistic view of
what was happening led to solutions which were not
solutions, and from thence to critiques of public programmes which missed the point.

To by-pass and to subvert the 'exploitative'
position of middlemen-brokers the government of India,
both before and after independence, sent several kinds
of lower level officials into the villages: co-operative society secretaries, extension officers, village
level workers, and panchayat secretaries. Disappointment followed: money-lenders continued to thrive while
co-operative societies failed, or at best expanded
slowly; new techniques and tools were adopted much more
slowly than had been hoped; the members of the dominant
castes who had supplied the headmen and run the old
caste panchayats took over the management of

co-operative societies and new organs of local government. Along with disappointment came charges of incom-
petence and corruption. Certainly a significant number
of lower level officials were technically poor at their
jobs. They did not know enough about the *whats* and
hows of agricultural techniques, did not understand how
the individual measures of improvement must be fitted
together to make an economically worthwhile whole, and
did not grasp the scientific bases of the improved
technologies. But this was only a part of the problem:
when right, when technically competent, when knowledge-
able about why the improvements should be made, these
officials were nevertheless often unable to convey the
ideas and unable to teach the cultivator how to acquire
and to use the new techniques. The reasons, I submit,
were not the ignorance or stupidity of cultivators -
and, in any case among social scientists, this interpretation has been largely dropped in the last two
decades [16] - nor by any means entirely a failure to
appreciate some one or more specific elements in the
local situation (although such was frequently the
case), but rather that the extension officer operated
and discoursed in the modes and phrasings, and with
the perceptions of cause-and-effect and of reward and
punishment, of the modern urban world. The cultural
idioms as well as the procedures of the urban world
were by no means wholly meaningful in the world of
village India, and this lack of meaningfulness reinforced villagers' already well-developed distrust of
government agents.

Reformers and developers assumed that what was
needed to develop the villages and to change the villages was access to more resources and new techniques
at lower costs. They were right in that without more
wherewithal of inputs and more knowledge of how-to-do
there would be no development. But they were in
error in thinking that *access* meant the establishment
of modern institutions willing to provide credit,
information, tools, cement, and services at lower cost
than money-lenders and merchants had been charging.
Like nitrogen for plants, new inputs for villagers
must be in an 'available form'. Brokering is putting
resources and extra-village organizations into an
'available form'. When the organizations are structured in a modern mould and staffed with personnel who
live, or try to live, or want to live, only in the
modern style, then the new elements of modern scientific society are not transmitted to the participants in

172

the small, village societies. Furthermore, insofar as
people entering a brokering role did have the trust of
the villagers, '... in virtually all cases this trust
[was] withdrawn if the broker [was] seen to be a mis-
sionary for modernization'.[17]

Indian leaders and administrators conceived of
extension officers and panchayat and co-operative
secretaries as efficient, honest, 'economic' middlemen,
but the officers and secretaries failed in these roles
in significant part because what was needed were brokers who could translate new knowledge and opportunities into the social idiom and perceptions of the
villagers. In the absence of new officials good at
brokering the new technologies and organizations,
'private entrepreneurs-in-folkview-translation' continued to thrive: men who could operate in two subcultures became political brokers who effectively took
over the substance of the roles of the panchayat and
co-operative secretaries while the money-lender still
lent at 40 per cent to villagers who would pay 'extra'
for access on terms understandable and acceptable in
their own view of how-the-world-works.

Were this the whole story the efforts at development would have been a complete failure: but, in fact,
they were not. Quite the contrary. The long-run rise
in agricultural output since the 1950s, at about three
per cent per year, was ample evidence of more than
minimal success. Furthermore, while results were always less and later than planned, the extension efforts
of the Indian government did contribute to change in
the villages and to the creation of effective linkages
between the sectors. One might liken the process to
the effect of water pounding upon the lip of a water-
fall: nothing appears to happen until suddenly a large
piece gives way. Similarly, there appeared to be no
revolutionary change in rural India for 15 to 20 years
after independence, and then the 1970s saw many changes.

One of the first evidences of change was corruption
in the development services. Curiously, from the view-
point presented in this essay, one important way in
which extension officers were corrupted involved brokering. Bribing officials could occur only because
cultivators wanted the new inputs, but if corruption
in the development services was a mark of the success
of the services in creating demand for new inputs, it
was also a measure of the failure of the services to
create properly *public-service* brokers. This failure
was manifested in that common form of corruption

whereby a development officer held up validation and transmittal of forms for government subsidy or for the supply of new farm inputs until a few rupees found his pocket. The way in which this kind of transaction was conducted illustrates the importance of brokering: the villager often did not himself go to the official, but rather a manufacturer or seller of inputs himself approached the validating official. This seller had already reached an agreement with a villager who wanted the new inputs and had already helped the villager to fill in the forms. [18] He too was a broker who could deal with both the villager's culture and the bureaucracy's culture.

There have been other changes reducing the need for culture brokers and the opportunities for culture brokering. The village headman or zamindar is no longer the focal point for revenue collection. During the 1960s the members of district zilla parishads and members of the legislative assemblies became the people who represented the villagers to officialdom.

The efforts of community development officers over 20 years and experience of political activity at block, district, and state levels, reinforced by the opportunities provided by the Green Revolution, changed the villagers, or at least those villagers who had accustomed themselves to the new technologies and expanding markets. Sugar farmers in Maharashtra and wheat and now rice farmers in Punjab, Haryana, and western U.P. are not only willing and able to approach representatives of the modern or urban culture - they even barge into the offices of professors of agriculture. The village money-lender is now facing effective competition from the banks, which have, since nationalization, been required to achieve lending targets in the rural area. Perhaps legal necessity was the mother of cultural invention by bank managers, but similar instructions to the State Bank of India 15 years earlier were not nearly so effective. More likely the 'lead banks' - one in each district responsible for seeing to it that the banks in the district do lend the target amounts - have met a more responsive clientele. In either case, the money-lender is being replaced by the banks when loans are wanted for productive purposes.

It is possible that culture brokers will survive for some time yet because there is still a lot of difference between the world as understood by the landless labourer and the Harijan and the world as understood by development administrators and the political organs of the nation and the states; but it is perhaps equally likely that political and labour organizations will eliminate the need for culture brokering between the dispossessed and the rest of Indian society.

Culture brokers arise when two groups wish to deal with each other but find that they 'word the world'[19] so differently that they cannot reach mutual accommodations. The culture broker always has a substantive function - the achievement of one of the mutual accommodations which the two groups wish - but the key to his position and power is not his technical expertise in the substantive function but his ability to word the world differently, and intelligibly, to the members of the two groups. In India he often appeared corrupting and exploitative because he enjoyed more income or power than seemed justified by the particular accommodations - loans, access to officials - he made possible; and because he violated the law or the ethics of one or both of the cultures he served to connect. He was certainly corrupting of the administration and was probably exploitative of the villagers with whom he dealt - at least, he certainly took advantage of his position and was less than averagely sensitive to the standards of law and equity as commonly understood in India. However, such behaviour was necessarily inherent in his role, which was to act between and therefore outside as well as inside both cultures, and therefore to some degree independently of the ethical standards of both. It is understandable that he tried to maintain his role in the face of the efforts of reformers, adminstrators, and statesmen to replace him with other, less costly and more equitable agencies. If some of his gains were ill-got, not all were; for the very situation of cultural diversity must share some of the blame.

The Indian brokers' roles originated in the difference, in a phrase popular in the 1950s, between the 'little traditions and the great tradition'. In particular, as British commercial practice and law became more important in India, the numbers, wealth, and powers of the culture-brokering money-lender and lawyer grew. It has only been very recently, perhaps only in the last decade on any significant scale, that the village farmer and those representing the city and the nation have come to understand each other's cultural idiom well enough to do without culture brokers.

Neale, 'The role of the broker in rural India'

The line of argument in this essay originated in a
paper of the same title delivered to the Annual Meeting of the American Association for the Advancement
of Science, New York City, 30 December 1967.

1. Fourth edition (London 1947).
2. Bombay 1954.
3. That many or all money-lenders did these
things was probably true; but the point of the argument which follows is that these facts do not exhaust
the important truths about money-lenders (or about
other rural brokers).
4. The point was made at the SOAS Conference in
December 1980 that a great deal of lending in India's
villages was by richer villagers to poorer villagers
in kind, especially in foodstuffs; and that such lending probably constituted well over half of total lending within India's villages - perhaps, it was
suggested, amounting to three-quarters of all village
lending. The Report of the All-India Rural Credit
Review Committee(Bombay: Reserve Bank of India 1969),
p.100, says that professional money-lenders provided
43.8 per cent and traders and commission agents 6.1
per cent of the total borrowings by rural households
in 1950-52. The comparable figures for 1962 are 12.7
and 10.1 per cent. Landlords and 'agriculturist money-
lenders' provided 26.8 per cent in 1950-52 and 34.6
in 1962 (relatives provided 14.4 and 8.8 per cent).
But, because no one knows either the total amount of
lending nor the amount in kind, it is impossible to
state with any precision the 'proportional importance'
of the money-lenders' activities within the villages.
However, the point of this essay does not depend on
the relative importance of the money-lender, but only
upon the fact that he did have a significant role -
and if his lending amounted to only a fifth of total
lending, his role would still have been significant.
The much reduced proportion of rural credit attributed
to the money-lender in 1962 may reflect the decline in
the importance of his role as culture broker, a decline
discussed toward the end of this essay.
5. Henry S. Maine, 'Prices and Rents', in *Village
Communities in East and West* (3rd, author's edition,

New York 1876).

6. I believe that Eric Wolf introduced this concept. See his 'Aspects of Group Relations in a Complex Society', *American Anthropologist* 58 (December 1956), pp.1065-78.

7. Sydel F. Silverman, 'Patronage and Community-Nation Relationships in Central Italy', *Ethnology* 4 (April 1965), pp.172-91.

8. Wolf, op.cit., pp.1071-2.

9. Clifford Geertz, 'The Javanese *Kijaji*: the Changing Role of a Culture Broker', *Comparative Studies in History and Society* 2 (April 1960), pp.228-49. The literature on culture brokers is larger than the citations here might indicate. However, an effort at much wider citation or further illustrations does not seem necessary, or even advisable, in this essay, in which I wish to borrow the concept and offer it as a possible explanation of some of the traits of those dealing with Indian villagers. Those interested in further discussions of the meaning, significance, types, and case studies might consult B. Kapferer, ed., *Transaction and Meaning* (Philadelphia: Institute for the Study of Human Issues 1976), especially the references in A.P. Cohen and J.L. Comaroff, 'The Management of Meaning: On the Phenomenology of Political Transactions' (pp.87-107), pp.105-7; or Irwin Press, 'Ambiguity and Innovation: Implications for the Genesis of the Culture Broker', *American Anthropologist* 71, 2 (April 1969), pp.205-17, which relates the concept of the broker to the concept of 'the marginal man'.

10. In his discussion of the seemingly analagous roles of Indian politicians and officials, Bailey says that these people 'are not ... "culture brokers" in the sense of providing a communication of ideas and a meeting of minds: on the contrary .... By providing pragmatic contacts they render unnecessary normative communion'. F.G. Bailey, 'The Peasant View of the Bad Life', *Advancement of Science* 23 (December 1966), pp.399-409. However, it seems possible to view Silverman's broker as making commercial and legal understanding unnecessary, and Geertz's broker as making orthodox understanding of Islam unnecessary (opp.cit.).

11. See Adrian C. Mayer, 'Patrons and Brokers: Rural Leadership in Four Overseas Indian Communities', pp.167-88, in Maurice Freedman, ed., *Social Organization: Essays Presented to Raymond Firth* (Chicago 1967), which contrasts the broker with the patron as 'ideal types': 'The patron recruits followers by his power to

dispense favours. The broker, on the other hand, is
a middleman attracting followers who believe him able
to influence the person who controls the favours ....
[W]hereas the client of the former is only interested
in his relation with the patron, and does not care
about the source of the patron's power, the client of
the latter has a relation with the person with whom
the broker is in contact, and indeed has called in the
broker to influence that relation to his advantage'
(pp.168-9). The point is important in respect to
roles, for both roles can be adopted by a single person
in respect to another person. Silverman's brokers (op.
cit.) illustrate how patrons can use knowledge as well
as favours-to-grant, and be both patrons at home and
brokers with the outside world. The culture broker in
India, as argued in this essay, not only influences relations with outsiders - there may be only the most
tenuous relations with outsiders in the absence of a
culture broker.

12. See F.G. Bailey, *Politics and Social Change:
Orissa in 1959* (Berkeley 1963), pp.136-57, for a discussion of politicians.

13. Bailey, 'The Peasant View of the Bad Life',
p.404.

14. I am indebted to F.G. Bailey for the proposition that in 'simple' societies relationships are 'complex', whereas in 'complex' societies relationships
are 'simple'.

15. I have not seen such statements in the scho-
larly literature but Indian officials and MLAs made
this 'complaint' and some other people familiar with
rural India have expressed agreement.

16. At least in its overt form; but I suspect that
it has crept back in the covert forms of 'the importance of education' and 'investment in human capital'.

17. Bailey, 'The Peasant View of the Bad Life',
p.405.

18. I know of no literature which supports this
assertion with citations of specific cases, but Indian
and foreigner alike, who have worked in community development blocks, agree that this was a common form of
corruption - as did sellers of such equipment whom I
have interviewed.

19. For this phrase too I am indebted to F.G.
Bailey, in comments he made at the Interdisciplinary
Conference on Processes of Change in Contemporary Asian
Societies at the University of Illinois at Champaign-
Urbana, 5-7 November 1970.

TWO KARNATAKA VILLAGES AND THE OUTSIDE WORLD: INTERNAL CHARACTERISTICS, MOVEMENT LINKAGES, AND STATE OF DEVELOPMENT

H.G. Hanumappa and John Adams

Introduction

For over one hundred years India's villagers have been increasingly drawn into and had their lives affected by external developments. In the late nineteenth century railroads were laid down, the road system was repaired and extended, port and dock facilities were put in place, and telegraphic links were established within India and overseas. These infrastructural improvements were associated with an increased use of money and the spread of product and factor markets, and these phenomena were in turn connected to the dramatic gains in exports and imports of the 1860-1910 period.[1] It is still an open question as to whether there was any uptrend in average incomes during this time, but there is no doubt that the degree of economic, social and political change in the villages was profound. These forms of change, and the concomitant expansion of the infrastructure and market system, have continued to move in tandem right down to the present.

From the village perspective, rather than that of the economic historian, the interactions of village life and these external dimensions of change have been catalogued and assessed by several generations of field workers.[2] These anthropologists and other researchers provide ample documentation of the myriad changes in the villages. They usually describe the physical and infrastructural setting with care, stating precisely how far roads, rail stations, market towns, and other features of importance are from the villages and what links there are to them. What is often deficient in these studies, however, is the failure to expound in any detail upon the frequency with which villagers utilize these aspects of the village's external environment. Nor is there any systematic analysis of which strata of villagers use which external features and for what purposes. There is thus a yawning hiatus between the carefully sketched infrastructure on the one side and the copiously depicted pattern of village structure and change on the other. Actual connections and movements between these two spheres are described

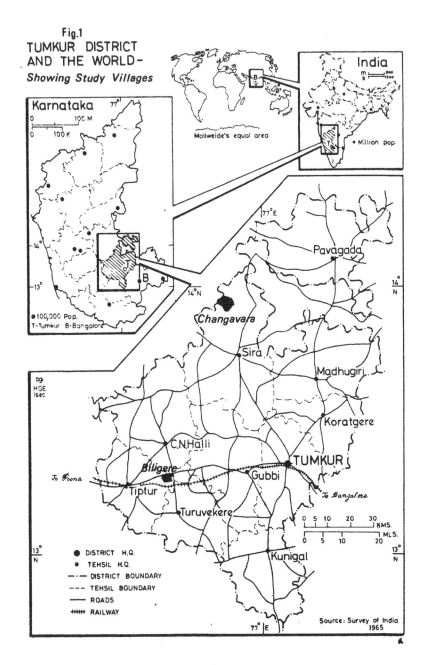

Fig.1
TUMKUR DISTRICT AND THE WORLD-
Showing Study Villages

only anecdotally or in a fragmented way.³ An interest of this paper is to use the method of reversing
the usual anthropological procedure and to quantify
and analyse movement patterns at the village level, as
the first emphasis, with village conditions being described only when relevant.

Evidence collected in detail as part of a large
sample survey of the villages of Tumkur district,
Karnataka state, and via field visits provides considerable insight into the nature of movements and inter-
actions between two South Indian villages and the outside world as tangibly manifested in neighbouring villages, hobli and district headquarters and market centres, and the state capital, Bangalore.⁴ Furthermore,
it is possible to relate the frequency of visits from
each of the two villages to these various places to
the social and economic characteristics of the travellers. It is also feasible to sort visits by purpose. Although two villages cannot be used as a basis
for wide generalizations about patterns over all India,
or even within Tumkur district, the novelty of this
exercise makes it of intrinsic interest and may serve
as a stimulant to parallel investigations.

Movement patterns in rural India take many forms.
People may migrate permanently to other villages or
exit from the rural sector to towns and cities. The
concern here is, however, with transient movements of
short duration, after which the visitor returns to the
home village. Such movements may be habitual, as going
into town to work each day, or essentially sporadic,
arising out of special needs, interests, or circumstances. Whether habitual or sporadic, the frequency
and purpose of external movements are likely to be
closely related to a number of factors. The physical
and economic base of the village and its occupational
and demographic structure will influence a settlement's
mobility patterns. The movements of a village's residents will be affected by its level of development, the
location of the village in relation to neighbouring
markets, administrative centres, educational facilities, clinics, extension offices, and other things
such as cinemas or co-operative offices. The quantity
and quality of bus, road, and other infrastructural
links will condition the frequency and timing of such
visits. Political involvement and the aggressiveness
of local leadership in seeking extension or other contacts will be important. Kinship ties, such as those
involving marriage networks, and the pull of religious

centres may shape travel patterns. Insofar as possible the impact of these various influences on the
movements of villagers in the two selected Tumkur villages will be assessed. Following the example of Epstein and others who have used a comparative method-
ology, the two villages were chosen because they had
different characteristics. It will be shown how these
differences are related to the quite striking contrast
in movement patterns between the two.

While a tracing of the elaborate movement patterns
of two sets of Indian villagers, viewed against the
backdrop of their respective ecological, economic, and
demographic milieux, is not a trivial gesture, it would
be overly mechanical and simplistic if matters were
left thus. The argument to be made is not only that
movements are outgrowths of the underlying village conditions but that they are connected with salient social
and political features of the villages. In particular,
many movements follow lines of social and political
interaction between key village groups and individuals
and the outside world. These connections to the larger
political and administrative system of the region,
state, and nation are highly instrumental in changing
the economic base and ultimately the level of development of a village. Or, where such connections are weak
or absent, the village base is static or eroding. A
key intervening variable may be styled 'leadership' or
'manipulative ability', which is associated with a particular caste structure. There is, in sum, a triangu-
lar relationship among movement, the economic base and
its development, and political and administrative
gamesmanship. Infrastructural links, the village's
ecological base and resources, basic demographic patterns, are conditioning factors but are not decisive.

*The Setting: District, Tahsil, and Village
Characteristics*

Karnataka state may be divided along two axes into
north-south and west-east dichotomies.[5] The northern
zone features black soils utilized extensively for
cotton. The south is typified by ragi, small stock,
and little irrigation. The west, along the coast, is
a high rainfall, rice-oriented area.[6] Although it
falls in the southern and eastern regimes, Tumkur district is not an extreme case of either melange of
characteristics. Still, ragi occupies about 29 per

cent of the net area sown and is the most widely cultivated crop.[7] Sheep and goats are significant in the
rural economy.

The two villages chosen are located in Sira and
Tiptur taluks. The economies of these two microregions
of Tumkur district have somewhat different features,
although they share the limitations of light Deccan
rainfall. Figure 1 shows the locations of Karnataka,
Tumkur, the two taluks, and Biligere and Changavara
villages, located respectively in Tiptur and Sira
taluks. Railways and major roads are drawn in. The
two taluks, which form the immediate economic and
political context for life in the two villages, represent variations on the traits typical of Tumkur. About
62 per cent of the area of Tiptur is cultivated, versus
47 per cent in the district and only 27 per cent in
Sira. About one-third of the arable in Tiptur is devoted to ragi, which is about the district average;
this contrasts with only 12 per cent in Sira. The
chief sharply-defined aspect of Tiptur is that 28 per
cent of its cultivated land is in coconut plantations.
Sira has a diversified agriculture, because of canal,
well, and tank irrigation covering 19 per cent of its
arable. Minor millets are grown on one-quarter of the
land, and pulses occupy 21 per cent. Cash cropping
takes the form of groundnuts (11 per cent), coconut
(3 per cent), and areca nut (3 per cent). About 23
per cent of the district's sheep are in Sira taluk.

The two villages, Biligere of Tiptur taluk and
Changavara of Sira taluk, were selected in part because
they represent the modes of agriculture of the region.
Table 1 shows the land-use patterns in Biligere and
Changavara. For reference, the respective populations
of the two villages as of 1971 were 1538 and 1765.
Despite their rough equality in population numbers,
Changavara has over three times the total area of Biligere, but the large area unsuited for agriculture,
and scant irrigation, mean that Changavara must focus
its agriculture on dry cropping. In contrast, the farm
land of Biligere is 30 per cent irrigated from tanks
and wells and over 40 per cent of the gross cropped
area is devoted to wet land and garden agriculture,
with coconut tracts dominating. Ragi is the most
important grain crop in Biligere; there are smatterings
of other millets and pulses. Ragi is important, too,
in Changavara, but there is an even more diverse mix
of various millets and pulses. Some irrigated paddy
and dry and irrigated tobacco are grown.

In addition to their agricultural contrasts,
Biligere and Changavara have exhibited radically
different demographic trends in the 1951-71 period.
According to table 2, over the two census periods,
India, Karnataka, and Tumkur district have all experienced positive population growth in the range of 19
to 25 per cent. Tumkur district is at the bottom end
of this range, but Biligere is toward the top. The
divergent case is Changavara, where growth at about
one-third the district's rate in the 1951-61 interval
was followed by an absolute and rapid decline of 19.4
per cent in 1961-71. For this reason Biligere can be
called a 'growing' village and Changavara a 'declining'
village; of course, these designations do not imply
anything about average income trends although they may
be related to them.

The demographic structure of the two villages is
broken down in table 3. In Biligere, the uptrend in
population is more or less matched by an expansion of
households, although there is a rise in average household size from 5.0 to 5.8 persons. The male/female
ratio has climbed between 1951 and 1971, perhaps reflecting some in-migration of males. The shrinking
village has experienced a decline in the number of
households from 336 to 218. The sex ratio has risen
somewhat but the source here may be high female infant
mortality connected with dimmer local prospects rather
than selective in- or out-migration. A particularly
interesting phenomenon is the elevation of household
size from 6.1 to 8.1 persons with most of the increase
coming in the last decade of falling population.
Either small domestic units have found it easier to
emigrate, or having fewer resources have been more
driven to. The lack of scheduled caste out-migration
on a proportional basis, however, weakens both of
these propositions because their household size would
normally be low. Since the availability of housing
would be enlarged as population shrivels, this could
be presumed to lead to some domestic fragmentation and
dispersion. In Changavara, however, a number of
houses stand empty suggesting that social or economic
factors are controlling household size, rather than a
shortage of housing.

The taluk and village agricultural bases do not
permit any easy generalizations about relationships
between the economy and demographic and mobility patterns. The irrigation of a high proportion of village
land and concentration on coconut farming has provided

184

an impetus to population growth above the regional
average for Biligere. The dry farming of Changavara
has been less successful. It is clear, however, that
other factors need to be considered in order to ascertain why emigration has been so high in Changavara.
It may be anticipated that transient movements will
also differ, reflecting the known differences in the
ecological and economic situations of the two villages.
      Biligere and Changavara should manifest differ-
ences typical of growth and expansion on the one hand
and stagnation and decline on the other. This supposi-
tion is confirmed by obvious differences in literacy
and in the amenities available in the two villages.
Tables 4 and 5 summarize these contrasts. The literacy
rate is a good measure of childhood contact with educational institutions in rural India. Looked at dynam-
ically, a high and rising rate indicates that villagers
are reaching out for educational opportunities and
possible economic advantages. In turn, educational
exposure may make villagers more open to outside ideas
and more able to cope with the increasing demands of
a modernizing society. Such developments are of high
salience and influence when women's education is involved. The literacy rate in Biligere has been high and
rising during the 1951-71 period (see table 4).
Changavara's people had low literacy rates through
1961, after which some gains are noticeable. The position of women in Biligere rapidly shifted in the non-
traditional direction after 1951 so that their literacy
rate is actually as high as that of Changavara's men.
Female literacy in Changavara is quite low although
some gains have been made in the last decade. These
findings imply that Changavara is at once more conven-
tional, less receptive of educational involvement,
especially for girls, and not as participatory in the
ladder of schools of the region.
      The labour participation rates for 1961 and 1971,
included in table 4, do not convey much insight. De-
finitional changes make strict comparisons between the
censuses impossible, but for the two years Changavara
has higher male participation rates. The female workers of Changavara appear to have been marginally employed in agriculture in 1961, and with the defini-
tional change of the 1971 census this peripheral activity was not sufficient for them to be counted as
workers.
      To highlight further the image of Biligere as more
progressive and more involved in interaction with

regional economic and political developments, the
facilities or amenities available in the villages are
identified. The argument is put in terms of a reci-
procal interaction between an outward-looking village
and its milieu, the result being progressive or modern
behavioural patterns. Conversely the declining village
is less keyed into surroundings - there is less social,
political-administrative, economic interaction - with
the result that it is less progressive or modern. Its
residents may face more 'leave-for-good-or-else' decisions once dead-ends are reached. They lack the ability and opportunities for more complex responses to
India's changing rural setting. Superior amenities in
Biligere are both a sign of wider involvement and more
successful manipulation and a base for the expansion
of a village's relationships with the outside world.

Table 5 makes amply plain the superior development
of facilities achieved by Biligere, a differentiation
especially notable given that both villages are of
roughly the same size. While both have electricity,
Biligere has piped water, a primary health centre, and
a family planning clinic. Changavara does not even
have a small dispensary. The consciousness of the
desirability of piped water and of the benefits of
medical attention, not to mention receptivity to family
planning, attest Biligere's orientation towards the
securing of manifestations of modernity, valued either
for their own sake or as tokens. Post-secondary education is even available in Biligere itself in the form
of a junior college. Changavara has the usual amenities of an Indian village in 1980: wells, electricity,
schools, road and bus services, and a post office.
Biligere has gone beyond what has become the usual to
have such novelties as chlorinated water, superior
health facilities, and a junior college.

Movement Patterns: Interaction with the Outside World

On balance, it is accurate to say that Biligere has
somewhat better access to its taluk headquarters (Tiptur) than Changavara does to its (Sira). Biligere is
also near the Bangalore-Poona railroad. The villagers
of Biligere enjoy somewhat easier access to Tumkur,
the district headquarters, than do those of Changavara,
and can also more easily visit Bangalore, the capital
of the state. Nonetheless, these advantages are not
so significant as to account for the dynamism of one

village and the retrogression of the other. The economic resources of a village are susceptible to management and it is unclear why a previously adequate base
should have declined to the point that out-migration
would have been forced on so many, as has happened in
Changavara. There is a considerable scope to push beyond these undeniably important but still not fully
convincing factors to others.

On the basis of its more cash-oriented economy
centred on the coconut, and because of its long-stand-
ing interest in securing better education and better
facilities for itself, it may be argued that Biligere
will have a wider network of contacts with outside centres than Changavara. Such connections will involve
not only market links, but also visits to relatives,
religious centres, and political seats. Rural Indians
build alliances and seek support through a variety of
relationships; they receive information about technology, occupational opportunities, and political payoffs through many channels. Visits to relatives or
religious sites must not be seen merely as leading to
frivolous or purely social encounters. Similarly,
travel to markets may involve much socializing, casual
political action, and information-gathering and idea-
exchanging.

Table 6 illustrates visits of the residents of
Biligere and Changavara to their relatives over four
different distances. As expected, the rate of visitation is lower the greater the distance involved. Not
only cost and time are relevant, because the distribution of kin must be considered. Since the two villages
are of roughly equal population size, the number of
visits is a reasonable raw measure of interaction with
the outside world (for kin, physically 'outside' even
if socially 'inside'). Regardless of distance, the
villagers of Biligere far exceed those of Changavara
in travelling to meet with kin. Two anomalies concerning Changavara require some explanation. Changavara
is located at the western edge of Tumkur district but
is still close to Andhra Pradesh on the east. Visits
to kin draw villagers outside the district to the west
and into Andhra on the east; hence, the number of such
journeys within the state exceeds the number within
the district and the number of visits outside the
state is higher than for Biligere.

The total number of visits to kin is 2,022 for
Biligere and 481 for Changavara or a difference of
over 4.2 times. More persons (556) travel for this

purpose from Biligere than the number (248) from
Changavara, although the ratio is only 2.2. At all
distances the frequency of visits per person is higher
for Biligere than Changavara, with the total averages
being 3.6 and 1.9 visits per person respectively. Not
only does Biligere have more people visiting relatives
in and outside the taluk, but they do so almost twice
as commonly.

Visits to religious centres have their own intrinsic motives, but also afford opportunities for political and economic opportunism and for discussions with
caste or sect peers. Such visits require some affluence and manifest religious fervour and a traditional
outlook. These several influences are reflected in
table 7, in which the less progressive, declining
village is found to have made more religious visits
in one year than did the other. Only three of these
visits took residents of Changavara outside the district, however, compared to 68 such visits (49 per
cent) for Biligere. The average frequency of visits
per pilgrim is about one per year in all cases. The
villagers of Biligere may be typified as somewhat less
disposed to religious travels than those of Changavara,
but true to form their inclination is to longer distances. These results show a more parochially-oriented
exposure to regional religious visitation on the part
of Changavara and more cosmopolitan participation in
pilgrimages by the villagers of Biligere.

Many young rural Indians must, every morning and
afternoon, make the trip to and from school. Indians
of any age, and at virtually any time, are on the roads
and tracks between villages and local markets. Table
8 summarizes the movements to and from educational
centres for the two villages. Given its endowment of
educational insitutions, Biligere's children largely
remain within the village, but 40 students voyage
within the taluk or further to attend schools (the
response concerned 'daily' travel but the longer distances may necessitate weekly or other periodic movement). Changavara does have some students who are
being educated outside the village, but its low overall
commitment to education is consistent with its low
literacy rate and lack of advanced facilities.

Both villages have products - coconut in one case
and tobacco, small stock and ragi in the other - that
must be taken to market; and, both villages need to
purchase consumption goods and agricultural inputs.
Table 9 shows the monthly frequency of market visits

and their purpose for the two villages. Insofar as
the purchase of consumption items is concerned, Changavara actually exceeds Biligere in the number of visits
outside the village. Biligere's location on a main
road between the taluk and district headquarters, and
its nearness to a north-south road and the Bangalore-
Poona railroad, have encouraged the establishment of
shops. Purchases of consumer items in the village are
convenient and longer trips are unnecessary. Differences between the two villages in movements for marketing become more acute when farm sales are examined.
Biligere does more travelling for farm sales than does
Changavara; the same is true when the purchase of farm
inputs is the purpose. The vitality of the coconut
economy of Biligere and its related non-farm activities
shows up clearly in the large numbers of visits to
taluk headquarters for the selling and buying of farm
and non-farm products. Most marketing for both villages is done at the taluk headquarters, which is an
interesting comment on their efficacy as regional economic centres - both appear capable of bearing the
demands placed upon them by client villages. While
there is not by any means a trivial degree of market
interaction between Changavara and the outside world,
Biligere has a quantitatively greater rate of market
participation and that participation covers a broader
array of activities.

Apart from education and marketing, the kind of
work a villager does, and the place where it is done,
will guide regular movements outside the village.
The occupational structures of the two villages are
given in the first four lines of table 10. The chief
differences in the two villages are that Changavara
has more agricultural labourers but fewer small and
medium farmers. This contrast is not of great import,
however, since landholdings in a wetter village are
likely to be smaller than in a dry village. The
greater variety of occupations in Biligere is shown
by a somewhat larger number of workers in the 'other'
category, which includes shopkeeping, modern crafts,
carting and driving, and metal work. All in all, the
occupational structures of the two villages are not
radically different. Once again, however, the greater
regional involvement of Biligere is shown by the number
of workers who live in the village but spend some
appreciable part of their typical workday some distance
away. There peripatetics are drawn not only from the
more mobile artisans and other groups but from middle

and other farmers. The ability of these farmers to
cultivate lands outside their own village, lands in
some cases that are even outside the district, is testimony both to their managerial and entrepreneural
abilities and to their skill in handling the often
difficult role of outsider in a foreign village community.

The caste composition of the two villages varies
profoundly. Changavara has quite diverse social divisions. The major landholding castes are the Kuruba
and Golla households, 45 in number.[8] Nineteen each of
Lingayat and Vokkaliga families have land. There are
42 scheduled caste and 33 scheduled tribe families.
The larger landowners are from all three of the farm
household groups and smaller landowners are mostly
Kurubas and Gollas. In Biligere, there is a patently
dominant group of Lingayat farmers, who are formed
into 144 households with small and middle-sized holdings. There are 44 scheduled caste and 14 scheduled
tribe families. In both villages there are representative artisan, service, and twice-born castes. In
Tiptur taluk, where Biligere is situated, almost 40
per cent of the population identifies with the Lingayat
group so the village is tied into the locally most
numerous castes. Only 15 per cent of the population
calls itself Vokkaliga and this is the second lowest
proportion in the district's 11 taluks. In Sira taluk,
about 31 per cent of the population is Vokkaliga and
only 2.2 per cent is Lingayat. This district does
have the largest Golla-Kuruba proportion in the district at about one-fifth. Changavara's population is
not clearly affiliated with its taluk's plurality
caste, the Vokkaligas, although its Gollas and Kurubas
would appear to have some comparatively strong external
attachments within the district. Changavara has an
untypically high share of scheduled caste and scheduled
tribe families, and particularly many of the latter
disadvantaged group. There is therefore a sharp contrast between the classically shaped social structure
of Biligere, featuring as it does a cluster of Lingayat farmers in the midst of a regionally numerous and
influential amalgam of castemates, and that of Changavara, showing another face of rural India, namely a
village with no clear elite and a large number of
socially marginal families. These contrasting caste
distributions, and the potentials for extra-village
connections that they stimulate or inhibit, contribute
to the differential ability of each village's

population to interact effectively with its social and political surroundings. The identification of a common interest or interests and the leadership of Changavara's diverse array of people is more likely to be a formidable, if not impossible and fruitless task, while Biligere offers a situation ripe for the emergence and management of an effective caste spokesman, unless lineage or other rivalries disunite the preponderant Lingayats.

A summary of movement patterns by occupational group is provided in table 11. Since the occupational ranks are associated with caste status, inferences about differences across castes may be made. This large table provides a synthetic overview of extravillage visits. The evidence firmly reinforces the line of argument being developed: that the more extensive and more frequent contacts of Biligere tie it into intertwined social, political, and economic networks in the region and state; that these movements are important evidence of this progressive village's efforts to gain information, secure economic advantages, and enhance the village's payoffs from the taluk, district, and state political-administrative systems; that the declining village, Changavara, has been less skilful in forging such links, with consequent backwardness in education and amenities.

The parochial nature of Changavara's connections is exhibited in the dominance of visits per month to neighbouring villages rather than more distant targets. A total of 682 visits by 153 persons to nearby communities was made in an average month for a per person visit rate of 4.4. This rate is pretty well constant across occupational categories. Biligere visits neighbouring villages less commonly but more persons (191) make such visits, albeit at the low average rate of 1.9 visits per person. So, in a given month fewer of Changavara's people will travel to other villages and, while they will do so with double the frequency, they are therefore as a group less exposed to the circulation of ideas and information in their immediate vicinity than those of Biligere. The pattern is much the same for 'within taluk' travel: movement within the adjacent rural areas rather than to regional economic and political centres, carried on by a few relatively active people in Changavara, and more numerous, but less frequent travellers from Biligere.

Final Evidence and Conclusion

The two villages are remarkably at variance in the
frequency with which their residents visit regional
centres: the hobli, taluk, and district headquarters.
No single part of the evidence more reinforces the
view of Biligere as actively pursuing its interests
through systematic manipulation of the local economy
and political system. The broad pattern is that more
of Biligere's villagers, from more occupational groups,
visit these centres more regularly than do those of
Changavara. One hundred people of Biligere visit their
hobli headquarters for every one from Changavara. Four
times as many people make four times as many visits to
the taluk headquarters; 40 people average 1.8 visits
per month to the district headquarters, versus three
people making three visits from Changavara. The occupational differences in mobility between the two villages are revealing. Wherever the numbers are large
enough to mean anything, each of Biligere's work
groups makes more visits on average than do Changavara's. For Biligere, it is the medium farmers that
dominate in absolute numbers the movements to regional
centres. *Most critical, however, is the telling observation that for each of the three centres the size of
holding and higher social status and greater political
power in the village are perfectly correlated with the
frequency of such visits.* On an annual basis large
farmers who make such journeys undertake 30 visits to
the hobli headquarters, 36 visits to the taluk headquarters, and 29 visits to the district headquarters.
Middle and small farmers in the aggregate make more
total visits to the three types of centre but their
rates of doing so are lower. The villagers of Biligere
visit the state capital more than do those of Changavara, further demonstrating their aggressive reaching
out for gain and advantage.

Field visits to the two villages have provided
further support for the thesis attributing Biligere's
growth to the interaction of favourable internal economic conditions, an aggressive, questing, and manipulative leadership, identifiable with the farming
groups (but not exclusively), better education and
facilities, and a modestly advantageous location in
relation to infrastructure. Biligere has a group of
local leaders that in the last 15 years has been responsible for the obtaining of a junior college, a
primary health centre, and piped water. The village's

location on the state highway has been exploited at every possible opportunity by this leadership. A favourite ploy has been to meet with political figures and senior government officials passing up and down the road, encouraging them to detour into the village proper. This behaviour is largely absent in Changavara where there is an absence of such local initiative. Consequently, schooling and other amenities are undeveloped and there has been demographic decline through permanent out-migration. The more isolated location of Changavara and its dependence on extensive dry-land farming are doubtlessly factors in its population recession, but it is undeniably further disadvantaged by poor human resources, a weak orbit of contacts throughout its region, and a dearth of entrepreneurial and manipulative farmers.

Throughout its recent history Biligere has been led by a remarkable and sagacious panchayat chairman. He has vigorously pursued caste and village interests and has been responsible for the bringing of many amenities and development schemes into the village. He has been chairman of the taluk development board and in an oversight position for local planning and distribution of resources. He has made a full lifetime commitment to the idea that payoffs are to be had by capturing and manipulating the local political and administrative apparatus and using it for the benefit of the village. Recognizing that it is not a perfect system, this is nonetheless how rural India is supposed to work and how in the present institutional setting a village is supposed to develop itself in alliance with external powers and aid. This village leadership is provided by an individual who happens to be in the neighbourhood of 75 years old. Whether his sprat of a protégé (who is about 40) will ultimately continue this adroit management is not certain, but conditions are favourable.

The identification and analysis of extra-village contacts focus attention on a measurable behavioural dimension of the process of change and development in south India. Too often villages have been analysed only by the description of internal economic, political, and social relationships. The infrastructure has been regarded as important and it is frequently specified and mapped at the beginning of village surveys; market towns and administrative centres are normally mentioned. The evidence from Biligere and Changavara convincingly demonstrates, however, that a detailed examination of interactions between village populations and their regional context can shed considerable light on internal development patterns, including their demographic profiles, and the availability of electricity, schooling, and other beneficial elements.

The finding that the farmers, especially the large farmers, are more intensively involved in the interchange between village and local economic and political centres, is consistent with much recent discussion of rural India. Large and middle farmers are perceived as the leading groups in more progressive areas in reaching out to, manipulating, and even 'capturing' local political and administrative agencies capable of providing farm inputs such as seeds or fertilizer, irrigation and power, extension advice, credit, or public goods such as schools, roads, wells, or clinics. A question not opened in this discussion of such links is whether these activities lead to a skewing of these benefits in favour of the already comparatively rich and powerful. The breadth of Biligere's ties to the outside world, encompassing as it does all occupational groups, implies there is at least some catholicism in the process, but this issue cannot be faced with the evidence in hand.

Insofar as the future is concerned, further development and modernization, along with deepening politicization of the rural populace, will enchance the importance of the kinds of personal contacts nurtured by Biligere. To some extent the transient migrations of Biligere - to work as well as to bring benefits to the actors and the village at large - may be perceived as a substitute for permanent out-migration of the type found in Changavara. Facilitating, anticipating, and determining how to control - rather than being controlled by - such transient and opportunistic migration and movement may be essential for an administration desirous of working effectively and achieving its particular mission in the Indian rural setting. The lesson of Biligere is that an alliance between capable village leadership and local development agents can put into place effective schemes in such fields as schooling, health and family planning, dairying and modern farming, clean water and sanitation, and others. The lesson of Changavara may be that a divided village lacking caste consensus and leadership may have significant difficulty in reaching out to local political and administrative networks. Able and achieving

individuals in such circumstances may opt out via
education and migration. Changavara has generated a
number of college graduates but most have moved away,
one as far as Canada where he practises medicine. If
Changavara is to restore any dynamism to its economy,
very strong pressures and positive opportunity creation
from outside may be required.

TABLES

1. AGRICULTURE STRUCTURE IN ACRES

	Biligere Area	%	*Changavara* Area	%
Total area	1948	–	6540	–
Area not available for cult.	199	–	633	–
Total cultivable area	1749	100.0	5907	100.0
Irrigated area	526	30.1	424	7.2
Unirrigated area	708	40.5	4844	82.0
Cultivable waste area	515	29.4	639	10.8
Gross cropped area	1234	100.0	5268	100.0
Dry land	708	57.4	4844	92.0
Wet land	83	6.7	323	6.1
Garden land	443	35.9	101	1.9

Sources: 1. Census of India, District Census Handbooks,
    Tumkur District, 1951, 1961, 1971.
  2. Personal field visits.

2. GROWTH OF POPULATION, 1951 to 1971: PERCENTAGES

Decades	India	Karnataka	Tumkur Dist.	Biligere	Changavara
1951-1961	21.5	21.6	18.8	23.7	5.9
1961-1971	24.8	24.2	19.0	24.4	-19.4

Sources: Census of India, District Census Handbooks,
    Tumkur District, 1951, 1961, 1971; General
    Population Tables, Part IIA(i), All India,
    1961, 1971.

3.   DEMOGRAPHIC STRUCTURE: BILIGERE AND CHANGAVARA

	Households					*Population*			H'hold
Year	Total	% Change	Male	Fem.	Males Fems.	Total	% Change	SC/ST (%)	size (av.)
BILIGERE									
1951	198	–	500	499	100	999	–	NA	5.0
1961	234	18.2	652	584	117	1236	23.2	14.1	5.3
1971	262	12.0	814	724	112	1538	24.4	14.7	5.8
CHANGAVARA									
1951	336	–	1079	990	109	2069	–	NA	6.1
1961	370	10.1	1158	1033	112	2191	5.9	14.1	5.9
1971	218	-14.1	956	809	118	1765	-19.4	14.7	8.1

Key: NA Not available SC/ST SC/ST population to total
                                  population
Source: Census of India, District Census Handbooks,
        Tumkur District, 1951, 1961, 1971.

4.   LITERACY AND PARTICIPATION RATE IN BILIGERE AND
     CHANGAVARA

Year	Male	Female	Total	Male	Female	Total
BILIGERE						
	Literacy			*Percentages*		
1951	167	42	209	33.40	8.42	20.92
1961	337	117	454	51.69	20.03	36.73
1971	485	246	731	59.58	33.98	47.53
	Workers			*Participation rate*		
1961	362	154	516	55.52	26.37	41.75
1971	442	84	526	54.30	11.60	34.20
CHANGAVARA						
	Literacy			*Percentages*		
1951	190	16	206	17.61	1.62	9.96
1961	200	8	208	17.27	0.77	9.49
1971	174	351	425	34.70	9.15	24.08
	Workers			*Participation rate*		
1961	1320	547	1320	66.75	52.95	60.25
1971	599	64	663	62.66	7.95	37.56

Source: See table 2.

5.   AMENITIES BASE

Amenities	Biligere	Changavara
1. *Drinking Water*		
Wells	Yes	Yes
Piped Water	Yes	No
Tanks	-	-
2. *Electricity*		
Domestic	Yes	Yes
Irrigation	Yes	Yes
3. *Health*		
Primary Health Centre	Yes	No
Dispensary	-	No
Family Planning Centre	Yes	No
4. *Education*		
Primary School	Yes	Yes
Middle School	Yes	Yes
Secondary School	Yes	Yes
Junior College	Yes	No
Others	-	-
5. *Roads*		
Type of Road	'Pucca'	'Pucca'
Bus Stop	Yes	Yes
6. *Post Office*	Yes	Yes

Source: See table 2; field survey.

6.   VISITS TO RELATIVES (ANNUAL)

	Visits (No.)		Persons (No.)		Frequency per person	
	B	C	B	C	B	C
Within taluk	1023	362	236	163	4.3	2.2
Within district	550	25	170	20	3.2	1.2
Within state	438	73	146	48	3.0	1.5
Outside the state	11	21	4	17	2.7	1.2
Total	2022	481	556	248	3.6	1.9

Key: B Biligere   C Changavara
Source: Tumkur District Study.

7.   VISITS TO RELIGIOUS SITES (ANNUAL)

	Visits (No.)		Persons (No.)		Frequency per person	
	B	C	B	C	B	C
Within	71	162	63	142	1.1	1.1
district	*51*	*98.2*	*52.5*	*98*		
Within state	53	3	43	3	1.2	1.0
	38.2	*1.8*	*35.8*	*2*		
Outside the	15	–	14	–	1.1	–
state	*10.8*	–	*11.7*	–		
Total	139	165	120	145	1.1	1.1
	100	*100*	*100*	*100*		

Note: Figures in italics are percentages.
Source: See table 6.

8.   MOVEMENT FOR STUDY (REGULAR)

	Persons (No.)	
Places	*Biligere*	*Changavara*
Within village	354	61
Neighbouring villages	–	5
Taluk headquarters	7	–
Within taluk	2	–
Within district	17	12
Within state	14	6
Total reported	394	84

Source: See table 6.

9. TRAVEL FOR MARKETING (PER MONTH)

	Sale of prods.				Purchases (I)				Goods for Consumptn.	
	Farm		Non F		Farm		Non F			
	B	C	B	C	B	C	B	C	B	C
Within village	-	6	-	3	2	17	9	1	82	24
Within taluk	144	93	141	2	116	83	200	7	123	154
Within district	-	3	2	-	-	3	3	-	1	3
Within state	1	-	1	-	-	-	-	-	-	-
Total	145	102	144	5	118	103	212	8	206	181

Key: B Biligere C Changavara F Farm I Inputs
Source: See table 6.

10. MOVEMENT FOR WORK BY OCCUPATION GROUPS (REGULAR)

Occupations

		a	b	c	d	e	f	Oth.	Tot.	Row %
Total.	B	68	30	43	77	170	26	89	503	100
		13.5	*6.5*	*8.5*	*15.3*	*33.8*	*5.2*	*17.7*	*100*	
	C	137	25	40	38	105	40	50	435	100
		31.5	*5.7*	*9.2*	*8.7*	*24.1*	*9.2*	*11.5*	*100*	
Within	B	66	24	37	65	130	21	75	418	83.1
vill.		*15.8*	*5.7*	*8.9*	*15.6*	*31.1*	*5*	*17.9*	*100*	
	C	135	23	38	36	100	40	46	418	96.1
		32.3	*5.5*	*9.1*	*8.6*	*23.9*	*9.6*	*11*	*100*	
Neigh.	B	-	2	3	4	13	-	3	25	5.0
vill.	C	-	-	1	-	2	-	1	4	0.9
Taluk	B	-	-	-	-	2	1	1	4	0.8
HQ	C	-	-	-	-	-	-	1	1	0.2
Within	B	1	-	1	2	4	-	5	13	2.6
taluk	C	-	2	1	-	3	-	1	7	1.6
Within	B	-	-	1	-	9	1	3	14	2.8
dist.	C	-	-	-	-	-	-	-	-	0
Within	B	1	4	1	6	12	3	2	29	5.8
state	C	2	-	-	2	-	-	1	5	1.2

Note: Figures in italics are percentages.
Key: B Billigere C Changavara a labourers b artisans
        c marginal farmers   d small farmers
        e medium farmers   e large farmers
        Oth. others   Tot. total
Source: See table 5.

11. VISITS TO DIFFERENT PLACES BY OCCUPATIONAL GROUPS (MONTHLY)

Occupations	Visits B	Visits C	Persons B	Persons C	p.Per. B	p.Per. C	Visits B	Visits C	Persons B	Persons C	p.Per. B	p.Per. C
	Neighbouring Villages						*Hobli Headquarters*					
Labourers	59	240	22	55	2.7	4.4	80	-	50	-	1.6	-
Artisans	46	22	15	6	3.1	3.6	36	2	16	1	2.2	2.0
Marg.Fmrs	29	83	17	21	1.7	3.9	44	-	29	-	1.5	-
Small Fmrs	52	90	32	18	1.6	5.0	63	-	45	-	1.4	-
Med. Fmrs	127	134	81	28	1.6	4.8	135	1	74	1	1.8	1.0
Large Fmrs	17	73	9	15	1.8	4.8	30	-	12	-	2.5	-
Others	15	40	10	10	1.5	4.0	91	1	55	1	1.6	1.0
Total	376	682	191	153	1.9	4.4	479	4	281	3	1.7	1.3
	Taluk Headquarters						*District Headquarters*					
Labourers	7	12	5	8	1.4	1.5	-	-	-	-	-	-
Artisans	18	1	10	1	1.8	1.0	-	-	-	-	-	-
Marg.Fmrs	28	6	15	5	1.8	1.2	-	3	-	3	-	1.0
Small Fmrs	64	4	38	2	1.7	2.0	3	-	3	-	1.0	-
Med. Fmrs	167	20	75	12	2.2	1.6	33	-	18	-	1.8	-
Large Fmrs	24	9	8	7	3.0	1.3	12	-	5	-	2.4	-
Others	88	43	47	20	1.9	2.5	22	-	14	-	1.6	-
Total	396	95	198	55	2.0	1.7	70	3	40	3	1.8	1.0
	Within Taluk						*Within District*					
Labourers	1	28	1	6	1.0	4.6	-	-	-	-	-	-
Artisans	-	4	-	1	-	4.0	-	-	-	-	-	-
Marg.Fmrs	1	4	1	1	1.0	4.0	1	1	1	1	1.0	1.0
Small Fmrs	5	7	5	2	1.0	3.5	2	2	2	2	1.0	1.0
Med. Fmrs	8	-	5	-	1.6	-	-		-		-	
Large Fmrs	-	-	-	-	-	-	-		-		-	
Others	-	1	-	1	-	1.0	-	-	-	-	-	-
Total	15	44	12	11	2.4	4.0	3	3	3	3	1.0	1.0
	Within State						*State Capital*					
Labourers	-	-	-	-	-	-	-	-	-	-	-	-
Artisans	-	-	-	-	-	-	-	-	-	-	-	-
Marg.Fmrs	-	-	-	-	-	-	2	-	1	-	2.0	-
Small Fmrs	1	1	1	1	1.0	1.0	4	2	3	1	1.3	2.0
Med. Fmrs	1	1	1	1	1.0	1.0	22	1	10	1	2.2	1.0
Large Fmrs	-	-	-	-	-	-	8	2	4	1	2.0	2.0
Others	-	-	-	-	-	-	27	2	12	2	2.2	1.0
Total	2	2	2	2	1.0	1.0	63	7	30	4	2.1	1.4

Key: B Biligere   C Changavara   *p.Per* Visits per person
        Marg. Marginal   Med. Medium   Fmrs Farmers
Source: Data collected through field visits and from
         the Institute for Social and Economic Change,
         Bangalore.

Hanumappa and Adams, 'Two Karnataka villages and the
outside world: internal characteristics, movement
linkages, and state of development'

The authors wish to thank the authorities of the Tumkur
Project, the Institute for Social and Economic Change
(ISEC), for permitting them to use data from that study
in writing this paper. Hanumappa has worked as a member
of the team conducting this on-going project. Professor
V.K.R.V. Rao, Honorary Director of the project, has provided general guidance to all aspects of its research
and early recognized the importance of examining rural
movement patterns. The authors are thankful to Professor V.M. Rao of the Rural Economics Unit, ISEC, and
Dr S. Seshaiah of the Sociology Unit, ISEC, for comments
on a draft of the paper. The authors remain responsible
for the interpretation and analysis of evidence in the
study.

1. Vera Anstey, *The Economic Development of India*
(London 1936), chs.VI, XII, and XIV, remains for better
or worse, the best overview. Also see John Adams and
R. Craig West, 'Money, Prices, and Economic Development
in Late Nineteenth Century India', *Journal of Economic
History* XXXIX (March 1979), pp.55-68.
2. The standard comprehensive bibliography is
*Village Studies, Data Analysis and Bibliography, Vol.1:
India, 1950-1975* (Brighton 1976), compiled by Mick
Moore, John Connell, Claire M. Lambert, edited by
Claire Lambert; also see, for a description of some of
the older studies, John Adams and Uwe J. Woltemade,
'Studies of Indian Village Economies: A Bibliographical
Essay', *Indian Economic and Social History Review* VII
(March 1970), pp.109-37.
3. This is true of even detailed studies recognized
to be among the most thoughtful and comprehensive of
their type. Examine F.G. Bailey, *Caste and the Economic
Frontier* (Manchester 1957), T.S. Epstein, *Economic Development and Social Change in South India* (Manchester
1962), S.C. Dube, *Indian Village* (Ithaca 1955), or M.N.
Srinivas, 'The Dominant Caste in Rampura', *American
Anthropologist* LXI (February 1959), pp.1-16, and his
related papers.
4. The Tumkur survey covered 252, or 10 per cent
of the district's villages and over 30,000 rural

households. The villages were randomly selected but for each village all households were surveyed. Hanumappa visited the two villages selected for study several times in the summer of 1980 to check and expand the originally gathered material. Hanumappa was at the University of Maryland in 1979-80; Adams visited ISEC in 1980.

5. R.L. Singh, ed., *India: A Regional Geography* (Varanasi 1971), pp.791-828 and 907-31.

6. John Adams, 'Regional Patterns of Development in Karnataka', *The Journal of Developing Areas* 12 (July 1978), pp.439-48.

7. Data on Tumkur district and Sira and Tiptur taluks employed in this and the next few paragraphs are drawn from Government of Karnataka, Bureau of Economics and Statistics, *Tumkur District at a Glance, 1974-75*, issued by the District Statistical Officer, Tumkur, n.d. For a survey of the distribution of castes in Tumkur district, and their association with landholding, quality of housing, and other economic factors, see John Adams and H.G. Hanumappa, 'Caste and Economic Structure in Tumkur District, Karnataka state, India', presented at Association for Asian Studies, Southeast Regional Conference, Columbia, South Carolina, 25 January 1980; issued as working paper 12 (1980), Department of Economics, University of Maryland; also in the *Annals*, vol.II, Association for Asian Studies, SERC, 1981, pp.74-81.

8. Village data are taken from field notes and the Tumkur survey. Taluk and district data are based on the survey. See Adams and Hanumappa, op.cit., for a summary of caste distribution by taluk.

'DECENTRALIZED' PLANNING IN A CENTRALIZED
ECONOMY: A STUDY OF SARVODAYA PROGRAMMES IN
A TALUKA

Ghanshyam Shah

More often than not anthropologists and sociologists
have studied Indian villages and tribes 'Behind Mud
Walls' - in isolation from the outside world. With a
few exceptions, their description is ahistorical, as if
mud walls were stronger than walls made of cement and
concrete, were iron curtains steadfastly facing hurricanes
generated by outside forces. 'Governments may come and
governments may go but village society remains undisturbed' is an oft-quoted phrase used to explain the
resilience of rural society.[1] Social scientists have
theorized about the uniqueness of the Indian social
system, namely the caste system, which is governed by
the ideology of homo hierarchicus as against the ideology of homo equalis that characterizes the Western
society. According to them, caste hierarchy maintains
harmony in the village society.[2] Some of the scholars
plead for the protection of village society from the
onslaught of 'Western' culture and industrialization.
That is possible, they hold, only through 'decentralization' of political power and economy. Some others
emphatically hold that it is only through decentralization that local people can be involved in 'development'
programmes, and thereby strengthen the Indian democracy.[3]
The concept of decentralization is in vogue among theo-
reticians, policy-makers and administrators in contemporary India.

To Mahatma Gandhi and his apostles 'decentralization' is the panacea for all the ills afflicting India.
Gandhi wrote, 'I suggest that, if India is to evolve
along non-violent lines, it will have to decentralize
many things. Centralization cannot be sustained and
defended without adequate forces .... Rurally organized India will run less risk of foreign invasion than
urbanized India, well-equipped with military, naval and
air force'. Without decentralization 'human happiness
combined with full mental and moral growth'[4] is impossible to attain. Gandhi pleaded for building a village
'republic', that is, a self-sufficient and autonomous
village. The village should be self-sufficient as far
as its basic needs - food, clothing and other necessities - are concerned. Its economy should be planned

with a view to provide full employment to all the adults of the village, so that no one is forced to migrate to towns. Gandhi opposed industrialization with a view to counter exploitation on the one hand, and to provide full employment to all on the other. He held that large-scale production requires marketing, which means profit-seeking. That develops an exploitative mechanism. Industrialization also replaces man-power and hence it adds to unemployment. Gandhians, therefore, mainly favour the development of village and cottage industries. Along with decentralization of the economy, comes that of the polity. All major decisions relating to every village should be arrived at in the village itself rather than in the state and national capitals. The policy-makers and planners of India have accepted the Gandhian concept of rural society - at least in principle. Several programmes have been launched by the government during the last three decades for 'building the roots of a tree'.[5]

On the other hand, the world economy is predominantly capitalist. So is India's economy which gives 'a lot of initiative to private capital'. As India is economically a backward country, it faces the problem of capital formation for the growth of its economy. This calls for centralized economy for the management of investment, accumulation, production and consumption. It invariably involves the countryside in production, not for use, but for exchange. It develops a nationwide market economy, linking the village market with the international market in which the latter generally dominates the former. The political system that India has adopted is also centralized and is conducive to the development of capitalist economy. Though India is a federal state, political authority is constitutionally centralized in New Delhi. Elections, political parties and administration link New Delhi with all the villages in all the parts of the country.

This creates a paradoxical situation for the Gandhian workers. They shoulder the responsibility for building a self-sufficient, self-reliant and self-governing village community in a centralized economy over which they cannot exercise any control worth the name. There are three types of Gandhian workers. One: the political workers, engaged in political activities; they are divided into various non-communist political parties. Two: constructive or Sarvodaya workers; they carry out 'constructive', that is, socio-economic, programmes to ameliorate the condition of the masses.

They do not directly participate in the activities of
the political parties. Three: constructive-cum-politi-
cal workers; engaged in constructive as well as political work. In 1948, after the assassination of Gandhi,
the constructive workers formed the Akhil Bharat Sarva
Seva Sangh. Its aim is to bring about social change,
especially in rural India, through the voluntary efforts
of individuals and communities. Since its inception,
the Sangh has provided a platform and organizational-
support base for constructive as well as political workers of Gandhian leanings. There are numbers of Gandhian voluntary associations, working in various parts
of the country for the reconstruction of rural society.
One of such associations is the Valod Group in Surat
district, Gujarat. Though it has been primarily engaged
in implementing socio-economic programmes, it is not
averse to participation in political activities. We
give below a descriptive account of the constructive
programmes that the Valod group formulated and carried
out in a relatively backward area. While doing so, we
shall highlight the role local initiative and local
resources play in such activities on the one hand, and
the influence outside forces exert in the formulation
and the implementation of the programmes on the other
hand.

Background

The area in which the Valod Group has been active for
the last three decades is the Valod taluka of Surat
district in Gujarat, Western India. It is a cluster of
40 villages with a population of 51,999. The land is
rocky and sandy, eroded in many places by heavy rains.
Though there are three rivers in this taluka, they provide little irrigation water for agriculture in summer.
The rivers flow from east to west. They are small,
narrow and seasonal. They are flooded in the monsoon
and become mere rivulets during the summer.

Scheduled tribes and non-tribals are two major
social groups of the taluka. The former account for
more than three-fourths of the total population. They
include Chaudhri, Gamit, Halpati and Dhodia tribes.
Caste Hindus include Brahmans and Banias, the higher
castes; Patidars and Kolis, the middle castes; and Sut-
hars, Hajams, Darjis, the intermediate castes. Bhangis,
Chamars and so on belong to the lower castes. There
are also some Muslims residing in this area. On the

whole, the dominance of higher and middle-caste Hindus
is striking. High-caste Hindus own a large proportion
of agricultural land. Banias, in particular, were
traditionally (and are still) engaged in trade and money-
lending. Patidars and Kolis are neo-traders and money-
lenders. Among the tribals, 20 per cent are landless,
46 per cent own less than five acres of land and 24 per
cent own more than five acres of land. [6]

Contacts between the tribals and the non-tribals
of this area can be traced back for three centuries.
In the past, the caste Hindus and Muslim traders, forest
contractors and money-lenders, took away the land
belonging to the tribals and enslaved them; they were
reduced to the status of agricultural labourers. They
appropriated farm and forest products. Though the non-
tribals had no desire to better the lot of the tribals,
the latter were influenced by the religious beliefs and
the life-styles of the former. The bhakti movement of
the seventeenth and eighteenth centuries influenced the
upper stratum of the tribals who adopted the rituals
and the life-styles of the caste Hindus.

The tribals came closer to the high-caste Hindus
during the freedom movement. A few disciples of Gandhi
coming from other parts of Gujarat settled in the village of Vedchhi in the 1920s to carry out Gandhi's constructive programmes. They started a residential school
or ashrama to provide education for the tribal boys. At
the same time, they introduced the production of khadi
as part of their programme to encourage self-reliance
as far as clothing was concerned. They also tried to
induce the tribals to give up liquor and non-vegetarian
food. The tribals were also mobilized and encouraged
to particpate in political activities directed against
the British raj. [7]

After independence the activities of the Vedchhi
ashrama became systematized. As early as 1948, the
ashrama hosted the all-India training camp for senior
'constructive' workers. The camp was sponsored by the
Gandhi National Memorial Fund, New Delhi. The participants resolved that the development of the country was
possible along strict Gandhian lines. They decided to
concentrate their efforts on developing villages
accordingly. The camps prepared a development programme
for the village Vedchhi, 'which if successfully implemented would be transferred to every village throughout
India'. The Vedchhi plan emphasized the importance of
utilizing 'local resources and talent'. However, it is
beyond the scope of this paper to analyse the plan and

the method of its implementation or to assess how far
it was successfully carried out. Suffice it to say,
that the ashrama has continued to carry out several
socio-economic and educational programmes during the
last three decades.

The Valod group is an off-shoot of the activities
of the Vedchhi ashrama, though initially it developed
independently. It was formed by some of the natives of
Valod, the headquarters of the taluka, which is about
four kilometres from Vedchhi. The group consists of
six persons. Born in the late 1920s, they all belong
to the same age-group. They played and studied together
in the schools situated in and outside the village.
They are the sons of Banias and Brahmins whose fathers
were absentee landlords or money-lenders-cum-traders.
Like many school boys of those days, they were influenced by Gandhi and the freedom movement. They organized student activities, such as distribution of books,
performances of drama, cleaning of the streets, and
celebration of Gandhi Jayanti (Gandhi's birthday).
Like many other Gandhian youths, they romanticized
village life and decided to settle in Valod itself to
reconstruct the village according to the Gandhian model.

However they could not afford themselves to engage
in full-time voluntary work without financial support.
Hence they had to take to some employment to enable
them to earn their livelihood. For this purpose they
could either take up the traditional family occupation
- agriculture, business and money-lending - or they
could become teachers in the village school. Business
and money-lending were automatically ruled out, because
the young boys thought that these occupations were exploitative. On the other hand, they lacked the knowledge and experience which are necessary for pursuing
agriculture as an occupation. The only other alternative was service in the village school. Teaching would
give them a living and at the same time enough leisure
to enable them to pursue constructive activities.

There was only one primary school in the village,
managed by the District School Board. The three members
of the Valod group approached the office-bearers of the
Board and offered their services. The Board were convinced about their ability and sincerity in wishing to
develop the school, and were willing to appoint them as
teachers. But the local village leaders did not want
competitors in the public life of Valod and therefore
succeeded in preventing the Board from giving over the
responsibility of running the school. At this juncture

one of the leaders of the Vedchhi ashrama, Jugatram
Dave, who was in touch with the young men, came to
their rescue. He invited them to join the ashrama as
teachers. Two members of the Valod group immediately
accepted the invitation and joined the ashrama in 1948.
The other four joined at a later stage. While working
in the ashrama, they received lessons in Gandhian ideology and programmes. The ashrama helped them to establish contacts with Gandhian workers who were taking
part in the constructive and political activities in
various parts of the country. Slowly, the Valod group
began to feel that their employment as teachers did not
offer them a wide enough field of activities. They
were, therefore, in search of an opportunity to get
involved in rural economic development programmes.

At this time (1951), the Planning Commission prepared the first five year plan for the whole of India.
The plan adopted the Community Development (C.D.) and
the National Extension Service (N.E.S.) programmes for
rural reconstruction. The first programme owes its
origin to the West. It was influenced by the 'extension work' programme of the U.S.A. and the 'village uplift'
movements of Great Britain. The programme is based on
'self-help' and on the utilization of local human and
natural resources.[8] It had been started symbolically
on Gandhi's birthday, 2 October, in 1952, with 'American
Technical and Financial Assistance'.[9] The Khadi and
Village Industries Commission, managed by Gandhian
constructive workers and financed by the government,
launched the Intensive Area Planning Scheme adopting
the Gandhian version of the C.D. approach in fourteen
blocks. One of them was Vedchhi, where the Commission
handed over the project to Jugatram Dave, the leader
of the ashrama. Dave asked the Valod group to carry
out the project. Under the guidance of Jhaverbhai
Patel of the Khadi Commission, the Valod group accepted
this responsibility in 1954. Later on, in 1957, the
Valod group set up the formal organization known as the
Vedchhi Intensive Area Scheme (V.I.A.S.) under the
chairmanship of Jugatram Dave. Under the main Scheme,
the Commission provided the funds necessary for the
payment of the salaries of the full-time workers. It
also provided a small fund for undertaking economic
programmes. The Scheme ended in 1961. Thereafter the
Vedchhi Scheme itself prepared five-year plans for the
taluka, plans entitled 'Building from Below'. To date
three such plans have been prepared and put into execution, and the fourth (for 1980-85) has already started.

The five-year plans have, by and large, coincided with
national plans. The Planning Commission, in New Delhi,
postponed its planning exercise at one stage; so did
the Valod group. The Planning Commission prepared a
'rolling plan' for 1977-78; so did the Valod group.
The Vedchhi five year plans set targets for the taluka
as a whole. The basis of planning that the Valod group
claimes to have adopted is *janashaktini jagruti*, that
is, consciousness of people's power. The plans aim at
using local resources and mobilizing people for participation in the execution of the programme. It is an
attempt at 'establishing a decentralized co-operative
economy' and thereby at building a sarvodaya society on
the Gandhian model.[10]
    Before we discuss the programmes, a word is in
order about the status of the Valod group and the influence it has been wielding in and outside the taluka.
From the beginning, the members of the Valod group were
associated with the Congress party. They took part in
the various activities of the Congress in the 1960s and
continued to do so till the mid-seventies. One member
became the president of the district Congress committee.
Another member of the group was the personal assistant
to the president of the state Congress committee. A
third one was appointed as the Chairman of the State
Khadi Board. One more member holds an executive post
in the Khadi and Village Industries Commission. (As
mentioned, Jhaverbhai Patel, their mentor, who taught
them the techniques of planning, was a member of the
Commission. Later, he was also a member of the International Labour Organization, Geneva.) The group has
contacts with academics in Bombay, Ahmedabad and Amsterdam, whose guidance and assistance were made available
in the preparation of the Vedchhi plans. After the
introduction of panchayati raj in 1964 one of the
members of the group became the president of the taluka
panchayat. Through its organizational network, the
group maintains links with village sarpanches (presi-
dents). The Valod group enjoys considerable influence
in the taluka, and carries weight with the administration as well as in the politics of the area.

Programmes

The Valod group has undertaken a variety of programmes
with a view to 'build rural society from below' during
the last two and a half decades. Space does not allow

210

us to examine all the programmes in detail here. We
shall, therefore, discuss in brief, only a few of the
important ones to show the relationship between local
and outside centres.

Education. The Gandhians believe that education is
the agent of social change. Gandhi believed that 'a
right type' of education was essential for building the
new society of his dreams and for its maintenance. He
formulated a new educational system known as *nai talim*,
that is, basic education, to counter Macaulay's system
of education, which was imparted in government schools.
The nai talim puts great emphasis on education through
work.[11]

The Valod group entertained the ambition to start
a nai talim school. However, whatever may have been
Gandhi's ideals, starting any kind of school requires
capital to buy a piece of land, and construct a building
on it which is big enough to house the students and
equipment, as well as income to pay the salaries of
teachers and other employees. The Valod group thought
of two ways of collecting funds. One was voluntary
donations by individuals or institutions, local or outside. The second was to get finance in the form of
grants from the government. The group did not make any
effort to tap local resources. It felt that because
the inhabitants of the area were poor, it was 'impossible' to raise funds locally - for recurring and non-
recurring expenses. The possibilities of raising funds
by way of voluntary donations from outside the taluka
were also limited, because in the 1950s, the group's
contacts with outside donors were confined to friends
and relatives of members. The group, therefore, turned
to the government for financing its educational efforts.
But the government had to work according to its own
rules and procedure. Hence there was no scope for
starting another primary or secondary nai talim school,
as there was already one at Vedchhi - a village in the
taluka. But the group found that there was a possibility of getting a grant for starting a high school on
the traditional lines; all that was required was a
building. At that time, the Valod group was in charge
of the Intensive Area Planning Scheme, under which there
was provision for constructing a godown. The group
made use of this provision. It purchased a piece of
land and immediately constructed a small building for
which it obtained the Scheme's financial support.
The building was then treated as a godown for the
Scheme and also as a school as far as the education

department was concerned. The V.I.A.S. utilized its
connections with the district education department and
secured permission and a grant to start a high school.
The school was opened in Kalam Kui in 1960.

To be eligible for the recurring government grant,
a school must have, on its rolls, a 'minimum' number of
students prescribed by the government from time to time.
But the population of the villages around Kalam Kui is
predominantly tribal, and not many of these tribals had
completed the requisite primary education. The number
of students who could attend the high school was below
the 'minimum' prescribed by the government. Efforts
were therefore made to attract the required number of
students from distant villages. But these students
needed lodging and boarding facilities. The V.I.A.S.
did not command financial resources which could have
enabled it to offer these to the students. It was,
therefore, again forced to look to the government for
help. It found that there was an arrangement for matching grants, whereby government offered three-fourths of
the funds needed for the construction of a building,
provided the voluntary organization raised the remaining
one-fourth as a 'people's contribution'. The V.I.A.S.
did not have at its disposal even that much, nor had it
the confidence and patience needed to raise the required
funds from local people. It, therefore, had to seek
external support. Through some friends in Ahmedabad,
it came into contact with international organizations
which were financing 'development' work. The V.I.A.S.
presented its case to Community Aid Abroad, Australia.
It emphasized that if Community Aid were to agree to
give Rs.15,000, the Indian government would give
Rs.45,000 for the construction of the hostel building.
Community Aid agreed, and the V.I.A.S. treated the
fund as a 'people's contribution' and received the
matching grant from the government. Similarly, the
V.I.A.S. received more funds from different foreign
agencies to start four other high schools in different
parts of the taluka.

The V.I.A.S. realised that it had failed to start
a nai talim high school; it, therefore, introduced in
the curriculum some subjects like agriculture, spinning
and craft, which have a Gandhian bias. However, as the
number of subjects taught in schools is fixed, the
V.I.A.S. schools gave less weight to English, mathe-
matics and science. But this was not appreciated by
the local population. Some of the tribal students and
their guardians who wanted to compete with the non-

tribal students resented the fact that they had to study subjects which have a Gandhian bias. They realized that it is necessary to learn English and science, for taking up higher studies. They openly said that they knew agriculture, and that they had no desire to take to cultivation after they completed their education: 'We want to become Sahebs (bosses) in government offices just like other non-tribals'. They alleged that non-tribals are seeking deliberately to perpetuate the low positions of tribals by giving them education in subjects like agriculture and crafts, training for manual and not for 'office' work. This charge levelled by the tribals reveals that well-to-do tribals are attracted to the education offered by non-Gandhian schools located in towns. Slowly but surely, as the years roll by, smaller and smaller numbers of students from the taluka join the schools run by the V.I.A.S.

The V.I.A.S. wanted the schools not only to impart education on Gandhian lines, but also to become centres of village development work. Each school has adopted a few villages in its vicinity for carrying out 'intensive' development programmes. School teachers are considered to be village-level workers also. They are expected to visit the villages and implement development programmes. The V.I.A.S. made its expectations clear to the teachers at the time of recruitment. But all teachers do not work according to the V.I.A.S.'s expectations. And the V.I.A.S. is helpless, as the teachers' service conditions are determined by the government department, which also pays their salaries; the V.I.A.S. has little control over them. In fact, even some of the senior teachers who have been with the V.I.A.S. for many years are now reluctant to take part in village development work. Thus, the role of these schools as extension centres is also declining with the passage of time.

Agricultural Development. Since its inception the V.I.A.S. has tried to implement an agricultural programme on a continuous basis in addition to its work in the field of education. Agriculture is the main source of livelihood for the rural people. More than 95 per cent of the working population of the taluka are either cultivators or farm labourers. Besides, on the whole, Indian agriculture was backward in the 1950s. Tribal areas were more backward, and faced many more constraints than the non-tribal areas. Additionally, as elsewhere in India, agriculture in the Valod taluka faced institutional, infrastructural and input problems.

213

Most of the non-tribal 'agriculturists' - Banias, Brahmans, Patidars and Muslims - were absentee land-owners and many tribals were their tenants. The non-tribals also owned a high proportion of the total cultivable land. During the 1950s the state government passed several laws with a view to abolishing absentee landlordism and giving land to the tillers. Though the Valod group was sympathetic to the 'radical' land legis-lation, it did not directly participate in the imple-mentation of these laws. It was rather the leaders of the Vedchhi ashrama who made the tenants conscious of their legal rights and helped them to get land from the landlords. Because of these efforts, a few tribals be-came owners of the land which they were cultivating as tenants. But that has not brought significant change in ownership, as far as the tribals and the non-tribals are concerned. The non-tribals even now own a far larger acreage than the tribals. The Valod group did nothing to change this state of affairs. What it did in the 1950s as a part of the Intensive Area Planning Scheme, was to build up the infrastructure - by the levelling of land, construction of embankments and irrigation. And these activities proved to be benefi-cial mainly to the non-tribal landowners.

On the other hand, as the government rhetoric be-came shriller, the western aid-givers became apprehen-sive of land reforms. The Ford Foundation's Report on India's Food Crisis and Steps to Meet It (1959) asserted that India would have to increase the production of food-grains by 200 to 300 per cent. The report impli-citly criticized the entire approach which treated institutional change as the keystone of an agricultural strategy. It favoured a technocratic approach based on offering price incentives to individual farmers to enable them to go in for higher (private) investment in modern inputs, especially fertilizers. The Draft Out-line of the Third Five Year Plan, therefore, projected a very large increase in the outlay on fertilizers - from less than Rs.30 crores in the Second Plan to Rs.240 crores in the Third Plan.[12] The government adopted a 'package' for agricultural development which involved the utilization of numbers of modern agricultural practices - improved seeds, chemical fertilizers, and pesticides - in selected areas which had a potential for growth. Surat was one of the districts selected for the implementation of this 'package'.

The Valod group found the 'package' very useful from their strategic view-point. It therefore decided to take it up even though the group did not know what the response of the farmers to modern technology and input would be. This is reflected in its first five year plan (1961-66) for the taluka prepared under the guidance of Jhaverbhai Patel, then associated with the Planning Commission. It hesitantly projected the use of some 1610 tonnes of different varieties of chemical fertilizers. However, the response of the local farmers to modern technology was greater than the V.I.A.S. expected. At the end of these five years farmers of the taluka used up almost three times the amount of chemical fertilizers recommended in the plan. Similarly the use of high yield variety seeds also increased considerably.

The distribution of these inputs - fertilizers, high-yield seeds, insecticides - has been arranged through the government departments. The V.I.A.S. has worked as a co-ordinating agency between the farmers and the government. In the 1970s the V.I.A.S. received aid for the distribution of improved seeds, and diesel or electric pump-sets for irrigation from Community Aid Abroad, Australia. The V.I.A.S. is now directly involved in distribution work. The field workers of the V.I.A.S. provide technical expertise regarding 'modern' commercial crops. Consequently, the area under food crops has decreased and the area under commercial crops has increased during the last ten years. Also, agricultural yield per acre has increased in the taluka, as it has increased elsewhere in Gujarat.

But the V.I.A.S. failed to organize the market to the advantage of small and marginal farmers. It made unsuccessful attempts to organize marketing co-operative societies so as to offer 'reasonable' prices to the farmers for their agricultural products. Such societies incurred losses, failed to compete with individual traders, and had to be closed. On the other hand, the V.I.A.S. did not put its weight behind the implementing of the Land Ceiling Act (1973) and Minimum Wages Act (1972). It may be noted that during this period the Valod group was close to the ruling party. However, it complained that since the farmers did not get 'reasonable' prices for agricultural produce, it was uneconomical for them to pay the minimum wages laid down by law. It opined: 'Our planners demand justice from the farmers, but deny the same justice to them. In the absence of this justice in the form of fair prices to the farmers, the implementation of the Minimum Wages Act would just squeeze the farmers to the extent of making farming

uneconomic'.[13] The V.I.A.S. felt helpless in this
matter and left the problem of doing 'justice' to the
planners in New Delhi. It opted for the softer course,
and tried to develop non-farm economic activities to
supplement the income of small farmers and farm
labourers, or to change their occupation.

Khadi. When the Vedchhi ashrama was started 50
years ago, the production of khadi was adopted as the
main plank of its programme. The ashrama persuaded
people to spin and weave, and it also imparted training
for the purpose. In the beginning, the programme was
devised with a view to serving the national aim of
attaining independence through developing self-reliance,
at least in the matter of clothing. Later on, khadi
became an occupation which enabled some people to earn
their livelihood. By the time the Valod group started
working independently, the enthusiasm for khadi as a
means of achieving self-sufficiency in clothing declined. It became a commodity, like any other, to be
sold in the market.[14]

In order to boost the production of khadi, the
Union Government formed the Khadi and Village Industry
Commission - an autonomous organization - in 1952. The
state governments also appointed Khadi Boards in their
respective states in the early 1960s. During the 1950s
the Khadi Commission gave grants to the V.I.A.S. for
the purpose of encouraging spinning activity. It also
gave charkhas (spinning wheels) at subsidized rates and
offered marketing facilities as well. The government
also subsidizes khadi to boost its sales. The V.I.A.S.
distributed charkhas either free or at a subsidized
price to the spinners. It also distributed ambar
charkhas, an improved model of spinning wheel, to
increase the productive capacity of labour. With the
financial support from the state Khadi Board, the
V.I.A.S. conducted several training courses for the
spinners and weavers.

Despite such a huge effort, financial support and
managerial skill, the khadi programme has not taken off
in Valod even after 50 years. At the end of the last
decade the number of spinners had not increased by more
than four hundred. Their number also fluctuates from
year to year. For instance, there were 106 spinners in
1974-75 in village Algadh, where the V.I.A.S. had organized the Khadi Centre in 1956. In 1977-8 the number of
spinners had gone down to only 52. Every year, some
spinners were recruited but some dropped out. Very few
have continued to work as spinners for many years. The

spinners who dropped out reported that they could not
spare any time for spinning. Almost all the spinners
have been, and are, cultivators. They can spin only
in their spare time. 'Why don't you take to spinning?'
we asked the agricultural labourers. Their invariable
reply was that it was tiring as they had to spin alone
in the house. Moreover, farm labour was more remunerative than spinning, and, in contrast to a spinner, a
farm labourer could hope to secure a loan from the farm-
owner in case of need. During the year 1975-6, a
spinner in Algadh earned, on average, only Rs.102,
whereas in Degama a spinner earned Rs.705 per year.
The difference between Degama and Algadh arises from
the fact that the spinning wheels supplied to these two
villages were not of the same model. In Degama the
spinners used the ambar charkha, whereas in Algadh they
used the traditional spinning wheel. Moreover, the
V.I.A.S. started a workshop in Degama, where all the
spinners spin together under one roof for eight hours
a day. Their work is supervised, and the spinning
wheels are repaired as soon as they go out of order.
(Despite these facilities of supervision and organization, a spinner does not earn even a subsistence income.)
  Weaving is linked with spinning, as it depends on
the availability of yarn. Spinners in the taluka do not
spin regularly, and do not produce enough yarn to provide employment to many weavers. Like spinning, weaving
is also not an attractive occupation as it does not
provide even a subsistence income. The weavers who
worked in their spare time earned, on average, Rs.379
in 1978-9 in Algardh. In Buhari where they worked as
full-time weavers, they earned, on average, Rs.1,349 in
a year. Consequently, weaving is not an attractive
substitute for agriculture. In the whole of the taluka
one could never find even 50 persons who had taken to
weaving as a full-time occupation. In fact, there is
no full-time weaver today. The V.I.A.S. has brought
weavers from Maharashtra to keep the organization running. It has now extended spinning and weaving
activities to neighbouring talukas and districts so as
to maintain the production centre. The consumption of
khadi has also declined in the taluka. Though old
freedom fighters continue to wear it, young persons
prefer to go in for mill cloth. The V.I.A.S., however,
exports khadi to Amsterdam, London, Aden and Geneva
through its contacts with aid-giving agencies.
  Dairy. Development of the dairy industry was on
the agenda of the V.I.A.S. from the very beginning.

217

During the 1950s, thanks to its strong Gandhian orientation, it emphasized the development of cows, more than
of buffaloes. The programme however remained on paper,
as financial assistance was not forthcoming to enable
the group to buy cows of good quality. Moreover, there
was no incentive for local farmers to take to the production of milk as a market for milk did not then
exist. Though there were three co-operative societies
in Surat which supplied milk to urban consumers, their
activities were confined to Surat and the area around
it. None of them had any means of bringing milk from
distant villages to the city.

During the 1960s, the Milk Co-operative Society of
Kheda district, known as the AMUL, came into prominence.
Following the establishment of the Amul, attempts were
made in Surat to merge the three existing co-operative
societies and to start a huge milk processing plant.
The result, in Surat, was a dairy named Sumul in 1968.[15]
During the 1960s, the V.I.A.S. made efforts to organize
Milk Co-operative Societies and to bring more milch
animals into the taluka. Its first two five year plans
put a modest target - the distribution of 215 and 400
buffaloes in the taluka in the first and the second
plans respectively. The targets remained unfulfilled.
The taluka purchased 65 cows as against its target of
125 during the first plan period. In the second plan
it purchased 32 cows against the target of 100 cows.
The gap between the plan and the performance became
glaring.

However, the National Dairy Development Board
launched the Operation Flood I Programme in July 1970.
Its aim was to develop the dairy industry in four
metropolitan cities and the milk-supply areas surrounding them. This obviously gave a fillip to a small
dairy like the Sumul Dairy which launched a programme
of expansion. Between 1968 and 1975, the village co-
operative milk societies attached to the Sumul increased
from 14 to 445. The Sumul built a chilling plant at
Bajipura in Valod taluka in 1975, and this facilitated
the collection of milk from the surrounding area. On
the other hand, the Small Farmers Development Agency
of the government started giving a 50 per cent subsidy
to small and marginal farmers to enable them to buy
buffaloes. The other 50 per cent came from the national-
ized banks as a loan. Community Aid Abroad, Australia,
also gave financial assistance to the V.I.A.S. to enable
it to advance loans to farmers who were unable to get
advances from the banks for buying buffaloes. The

workers of the V.I.A.S. organized milk co-operative
societies in villages to collect milk from the producers for the Sumul.

The V.I.A.S. carried out a cross-breeding programme
in the taluka similar to one which had been implemented
successfully in Maharashtra. With financial support
from a foreign agency, an effort was made to cross-breed
the Indian cows with exotic breeds like the Jersey.
This programme faced several difficulties. The cross-
bred cows require good care and fodder which the farmers
of the taluka could not provide. Hence the milk yield
did not increase significantly. Moreover, artificial
insemination was not properly carried out in time, and
much of the semen brought over long distances was
spoiled. The programme remained a non-starter in the
1970s, though the V.I.A.S. hopes to make it successful
in the 1980s.

As a result of the efforts of the V.I.A.S., the
number of buffaloes has almost doubled during the last
ten years. However, the quality of the milch cattle
has not yet improved. And despite the distribution of
fodder and the provision of veterinary services, production of milk per buffalo has not increased significantly. On an average, it is less than one pound per
buffalo per day. Consequently the economic returns
are not satisfactory. On an average a milk producer
gets less than Rs.700 per year. He spends between
Rs.300 to Rs.400 on fodder alone. The net profit is
thus found to be almost nil, even without allowing the
farmer some minimal return for his labour. What he
gets is the psychological satisfaction that 'ownership'
of milch cattle may provide. Moreover, prices of green,
dry and concentrated fodder have increased during the
last few years, whereas the price of milk has not increased correspondingly. Further, with an increase in
the number of milch cattle, the supply of milk has
increased, but the buying capacity of the urban consumers has not. Hence, the Dairies have started facing
a problem of marketing their surplus which may become
acute in the 1980s. Obviously, the V.I.A.S. can exercise no control over these market forces.

Lijjat Papad. The V.I.A.S. organized the Sales
and Purchase Co-operative Society in 1962. Its objec-
tives were to purchase farm products from the farmers
at a 'reasonable' price and sell them in the market at
a competitive price. In 1968, the co-operative society
purchased a large quantity of udad (a legume), paying
a slightly higher price than the merchants used to pay

to the farmers. But by the time it had stocked up, the market registered a sharp decline in the price of udad. The society found that it would not be able to recover even its purchase price; loss was imminent. The V.I.A.S. contacted a friend of theirs who was associated with the Shri Mahila Griha Udyog Lijjat Papad (M.G.U.), Bombay. Udad is an ingredient of papad, which is prepared by the M.G.U. on a commercial basis. The papad is a wafer-thin, dry, round product which has a diameter of about seven inches. It is crisp, salty, and hot in taste. It is either roasted directly on a charcoal fire or fried in an edible oil. It is eaten by the middle-classes and the rich with their meals.

The V.I.A.S. processed the udad with a view to selling it to the M.G.U. They would not buy it, however, as its quality was different from that of the udad they had been using. To convince the M.G.U. that their udad was not inferior, the V.I.A.S. prepared samples of papad and sent them to the M.G.U. for approval. The M.G.U. not only approved of the sample, but also agreed to provide technical expertise and equipment to the V.I.A.S. to enable them to organize a co-operative society for the manufacture of papad. Later, the Valod Papad Society became a branch of the M.G.U. and thus the problem of marketing papad was solved. The M.G.U. invested Rs.1,000 and the V.I.A.S. Rs.500. Community Aid Abroad, Australia, gave financial support through the V.I.A.S. to enable the purchase of a delivery van.

Though the Valod M.G.U. started with a small group of seven members who prepared papad, it was able to employ 150 members at the end of only six months. The number increased nearly three-fold, to 410, by the end of 1976-7. In the first six months, the sale of papad fetched Rs.42,000. After ten years the sale of papad fetched a sum of Rs.2,812,000. The society distributed Rs.10,000 as remuneration during the first year. During 1976-7 the remuneration amounted to Rs.608,000. The Lijjat Papad at Valod, now has an impressive two-storied building - much more imposing than any of the other buildings of the village. It has a number of vehicles at its disposal and its members are provided with other amenities besides.

The Lijjat Papad, Valod, drew its membership from all the social strata, though the proportion of members drawn from different castes varies. It has been able to recruit more members from high-caste Hindus than from the tribals and the scheduled castes. In 1977-8, 40 per cent of its members were Muslims and 23 per cent were tribals; the rest were caste Hindus. [16] However, only one per cent belonged to the lowest castes, the Harijans, known as untouchable. The Lijjat Papad, Valod, has opened a sub-branch at Golan, a tribal village, with a view to enrol tribals. In 1977-8 it had 43 members. More than 50 per cent of them, however, were non-tribals. The reason is that papad does not form part of the meals of tribals. Moreover, unlike caste Hindus, tribal women work on farms.

The average income of a woman worker was Rs.708 in 1968-9; it increased to Rs.1,470 in the year 1976-7. The average remuneration of an employee works out at Rs.4·90 per day. [17] A woman has to work for at least seven hours a day to earn this remuneration which is slightly more than a farm labourer earns. Middle-class women who are generally not engaged in any economic activity, take up the preparation of papad as a spare-time occupation.

The V.I.A.S. is however not happy with the functioning of the Lijjat Papad, Valod. It has mainly a commercial approach. The V.I.A.S. tried to persuade the M.G.U. to extend the papad-making industry to tribal villages, but the latter turned down the proposal, because the M.G.U. is concerned about marketing the product. The V.I.A.S. resented the high salaries paid to the managerial staff of the Lijjat Papad, Valod. The M.G.U. recently declared through the press that the Lijjat Papad, Valod, had no organizational or any other relationship with the V.I.A.S. It is now centrally administered from Bombay.

Diamond Cutting and Polishing. The V.I.A.S. invested its man-power and financial resources in the diamond cutting and polishing industry during the mid-1970s. The diamond industry is directly linked with the international market. The production of raw diamonds and their marketing are monopolized by a handful of international companies based in London, Amsterdam, Tel Aviv, New York and Antwerp. Raw diamonds have to be cut and polished before they are used in machinery or as jewels. The diamond cutting and polishing industry developed in India after 1960. Labour is costlier in the European cities than in India. After the devaluation of the rupee in 1966, Indian labour became cheaper still. On the other hand, during the 1960s India entered the world diamond market for the first time, as a lot of princely jewellery was put up for sale - one piece of jewellery was worth as much as

Rs.1 crore. A market for such costly jewellery existed only abroad. In order to promote exports, the Government of India set up the Gems and Jewellery Export Promotion Council in 1966. Against the export of jewellery the government allowed the import of raw diamonds. They were to be cut and polished in India and then re-exported. The demand for diamonds increased in foreign markets in the mid-1970s, as people lost faith in paper currency and there was a buying spree in gold, silver and diamonds. This boosted the price of gold. Consequently, exports of cut and polished diamonds from India rose sharply between 1970 and 1978. The exports which were of the order of Rs.28 crores in 1970-71 reached Rs.82 crores by 1975-6. The figure for 1977-8 was as much as Rs.43,522,000.[18]

Bombay is the only centre for the export of diamonds. As Gujarat is quite near Bombay, and as the Gujaratis enjoy a monopoly in the diamond business, the work of cutting and polishing of diamonds has developed mainly in Gujarat. Ninety per cent of all the diamonds processed in India are from Gujarat. More than 80 per cent of the diamond-processing units came into existence in Surat between 1966 and 1975.[19] With the spectacular rise in exports between 1973 and 1976, small entrepreneurs started diamond cutting and polishing units even in rural areas, including fifteen villages of Valod taluka. They employed about 2,000 workers, a majority of whom came from taluka other than Valod. These units were owned by non-Adivasis. This development had nothing to do with the activities of the V.I.A.S.

The V.I.A.S., however, did not want to be left out. In 1978, it claimed: 'having been involved in decentralized small scale village industry through its development work in the past 25 years, it decided to encourage in every way possible the growth of this particular industry, and especially for the poorer groups and in the more remote villages'.[20] It helped several individual entrepreneurs to get loans to start one or two units. It started one co-operative unit, and one unit exclusively for women.

However, before these units were off the ground, the diamond industry in India faced recession. De Beers Consolidated Mines, the biggest owner of diamond mines, raised the surcharge on rough diamonds by as much as 40 per cent. Moreover, the Diamond Trading Company of London which holds a world monopoly in the trade of rough diamonds not only raised the price of diamonds, but also arbitrarily cut the supply of diamonds to

India. The Company started developing new and alternative centres like China and Singapore for the processing of diamonds. Consequently, Indian exports
of cut and polished diamonds fell to Rs.22 crores in
December 1978 from 43 crores achieved in the previous
month.[21] Many of the small diamond-cutting units which
had sprung up in the previous five years had to shut
down because of the crisis. As many as 1.5 lakhs of
people lost their jobs owing to the closure of diamond
units. This unprecedented reversal in this export
business marked the end of the great diamond boom
started in 1975. The diamond processing units of Valod
faced the same fate. All the units started by the
V.I.A.S. were closed down within six months. The
V.I.A.S., however, is waiting for an opportunity to
revive them.

Paper Mill. The V.I.A.S., a protagonist of cottage
and labour-intensive industries, started manufacturing
hand-made paper in 1958 with financial support from the
Khadi and Village Industries Commission in the form of
50 per cent loan and 50 per cent subsidy. The total
investment in the industry was around Rs.50,000. On an
average it provides employment to eighteen persons -
including the manager and salesmen. The average pay
of an employee was only Rs.979 in the year 1974-5; that
is, it was no more than the income earned by a farm
labourer. The production capacity of the hand-made
paper plant is, however, limited. On the other hand,
the demand for paper for cultural (printing and writing)
and industrial uses (craft and other packing material)
has increased considerably during the last three decades. The per capita consumption of paper was 0.7
kilogram in 1951. It had increased to 18 kilograms in
1977. The production of paper has not increased to a
corresponding extent. During the period of the first
five-year plan ending in 1966, there was a shortfall
of 153,000 tonnes of paper. Therefore, in order to
boost paper production, the Indian government de-
licensed the industry producing paper boards and straw-
board paper used by the packaging industries in 1966.

Slowly, the number of paper plants in general and
mini-paper plants in particular increased in the 1970s.
Recently, 'there has been a sudden rush of proposals
for putting up mini-paper plants with daily capacity
ranging from 10 tonnes to 30 tonnes of paper and paper
board. The government has so far (1979) issued 129
letters of intent and industrial licences for a total
capacity of 821,265 tonnes per year for such paper

223

mills. These schemes are based on raw materials, such
as paddy straw, wheat, husk, jute waste, bagasse, rags,
linter and waste paper.'[22] Since paddy is one of the
main crops in Surat district, paddy straw is available
in plenty. Even in Valod, the area under paddy crop is
around 8,700 acres yielding 27,000 tonnes of straw.
Moreover, the scheduled commercial banks have also
started advancing loans to the paper and paper board
industries. They advanced Rs.19,704,000 to the paper-
manufacturing plants at the end of June 1977.[23] Thus
with delicensing, the availability of advances from
banks and of raw materials, eight mini-paper plants
came into existence in Bardoli taluka, the taluka adjoining Valod, by the end of the year 1978. They are
controlled by rich and middle non-Adivasi peasants.
The growth of paper plants in surrounding areas and
their profitability attracted the V.I.A.S. It may be
mentioned that 'between 1973-4 and 1975-6, the profitability of the [paper] industry remained above the
average profitability ratios for all industries'. But
the V.I.A.S. did not have the necessary capital to invest in paper plants and the Adivasi farmers were not
economically so well off as to be able to raise the
needed share capital.

The Netherlands Organization for International
Development Co-operation came to the rescue. One of
its associates encouraged the V.I.A.S. to prepare a
plan for a mini-paper plant. The V.I.A.S. immediately
collected preliminary information from the existing
factories of Bardoli taluka. It also hired the services
of an expert and assigned to him the task of preparing
a project. The Netherlands Organization immediately
sanctioned a sum of Rs.18 lakhs. With this working
capital the V.I.A.S. proposed to establish the Valod
Antyodaya Sahakari Paper Mills Limited at Dumkhal,
four kilometres from Valod. It procurred a loan of
Rs.61 lakhs from a commercial bank. Thus, the total
cost of the project came to Rs.79 lakhs. The paper
plant which thus came into existence has a production
capacity of ten tonnes a day. It aims at providing
employment to 500 persons when the plant starts working
at full capacity.

Within two years land was purchased, the building
was constructed and machinery installed. Production
was started in April 1980. This mini-paper plant
represents a major change in the approach of the V.I.
A.S. to rural development. It has now started establishing capital-intensive industries. At this juncture

it would be hazardous to answer the question as to whether the mini-paper plant of the V.I.A.S. will be able to face the competition offered by the larger plants which produce as much as 80 per cent of the paper produced in the country. But if the experience gained in running this plant is favourable, the V.I. A.S. may perhaps be tempted to go in for still bigger projects.

Conclusions

The foregoing analysis of the rural development programmes pinpoints many theoretical issues related to economic planning and political authority in a 'backward' society. It also highlights the futility of the so-called Gandhian approach to rural development aiming at 'building from below' in a centralized economy. But at the moment I shall refrain from discussing these issues. Here, let us draw some conclusions regarding the linkages between the 'localized' rural society and the larger society of which it is an undoubted part. The present-day Indian rural society does not function - for good or bad - in isolation, notwithstanding the Gandhian ideology and efforts the Gandhians put in to build village 'republics'. A tiny tribal hamlet is linked with the district, the state and the national capitals through political institutions and administrative machinery. Production and consumption in village society have increasingly been linked with the market economy governed from metropolitan areas.

The local intermediaries - the Valod group is a case in point here - work as active agents (though sometimes as catalysts) in the process that increasingly establishes links between the local rural society and 'outside' forces. The 'outside' forces are not monolithic. They are complex and often pull in opposite directions. The intermediaries do not get swept away by all kinds of outside forces. They try to be selective and strengthen certain forces. They dilute or modify some and ignore others. Their selection is guided by their 'ideology' and subjective interests. If the ideology is not well-defined or if it is utopian the intermediaries become more vulnerable to subjective interests and the forces conducive to them.

Precisely this has happened to the V.I.A.S. The V.I.A.S. was greatly influenced by national and international forces - the government policy, market and

the availability of financial assistance in formu-
lating the programmes - whether for khadi, or a paper
plant. Their preferences and priorities have been
dictated by the market, though in the 1950s they re-
sisted it without success. The V.I.A.S. had limited
options in the selection of the programmes. Whenever
it tried to ignore the market forces, the programmes
came to a standstill soon after they were launched; or
they remained non-starters. Besides the market forces,
the response of the local people also influenced the
V.I.A.S. programmes. In the beginning the local people
did resist the change which resulted from the operations
of forces operating from outside village society. But
once they realized the economic advantages that were
made possible by the new opportunities, they began to
take advantage of these opportunities. Thus, their
resistance against the outside forces was slowly
weakened. In fact, during the 1960s and thereafter
the people of Valod gave a cold response to programmes
which tried to keep them within the village boundaries.
Hence, the V.I.A.S. had no option but to accommodate
itself to the forces working outside the taluka. And
it has successfully accomplished that, within the limits
imposed by the given resources, constraints and response
of the local people.

Shah, '"Decentralized" planning in a centralized
economy: a study of Sarvodaya programmes in a taluka'

This paper is a part of the study on Vedchhi Intensive
Area Scheme, partly financed by NOVIB, Netherlands.
H.R. Chaturvedi is a collaborator in the project.

1. See B.H. Baden Powell, *The Indian Village
Community* (London 1896); Louis Dumont, 'The Village
Community from Munro to Maine', *Contributions to Indian
Sociology* (December 1966).
2. See McKim Marriott (ed.), *Village India* (Chicago 1955); M.N. Srinivas, *India's Villages* (Bombay
1960); Oscar Lewis, *Village Life in Northern India* (New
York 1965).
3. Rajni Kothari, *Politics in India* (Delhi 1970);
S.K. Sharma and S.L. Malhotra, *Integrated Rural Development* (Columbia 1977).
4. M.K. Gandhi, *Sarvodaya* (Ahmedabad 1954), p.36.
5. Ghanshyam Shah, 'Gandhian Approach to Rural
Development', *Ideas and Action* 125, 6 (1978).
6. Ten per cent of the heads of households are
engaged in non-agricultural occupations.
7. I.P. Desai, 'Vedchhi Movement', in I.P. Desai
and Banwarilal Choudhary, eds., *History of Rural
Development in Modern India* II (New Delhi 1977).
8. Norman Long, *An Introduction to the Sociology
of Rural Development* (London 1977).
9. Francine R. Frankel, *India's Political Economy,
1947-77* (Delhi 1978).
10. Vedchhi Sanghakshetra Samiti, *Valod Mahal
Kshetra Ayojan* (Gujarati), Valod, V.I.A.S. 1962;
Jhaverbhai Patel, 'The Constructive Approach', in
*Building From Below, Third Five Year Plan 1975-79,
Valod Taluka* (Vanasthali, Sarvodaya Planning and
Training Centre, n.d.).
11. M.S. Patel, *The Educational Philosophy of
Mahatma Gandhi* (Ahmedabad 1953).
12. Frankel, op.cit.
13. Jhaverbhai Patel, op.cit., p.12.
14. I.P. Desai, op.cit.
15. Babubhai D. Desai, *A Socio-Economic Study of
the Milk Producers of South Gujarat* (Surat: Centre for
Social Studies (Mimeo.) 1979).

16. Bhikhu Vyas, 'Participation of Rural Women in Income Raising Group Activities' (mss.), Valod, V.I.A.S., n.d.
17. Ibid.
18. Diamond Company, *The Economic Times*, 7 August 1978.
19. K.M. Desai, 'Hirane Paher Padavana Udyog - Surat Ane Navsari Vistar no Ek Abhyas', Surat: South Gujarat University 1979, (unpublished Ph.D. Thesis).
20. V.I.A.S., *Planning for Industry in Valod Taluka*, Kanjod: Sarvodaya Planning and Training Centre, 1978, (Mimeo.), p.22.
21. Indra Gidwani, Diamond Industry, *Economic Times*, 16 December 1978.
22. 'Paper Industry: Position and Prospects III', *State Bank of India, Monthly Review*, March 1980, p.110.
23. Ibid.

INTERNATIONAL RICE RESEARCH AND THE PROBLEMS
OF RICE GROWING IN UTTAR PRADESH AND BIHAR

Paul R. Brass

It is widely asserted that the 'green revolution' in India has been far more successful for wheat than it has been for rice. In fact, the use of the high yielding varieties (H.Y.V.s) in rice, with their associated technology, has also produced impressive results in the Punjab and south India. However, in the great paddy-growing belt of northern and eastern India, stretching from the eastern districts of Uttar Pradesh (U.P.) into the Bengal delta and Orissa, virtually no increases in productivity have occurred in the last 20 years. Whereas, between 1960-2 and 1972-4, the average yield of paddy for those three-year periods increased in south India from 2,007 kilograms per hectare to 2,582 and in the Punjab, Delhi, and Himachal Pradesh from 1,470 to 2,930 kg./ha., there was only a marginal increase in yields in Orissa and West Bengal from 1,427 to 1,513 kg./ha., in Bihar from 1,260 to 1,309 kg./ha., and in U.P. from 1,123 to 1,192 kg./ha. Yet, this region of northern and eastern India produced 44.11 per cent of the paddy harvested in the country, amounting to 26.6 million metric tons.[1] More rice is produced in this region of India than in any country in the world outside of India, except for the People's Republic of China.[2] In this area, the H.Y.V.s in rice were not widely sown. Only 30.19 per cent of the acreage sown with H.Y.V.s in rice in 1974-5 was accounted for by the rainfed areas of northern and eastern India.[3]

Many people who know little about agriculture and think they know a great deal about the different peoples of India are quick to jump to conclusions, based on these bare facts, such as that the farmers of the northern and eastern Indian paddy belt are less energetic, innovative, and willing to take risks than the proverbially enterprising Punjabi peasantry and the nearly as proverbially clever Tamils. In fact, however, many farmers in this region have adopted the new H.Y.V.s in wheat and have extended considerably the acreage sown to wheat during the past decade. For example, wheat acreage in Bihar increased from 809,000 hectares in 1966-7 to 1,815,000 in 1975-6, with the percentage under H.Y.V.s going from 3.1 to 96.4. In U.P., wheat acreage increased from 4,394,000 to 6,103,000 hectares, with

the percentage under H.Y.V.s rising from 8.3 to 73.7
in the same period.[4]

Moreover, the problems of northern and eastern
India paddy-growing are common to three-quarters of the
paddy-growing areas in Asia. When it became clear in
the late 1960s and early 1970s that the adoption of the
new seeds and the associated technology had peaked, in
terms of coverage, at approximately 25 per cent of the
rice-growing areas of Asia, it was generally assumed
that the principal limiting factor in the spread of the
H.Y.V.s in paddy was the availability of irrigation
which also was confined to 25 per cent of the cultivated paddy acreage in Asia. Although rice scientists
at the International Rice Research Institute (IRRI)
and elsewhere argue that the new H.Y.V.s in paddy will
do better than traditional varieties even in the upland
and drier areas, provided that fertilizers and pesticides are applied, it was clear that farmers were not
willing to take the risks involved in applying expensive
inputs for limited increases in yields in agricultural
zones where either the absence of irrigation or inadequate water control already made paddy-cultivation a
high-risk enterprise. In fact, it is believed at IRRI
that many farmers in northern and eastern India are
using the H.Y.V.s and applying fertilizer in the rabi
season and getting good yields, but 'are not putting
an ounce of fertilizer in the field(s) during the wet
season' when the risks of flood and/or drought threaten
to wipe out all investments in such high-cost inputs.[5]
These impressions are also held by persons in the Indian
Council of Agricultural Research, who point out that the
major increases in rice production and in rice yields
in India have occurred 'in non-traditional rice areas
or in non-traditional rice seasons'[6] when irrigation
can be applied and water-logging is not a problem.
However, in the rainfed areas and in the kharif season,
both the great risks of total crop loss and the somewhat less catastrophic risks of fertilizer loss through
leaching after heavy rains make the use of H.Y.V.s in
rice, with the associated technology, unattractive to
most peasants. Moreover, in the Philippines, farmers
were using the H.Y.V.s on irrigated land, but were not
achieving the yields expected. These problems in
India, in the Philippines, and elsewhere suggested that
the association between irrigation and the adoption of
H.Y.V.s and between absence of irrigation and the use
of traditional varieties did not necessarily imply a
simple causal relationship such that the spread of

irrigation would necessarily lead to the adoption of
H.Y.V.s. Consequently, in the early 1970s, IRRI
launched a research programme, led by its economists,
on constraints in the adoption of the new technology
in rice in order to discover precisely what were the
limiting factors in the further spread of the H.Y.V.s.[7]

At the same time in India, agricultural policy
makers concerned about the same questions and also
about questions being raised by political leaders as
to why there had as yet been no 'rice revolution' began
to turn their attentions to the special problems of the
predominantly rice-growing rainfed areas of Bihar,
Orissa, and West Bengal. Then, in 1977, when the
Janata party came to power, with its principal base of
support lying in north India and including all the
principal rainfed areas in that part of the country,
and with a clear commitment to give the highest priority
to agricultural and rural development, the time was
clearly ripe to assist the farmers of northern and
eastern India.[8] In September 1977, at the suggestion
of the Director-General of the Indian Council of Agricultural Research,[9] an IRRI team of economists and rice
scientists visited India and joined with a Government
of India team to tour the paddy-growing areas of eastern
India and to prepare a report on the strategies required
to increase rice production in those areas. That team
found that, in villages they visited, 'a negligible portion of the land' was sown with H.Y.V.s except in irrigated villages where H.Y.V.s were sown in the rabi
season.[10] The failure to adopt H.Y.V.s in eastern India
in the main kharif season was attributed to the fact
that the H.Y.V.s were simply unsuitable to most of the
region because of problems not only of availability of
irrigation, but of water control generally. For
example, rapid flooding in north Bihar would quickly
submerge the stiff and short-stalked IRRI type varieties. In other areas of eastern India, drought, rather
than excessive water, was a frequent problem. Some
areas often experience both flood and drought conditions in alternate seasons. In areas where canal irrigation was available in the kharif season, it was
found that its use caused 'excessive silting in farm
fields'.[11] Because of the short monsoon in this part
of India, the H.Y.V.s, which flower in September-Octo-
ber, and, therefore, require watering when the monsoon
is finished, are unsuitable for much of the region,
which requires instead 'short duration, non-photoperiod
sensitive varieties'[12] that flower early even under

monsoon cloud cover. In general, the IRRI study team
was impressed by the heterogeneity of environments
under which paddy was grown in this region, ranging
from drought to high water. Finally, given the high-
risk farming in most of these environments, especially
during the kharif season, and given the relatively
high price of nitrogen and the low market price of
paddy, the team found it not at all surprising that
neither the H.Y.V.s nor large quantities of inputs
were being used.

The team found it possible to identify what strategies needed to be followed in eastern India, but was
not particularly sanguine about the likelihood of
success in the near future. What was required, the
team suggested, was adequate water control, the replacement of photoperiod sensitive with short duration non-
photosensitive varieties in large parts of the region,
and an emphasis on high-stability rather than high-
yielding varieties in these high-risk farming areas.
However, adequate water control in much of this region
is hundreds of millions of rupees and many years ahead
because such control involves large-scale construction
of flood prevention and canal systems. With regard to
the development of new varieties suitable to 'the
drought and flood conditions common in Eastern India',
the IRRI team suggested that insufficient research was
being done to produce such varieties, that where
potentially suitable varieties were available at
research stations, adequate mechanisms were not available for their 'field testing', multiplication, and
'rapid and wide dissemination'. Moreover, it was
found that the development and release of new varieties
of rice in India took ten years, rather than the five
years normally required in the Philippines, and that,
even after ten years, once a 'variety is released,
there is no assurance that seed will be made available
to farmers'.[13] In other words, the adequacy of both
agricultural research and the linkage between research
and the distribution system in India was questioned.

Phrased in simple language, the report of the
IRRI-Government of India team could lead to only one
conclusion, namely, that there is not yet available
for most of the paddy-growing region of northern and
eastern India a suitable technology to increase or even
stabilize yields.[14] This rather sobering conclusion
raises several broad questions of strategy both for
international rice researchers in general and for Indian
agricultural policy makers in particular. First, given

232

the difficulties in the rainfed areas and the unlikeli-
hood of dramatic improvement in the near future, does
it make sense to divert resources to those areas that
might be used to increase production further in the
irrigated areas? If increased production is deemed
necessary to feed the population of India and Asia,
then why not continue to concentrate resources on
improving results in the irrigated areas through the
application of more inputs or of inputs applied with
ever more precision? It is estimated at IRRI, for
example, that only 17 to 50 per cent of the technology
that is available for the irrigated areas, including
fertilizers, pesticides, weedicides, and the like, is
actually being used and that the fuller utilization of
already available technology in the irrigated areas
might lead to a bigger increase in production than
efforts devoted to the rainfed areas. In fact, insofar
as India is concerned, the concentration of agricultural development resources in irrigation and inputs
in the Punjab has made it possible for farmers in the
Punjab, already famous for their output of wheat, to
produce substantial quantities of rice. The rices
grown in the Punjab are principally Java and IR-8.
The latter, which is not highly regarded because of its
poor taste, flavour, and texture, is not eaten in the
Punjab, but is shipped through the central government
procurement system to be processed and marketed in the
food-deficit paddy-growing regions of eastern India.
In this way, the prosperous Punjab farmers are benefited, the urban residents of Calcutta are fed, and the
small paddy-farmers of eastern U.P. and Bihar continue
to struggle along at a bare subsistence level, producing high quality, but low-yielding grains that they
are often unable to market even if they should produce
a surplus because either the price is too low or marketing facilities are not available. The value choice
here then becomes one of deciding whether or not to
divert financial and other resources to maintain the
poor subsistence paddy growers of U.P. and Bihar when
production and consumption needs might be better met
and the political dangers of discontented urban populations be more easily warded off by a policy that
maximizes the potential for immediate production
increases. Such a policy accepts that it may be necessary to introduce inequalities into the agricultural
economy to prevent the greater evil of an inadequate
food supply. For example, a policy maker at the Indian
Council for Agricultural Research, frustrated over the

criticism that the Intensive Agricultural District
Programme introduced into India in the 1960s under the
sponsorship of the Ford Foundation enhanced rural tensions between those farmers who acquired irrigation and
those who did not, responded:

> But then ... we have got 650 million people.
> We have got to feed them also. So, those
> who make these comments do not understand
> that we must also have enough food for everyone.[15]

If there is a single basic value assumption in
international agricultural research that underlies the
overall strategies that are followed and that sets
the boundaries for specific decisions and alterations
in policy, it is that increasing agricultural production must take precedence over all other considerations.
The whole world is familiar with the Malthusian arguments that justify the production orientation. Those
arguments have been so powerfully and widely presented
that they go virtually unchallenged as a basic premise
of agricultural research and policy making. Yet, it is
not at all clear that production, rather than distribution, is the more serious problem in the world as a
whole or in Indian agriculture in particular. For one
thing, there is no doubt at all that there was enough
grain in America, Australia, and the Soviet Union to
feed the people of the Sahel during the recent terrible
drought there. As far as India is concerned, American
food imports for 20 years filled the estimated gap
between production and consumption needs there. However, it is quite likely that there has nearly always
been sufficient food or production capacity in India
in the past two decades to feed the people of the
country provided either that all barriers to the free
movement of grain were removed or that governments were
willing or able forcibly to procure grain from surplus
areas to distribute to deficit areas. However, since
both policies presented political and/or economic
costs that the Government of India was not willing to
pay, it proved to be politically easier and also
cheaper economically to transport wheat from Kansas
to Bihar than from Punjab to Bihar and rice from
Louisiana to Calcutta than from Tamil Nadu to Calcutta.
When the Punjab began to produce a large marketable
surplus in both wheat and rice, the Government of
India found it politically expedient and financially
easier to procure grains at controlled prices from the

Punjab to ship to eastern India rather than either to
allocate the resources necessary or to provide the marketing facilities and price incentives to make it possible for the paddy growers of eastern U.P., Bihar, and
Bengal to feed themselves and to provide a surplus
for Calcutta.

The strategy of importing grain and procuring it
within India at a low price kept prices within reasonable bounds in India, thereby also preventing political
instability. It also benefited the production and
profit-oriented wheat farmers of Kansas and the Punjab.
The latter would have benefited even more from an open-
market policy in India, but they at least were permitted
to hoard surplus stocks and maximize their price by the
unwillingness of the government to squeeze them through
a harsh procurement policy. The production and import
strategy also ensured the dependence of India upon the
United States and of Bihar upon the Punjab.

Both the scientists and policy-makers at IRRI and
in India are well aware of the dilemma in which an
exclusively production-oriented strategy places them.
On the one hand, the IRRI scientists confront the real-
ization that the technology they have developed is
irrelevant to at least 60 per cent and possibly 75 per
cent of the rice farmers of Asia, but that a major di-
version of their own research efforts to developing an
appropriate technology for the rainfed areas might not
pay off for many years and that the ultimate pay-off
will, in any case, probably not be as great in terms of
yield increases as has already occurred and might still
be possible in the irrigated areas. On the other hand,
it is estimated that further efforts in developing
varieties, insect control and fertilizer use might lead
to production increases of a ton or two tons per hectare in the irrigated areas with the existing H.Y.V.s.
Moreover, a decision to shift a substantial part of
its resources to work on the diverse environments of
the rainfed areas raises considerable problems for IRRI
and carries greater risks. Although IRRI is financially
well-endowed and has adequate resources to carry on
research that is highly focused on a single, ideal
environment for rice-growing, it does not have the
resources to duplicate its research effort for a number
of different and less-than-ideal environments. Moreover, although it is possible to create an ideal
environment for rice-growing on a single research site
in the Philippines, it is not possible to create
several sets of adverse conditions that would duplicate

the varied environments in which rice is grown throughout Asia. Consequently, any major shift of emphasis at
IRRI towards research on the problems of rice-growing
under adverse conditions must involve IRRI much more
in collaborative research in different locations in
Asia.[16] In the face of these facts, IRRI policy makers
insist that the production emphasis was valid when IRRI
began and will continue to be valid in the foreseeable
future.

> The accusation that IRRI spent its early days
> working on irrigated rice exclusively ... [is]
> a very appropriate statement of what should have
> been done because the potential for increasing
> production [was unquestionably in] irrigated
> rice. And I think if [we] were sitting here
> twenty years from now, we'd probably say that the
> potential for increased production of rice between
> now and twenty years from now will be still very
> heavily oriented toward irrigated crops, so that
> there's no reason why IRRI shouldn't have done
> this. [17]

IRRI policy makers also believe that, if adequate
systems of irrigation and drainage were established in
the rainfed areas, the technology that has been emphasized at IRRI would then become appropriate for these
areas, though the yield potential in the rainfed areas
of north India, where the cloud cover is greater than
in other parts of Asia, would still be less than in
areas with greater radiation. Consequently, IRRI faces
a choice of whether to wait on the governments of Asia
to develop the water management that is desirable or
to try to develop a technology that would suit present
conditions without adequate water management. Since
IRRI policy makers do not foresee the widespread
development of good water conservation in most Asian
countries in the near future, they are

> not going down either road completely. We're
> still putting abut 40 per cent of our effort
> toward the irrigated situation and 60 per cent
> toward situations that might be changed but that,
> in some cases, will not likely be changed that
> much. [18]

Actually, the choices faced by IRRI scientists and
policy makers are more complex than simply choosing

between research in irrigated versus rainfed areas,
for the environments in which paddy is grown in Asia
are extremely heterogeneous. Each distinctive environment presents different problems, potentials, and value
choices. The apparently harmless, even noble goal of
providing a technology to maximize production of rice
in Asia, when translated into cost-benefit ratios, presents policy choices with quite different   value implications. Primary emphasis on increasing production
leads inevitably to favouring the already-favoured areas
and paying less attention to the less-favoured areas.
Moreover, since the more reliable forms of irrigation,
especially tube-wells but also canal irrigation, tend
to be made use of more by the larger farmers than the
small farmers, the production orientation also tends to
favour the bigger farmers and neglect the poorer. The
solution adopted at IRRI in the face of this dilemma
has been to continue emphasizing work on the technology
of irrigated rice, but to supplement it with work on
the problems of rice growing under adverse conditions.
In general, the attitude at the policy making level at
IRRI is that it is necessary and desirable that more
attention be paid to research on rice cultures in the
'adverse areas', but that 'once this is done, if we
find, for example, the potential ... in comparison to
what you could get in irrigated and other conditions is
insignificant, then you would phase out of a major input there and go ahead and put your money where it makes
sense in terms of potential change in production'. [19]
Moreover, the largest share of the research funds at
IRRI, approximately 41 per cent, continue to be allocated for work on irrigated rice, compared to 31 per
cent for the rainfed areas, and the remainder for other
adverse conditions (see table, p.238). This distribution reflects accurately thinking at IRRI about where
the next production increases are going to come. It
is believed that they are going to come first from
increasing production in the irrigated areas by improving the technology there and gaining better control
over insects and diseases that affect the new varieties
so that actual production will move closer to the yield
potential of the new varieties. The current feeling at
IRRI is that 'the feasible potential for increasing
rice production in rainfed wetland areas with reasonable
research inputs is second only to that in irrigated
areas'.[20] IRRI policy makers believe also that their
scientists will be able to develop new varieties that
will produce under adverse soil conditions and that will

withstand floodwaters, thus preventing catastrophe to the farmers in the high risk areas.[21] Through this particular mixture of research and results, it is believed that production in Asia will increase at a minimum of four per cent a year, enough 'to produce all the rice that is needed'.[22]

Table: Proportions of Paddy Land, IRRI
Research Budget and Anticipated Benefits

Environment	Area Sown to Paddy		IRRI	Anticipated
	Asia	*India*	Budget	Benefits
Irrigated	27	33	41	46
Shallow Rainfed	32	33	31	25
Intermed.Ditto	14	16		8
Deepwater	8	6	5	3
Dryland(Upland)	10	6	24	4
Other	9	6	–	13

Note: *Asia* refers to Asian developing countries except China. The table compares the proportion of land area sown to paddy in such countries and in India with proportions of the IRRI research budget devoted to research on different types of rice culture and of the anticipated benefits from future research inputs. The IRRI budget is the one for 1977; 'other' categories of environment were not separately classified there.

Source: *IRRI Long Range Planning Committee Report* (Los Banos, Philippines 1979), pp.20 and 45.

The allocations in the IRRI research budget have continued to be weighted heavily in favour of the irrigated areas. Moreover, reasoning in terms of expected returns in productivity from future research input in different types of environments, it is argued at IRRI that the weightage in their research allocations is an appropriate one. The table compares the allocations in the IRRI research budget in 1977 and the allocations that IRRI's Long Range Planning Committee feel are appropriate in terms of the criterion of productivity 'benefits from future research input' with the area sown with paddy in different types of environments in Asia. The table indicates clearly that IRRI planners have not been willing to consider seriously any criterion other than productivity as the primary basis for allocating research funds and that the distribution of their research budget has continued to reflect that orientation.

While IRRI policy makers do not deny that the benefits of the new technology have gone principally to the irrigated areas, they do not accept the criticism that the new technology has led to unevenness in income distribution or benefiting one group over another. At IRRI, the general response to this criticism is that the facts are not yet in, but that some of their own research on consequences in the Philippines suggests otherwise. However, the ultimate defence at IRRI to this set of criticisms also comes back to the production orientation, as the following quotation indicates.

> The ultimate beneficiar(ies) of all agricultural research ... are the people who eat the food and the ones that benefit the most are the low income people [who] eat that food because most of what we do ends up with a more efficient system and a lower price for food. ... And an institute like this ... that can help get these production levels up and keep those prices at a steady and reasonable level, the ultimate beneficiary is the poorest people in the country.[23]

For the Government of India, the policy choices that must be faced, given the limitations of the new technology in rice, are much more complex than those faced by policy makers at IRRI. For one thing, the Government of India must allocate research funds among different crops. The principal agency that determines the allocations for agricultural research in India is the Indian Council for Agricultural Research. It is apparent from the Research Council's current relative allocation of resources among the various crops grown in India and among the several non-crop-specific research projects it has funded that the historic neglect of rice research in India is not being rectified. Although most Research Council reports on crop improvement begin with rice and stress the fact that rice is the principal food crop in India, the relative allocation for rice research is nowhere near its relative importance in the country's agriculture. It is not easy to determine what proportion of the allocation for non-crop-specific research projects, such as those pertaining to soil management or agricultural engineering, ultimately benefit rice farmers, but there is no doubt that the proportion of funds allocated directly or

indirectly for rice research falls very short of the
nearly 80 per cent contribution of rice to the total
area sown with foodgrains production in the country[24]
or even the 27 per cent contribution of rice to the
total net sown area of the country.[25] In the Fourth
Five Year Plan, the allocation for rice in the Research
Council budget was Rs.16,000,000, a larger allocation
than for any other crop. However, this figure represented less than 30 per cent of the crop-specific
allocation for food and fodder crops, less than 13 per
cent of the total allocation in the budget for all
crops, and less than 5 per cent of the budget for all
projects.[26] In 1978, the allocation specifically for
rice research in the Research Council budget was less
than 3 per cent of the total.[27] Moreover, several of
the crop-specific agricultural research institutes in
India have been funded at higher levels than the Central
Rice Research Institute, including the Indian Grassland
and Fodder Research Institute, the Central Potato Research Institute, and the Institute of Horticultural
Research. In general, it has historically been the
case in South Asia that cash crops and specialized
crops grown for export markets, nearly all of them
requiring capital-intensive cultivation, have received
far more research support than the main food crops,
particularly rice. It is, for example, remarkable that
the Central Potato Research Institute is funded at a
higher level than the Central Rice Research Institute,
despite the fact that only half a million hectares of
land in India are sown with potatoes, whereas nearly
40 million hectares are sown with rice. Moreover,
the potato is a highly capital-intensive crop, 'quite
exacting in its requirements of inputs such as seed,
fertilizers, fungicides and pesticides and assured
irrigation'[28] and, therefore, not easily taken up by
'an ordinary cultivator', but grown mostly by specialized vegetable farmers or 'prosperous farmers'.[29]
        Although rice has clearly been neglected in com-
parison to other crops in India and in relation to its
contribution to the agricultural economy of the country,
it is not a fair criticism of the Indian Council for
Agricultural Research to consider only the relative
allocation for rice in relation to all projects sponsored by it. It is not only that many non-crop-
specific projects sponsored by the Research Council
benefit rice growers, but that there is some justifi-
cation for a non-crop-specific approach in general. At
the Council, the view is held that 'crops all fit ...

into a system because [the] farmer's life is a whole.
If he is growing wheat and rice [I] have to find a
solution to both the problems.'[30] On the whole, however, it does not appear to be the case that Research
Council projects are structured systematically from
the point of view of the specific mixed-crop patterns
of farmers in different agro-ecological regions of the
country. Rather, the overwhelming bulk of such projects
are either crop-specific or problem-specific, rather
than being focused upon different cropping patterns in
the numerous agro-climatic zones of India.

The neglect of rice has been most striking in the
rainfed areas of northern and eastern India, which are
only now beginning to receive substantial attention.
The 1977 report on Agricultural Research and Education,
after summarizing the work done on H.Y.V.s in rice in
India and noting their alleged 'significant impact'
in contributing to increased rice production in the
country,[31] concludes, however, that 'work on the monsoon rainfed rice is being intensified as the new rice
technology has not yet made a real impact in such
areas'.[32] There is not much evidence, however, that
such intensification has begun in earnest.

A more detailed statement of the problems of rice
production in the rainfed areas was presented in
another Research Council publication, titled 'Research
Highlights, 1977'. In this report, it was noted that
'the productivity and production of rice in low-lying
areas have remained stagnant' and that 'a large proportion of the rice-growing regions of West Bengal, Assam,
north Bihar, eastern Uttar Pradesh and Orissa have so
far been by-passed by the high-yield technology'.[33]
Referring to the joint Research Council - IRRI study
team survey of the problems of rice-growing in this
region, the report pointed out that 'since the performance and profit of the existing high-yielding
varieties with costly inputs are uncertain', it was
necessary for scientists to 'develop a technology which
combines good yield with reliability and security to
profit to farmers'. Recognizing that the problems
associated with the adoption of the new technology in
rice are particularly severe for the small peasantry,
the report went on to say that 'we need a high yield-
cum-high stability technology, if small and marginal
farmers are to be helped to take to such technology'.
However, the report concludes in a thoroughly ambiguous
manner with regard to how the new technology is to be
developed and, indeed, with regard to the suitability

of the existing technology for the rainfed areas.
After calling for the development of a high-yield high-
stability technology, the report concludes that the
problems of the 'rainfed upland areas ... can be
corrected with new material and technology available'
and the problems of the areas subject to periodic
flooding can 'also partially be corrected by popular-
izing flood-tolerant varieties'.[34] In order to achieve
these goals, three research projects were proposed to
be set up, 'one each for Bihar, West Bengal and Orissa'
to 'demonstrate the potentiality of the new technology
and high-yielding varieties suitable for problem
areas'.[35] Since, however, it is not even clear from
this report whether or not such a technology exists for
the rainfed areas, one cannot help but wonder how these
research projects are to be oriented and co-ordinated.
In the meantime, however, while the Indian Council for
Agricultural Research either makes up its mind whether
or not it has the technology - or whether or not to
admit that it *does not* have the technology - the extension agents of the agriculture departments of the U.P.
and Bihar, who are being led to believe that there is
a suitable technology for rainfed upland and flood-
prone areas, are going about 'recommending varieties
and techniques which, because the conditions are far
from perfect, are probably going to lose the farmer
money'.[36]

Another recent Research Council report, 'Present
State of Research and Education in Agriculture', is
more in tune with the conclusions reached by international rice research specialists in its admission that
'research has not yet been able to breed varieties for
very large areas experiencing heavy rainfall and conditions of water stagnation during the rainy season to
which the existing high-yielding dwarf varieties are
not adapted'. The report goes on to point out the specific problems of the dwarf varieties for the rainfed
areas, namely, inadequate 'resistance to pests and
diseases', and vulnerability 'to high rainfall and
water-logged conditions', which, when combined with
'the high cost involved in resorting to the plant protection measures recommended for these varieties',[37]
make it an extremely risky venture, especially for
small farmers, to adopt the H.Y.V.s in rice.

Once it is recognized that the technology is not
available to make the produciton of the H.Y.V.s in
rice 'reliably profitable' to the farmers[38] in the
rainfed areas and as long as the primary goal continues

to be to maximize the productivity of the land, then
the Government of India has three choices before it,
which are not necessarily mutually exclusive. One is
to allocate substantial research funds to the difficult
task of developing the high-stability varieties that
both IRRI and the Government of India feel are required
for the rainfed areas. However, while high-stability
varieties with low input requirements might please
cultivators, especially the small peasants, they do not
promise the dramatic increases in yield dictated by a
production orientation. The second alternative is to
alter the environment to suit the varieties available
through massive irrigation projects. This second
alternative, while obviously the most expensive one,
offers the prospect of predictability of results, since
it is known that the new varieties respond well to inputs if assured water is available, and maximal production increases. However, since the problems of the
rainfed areas concern water control generally, including
drainage and flood prevention, irrigation by itself
cannot satisfy the needs of all the paddy-growers in
the high-risk rainfed areas. A third alternative is
to move the paddy growers to withdraw from rice cultivation and to substitute crops such as maize, soybean,
and blackgram that require somewhat less water than
rice. The Report of the National Commission on Agriculture has proposed, in fact, that 3.27 million hectares of land constituting nearly 23 per cent of the
current rice acreage,[39] be withdrawn from rice in the
rainfed upland areas of U.P., Maddhya Pradesh and Bihar.
This proposal, which is supported also by the Indian
Council for Agricultural Research, has as its underlying premise the goal of maximizing production by
growing those crops that will give the best yield from
a given piece of land. It is also based upon the
assumption that, if yields of rice are increased from
lands that are suitable for rice-growing, the production needs of the country can be met from a reduced
acreage in rice. It is recognized at the Indian Council
for Agricultural Research that rice cultivation on marginal lands arises out of a 'farming system [that is]
based upon the home needs of the cultivator, not on the
basis of the marketability of the produce'.[40] Before
a marginal or small paddy-grower in Bihar can be persuaded to substitute soya bean, sunflower, or sorghum
for rice, he must be assured that his consumption
requirements for rice will be met. The ideal at the
Research Council is to produce enough rice from the

potentially highest yielding rice lands so that the government may procure enough rice to stock the fair price shops and thereby be in a position to provide a guarantee to the rice grower that, if he switches to another crop, he will be able to purchase his family's rice requirements at a reasonable price from the fair price shops. The National Commission on Agriculture has projected that the rice consumption needs of the country in 1990 can be met by a production of 60 to 70 million tons. It is believed at the Research Council that this projection may be too high but that, in any case, the goal can be met by bringing the yields in all the irrigated lands in India up to the Punjab level of 3 tons per hectare. Consequently, the favoured policy at the Council in relation to rice production is to increase the yields on the irrigated lands by continuing to apply and develop further the H.Y.V. technology, to substitute crops other than rice in the rainfed areas where rice is not 'the correct crop' in relation to the rainfall pattern, and to provide paddy growers who make such substitutions with rice through the fair price shops.[41] The Research Council approach, which is based upon the value of increasing production in the country as a whole by 'crop planning which will maximize the benefits of a given environment and minimize the environmental risks of that particular location'[42] conflicts with the existing values of both the small paddy-growers and several of the state governments as well, which emphasize self-sufficiency rather than maximal production. At present, the small paddy-grower does not wish to be dependent on sources other than his own land and labour to feed his family. Moreover, political leaders in Kerala and other states, where national policy favours increasing the acreage sown to plantation and other non-staple crops, do not wish to be dependent upon the central government to feed their urban populations and their rural poor.

Consequently, of the three proposals, the only one currently being pursued with some resoluteness is the second, which is the most conservative one under the circumstances. Provision of increased irrigation facilities is within the existing technological capabilities of government whereas the creation of high stability varieties is not. Moreover, it is far easier to build a state tube-well than to persuade peasants to change their cropping patterns, especially when it may not clearly be in *their* interest to do so. Provision of irrigation facilities to enhance the possibilities of adoption of H.Y.V.s in rice also is entirely consistent with the predominant production orientation.

The second alternative of developing suitable technology for the rainfed and other difficult areas also is being pursued, with the support of the Ford Foundation, which in 1975 agreed to provide $500,000 to fund research on agricultural technology for the adverse areas, including flood-prone, deep water, dry land, upland, and insect-infested areas.[43] However, it is questionable how serious the Indian Council of Agricultural Research is about pursuing vigorously the development of technologies and new varieties for adverse areas given their already noted ambiguity about the existence of such technologies and their desire to move a substantial proportion of rice area into other crops. There is, however, no major programme to implement the latter proposal. Nor are there any published documents that even discuss the likely consequences for farmers of such a major shift and the likely receptivity of cultivators to shifting to crops other than rice.

The proposal to shift nearly 23 per cent of the rice acreage in the rainfed upland areas to other crops raises strong doubts about the validity of the goal of increasing production as a reasonable guide for agricultural policy making. The individual cultivator is not interested solely in maximizing the quantity of foodgrains or other crops that can be produced from his fields, but has many other goals in mind which vary in importance also depending upon the size of his holding. The smallest peasants are most likely to be influenced considerably by the need to produce enough food to sustain their families, but even they are likely also to be concerned about a suitable mixture of crops such as would sustain an adequate variety of desired grains and vegetables to satisfy consumption needs. The cultivator may attempt to grow all or most of the food his family requires on his own lands or he may grow a mixture of foodgrains and cash crops and use the income derived from the latter to provide for his family's food consumption and other needs requiring cash. The larger the holding, the more likely is the peasant to grow a mixture of food and cash crops and to be motivated by considerations other than consumption, such as profitability and foodgrain quality, neither of which may involve an orientation to high yields.

The Ford Foundation, in a recent grant of funds to the National Council of Applied Economic Research for research on improving rice technology in adverse areas, has attempted to encourage further research on 'farmers' rice cultivation systems to identify socio-economic constraints' to the 'adoption of new technologies' and to focus more attention on 'the objective of increasing the profitability to farmers'.[44] However, the concern appears to be not with the profitability of the peasant's total operation and with what mixture of crops will maximize his economic return from his land, but with the more specific question of the profitability of the H.Y.V.s or any improved varieties of rice in relation to such factors as the relative price of paddy in the market, the cost of inputs, and the return in terms of increased production that the peasant gets in relation to the amount of paddy he must sell to buy the fertilizer that will increase his yields. These kinds of concerns arise naturally from the monocrop orientation of international and national agricultural research, which in turn is itself related to the production orientation that focuses on maximizing yields from particular crops. However, most farmers in north India grow a combination of cash crops and staple food grains. They are as much concerned with the technology for producing high-yield cash crops as they are with the technology for H.Y.V.s in rice. They are even more concerned with the market price for their cash crops and are very sensitive to fluctuations in the price of particular cash crops. The kinds of advice they require are not just how to grow H.Y.V.s in rice, but, given the available technology, irrigation facilities, and current and predicted market prices for various crops, what particular mixture of food and cash crops will maximize their opportunities to feed their families, to bring a sufficient return to marry their daughters, and to buy inputs - in that order of priority.

Although the Government of India has, in the past, shared with international agricultural research agencies a strong orientation towards increased production as a primary goal, this orientation has been modified in practice by the government's political concern to distribute food to the urban classes at a moderate price. The government's price policy, therefore, has put a damper on increased production of foodcrops. The failure of state governments in north India to provide adequate marketing facilities also has been a disincentive to production increases in the more inaccessible districts of the region. Pressure from the less

favoured regions and states for an equitable allocation of resources also has modified tendencies to concentrate resources in the more productive areas.

On the other hand, the entire orientation of
India's economic development policies in the Nehru era,
when rapid industrialization was the primary goal and
the needs of agriculture were slighted, retarded agricultural modernization in the rainfed areas. Resources
that might have been used to build extensive irrigation
networks and flood control systems and to extend hydro-
electric power to remote areas were directed instead to
industry. In recent years, however, particularly under
the former Janata government, there has been a shift in
emphasis in favour of agricultural development and
small-scale rather than large-scale industry. An
important component of this shift was the decision
under the Janata government to divert considerable
resources to irrigation, including a plan to irrigate
the whole of Bihar state in five years. It is difficult to believe that such a grandiose plan could be
brought to fruition in the time indicated, but the goal
at least was indicative of a major change in priorities.

Despite the recent indications that governments in
India plan to expend significant financial resources to
develop agriculture in the rainfed areas, it is not at
all clear that those resources will ultimately benefit
the small paddy-grower. In the first place, it is not
even clear that irrigation by itself, in the absence of
adequate flood control measures, would be used by paddy-
growers in these high risk areas or that they would or
could use the H.Y.V.s and the inputs required to get
good yields from them even with irrigation. Second,
it is also not clear that governments in India are prepared to devote the kind of resources necessary to confront the problems of developing the full range of
technologies required to grow more paddy under the
extremely heterogeneous conditions that exist *within*
the rainfed areas. Finally, it is least of all clear,
despite the creation of such organizations as the Small
Farmers' Development Agency and the Marginal Farmers'
and Agricultural Labourers Agency that the Government
of India is willing to make a commitment to preserve
and protect existing small farmers and to make marginal
farmers viable, for such a commitment would mean a
reorientation of the whole thrust of economic development policy for India away from the capital-intensive
industrialization strategy and the production emphasis
in agriculture to a labour- and land-intensive

Paul R. Brass

agriculture-oriented strategy with an emphasis on
extending the benefits of science and technological
change in agriculture to all farmers who can reasonably make use of it to improve their own well-being.

Brass, 'International rice research and the problems
of rice growing in Uttar Pradesh and Bihar'

This paper has arisen out of a project on Value Issues
in Technological Innovation and Social Choice: A Case
Study of U.S. Rice Production Technologies in South
Asia, on which I have been engaged for the past three
years jointly with Robert Anderson, Edwin Levy, and
Barry Morrison. Research for the project was funded
by the Ethical and Human Values in Science and Technology Division of the National Science Foundation. I
am solely responsible for all statements of fact and
opinion contained in this paper.

Abbreviations

ICAR   Indian Council of Agricultural Research
IRRI   International Rice Research Institute

1. Adelita C. Palacpac, *World Rice Statistics* (Los
Banos [IRRI] 1977), p.32.

2. Ibid., p.13.

3. Calculated from ibid., p.38.

4. Ibid., pp.39-40.

5. Interview at IRRI on 15 and 16 February 1978.

6. Interview in New Delhi on 23 March 1978.

7. Ibid.

8. Ibid.

9. Ibid. and interview in New Delhi on 20 March
1978.

10. Randolph Barker, *Socio-Economic Constraints to
the Production of Photoperiod Sensitive Transplanted
Rice in Eastern India* (Los Banos [IRRI] 1977), p.5.

11. Ibid., p.2.

12. Ibid., p.11.

13. Ibid., p.9.

14. Interviews at IRRI on 16 and 20 February 1978.

15. Interview, New Delhi, 23 March 1978.

16. Interview, New Delhi, 20 March 1978.

17. Interview, IRRI, 20 February 1978.

18. Ibid.

19. Ibid.

20. *IRRI Long Range Planning Committee Report* (Los
Banos, Philippines [IRRI] 1979), p.23.

21. Ibid.

22. Ibid.

23. Ibid.

24. Government of India, Ministry of Agriculture and Irrigation, 'Report of the National Commission on Agriculture' Pt.VI: *Crop Production, Sericulture, and Apiculture* (Delhi 1976), p.53.

25. Calculated from Government of India, Ministry of Agriculture and Irrigation, 'All India Report on Agricultural Census, 1970-1' (Delhi: Controller of Publications, 1975), pp.29-31.

26. Calculated from ICAR, *Agricultural Research in India: Achievements and Outlook* (New Delhi 1972), pp. 47-9.

27. Interview, New Delhi, 23 March 1978.

28. 'Report of the National Commission on Agriculture' VI, p.282.

29. Ibid., p.283.

30. Interview, New Delhi, 23 March 1978.

31. ICAR, *Agricultural Research and Education: Recent Progress* (New Delhi 1977), p.24.

32. Ibid., p.26.

33. ICAR, *Research Highlights, 1977* (New Delhi 1977), p.4.

34. Ibid., p.6.

35. Ibid., p.7.

36. Interview, New Delhi, 20 March 1978.

37. ICAR, *Present State of Research and Education in Agriculture, Animal Sciences, and Fisheries and Approach to Their Further Development During the Fifth Plan Period* (New Delhi 1978[?]), p.3.

38. Interview, New Delhi, 30 December 1980.

39. 'Report of the National Commission on Agriculture' VI, pp.65-7.

40. Interview, New Delhi, 23 March 1978.

41. Ibid.

42. Ibid.

43. Interview, New Delhi, 20 March 1978.

44. Ibid.

For Product Safety Concerns and Information please contact our EU representative GPSR@taylorandfrancis.com Taylor & Francis Verlag GmbH, Kaufingerstraße 24, 80331 München, Germany

Printed and bound by CPI Group (UK) Ltd, Croydon, CR0 4YY

08/05/2025

01864385-0001